THE
FAMILY TREE
TOOLKIT

THE
FAMILY TREE
TOOLKIT

A Comprehensive Guide to Uncovering
Your Ancestry and Researching Genealogy

KENYATTA D. BERRY
Host of *Genealogy Roadshow*

Skyhorse Publishing

Skyhorse Publishing books may be purchased in bulk at special discounts for sales promotion, corporate gifts, fund-raising, or educational purposes. Special editions can also be created to specifications. For details, contact the Special Sales Department, Skyhorse Publishing, 307 West 36th Street, 11th Floor, New York, NY 10018 or info@ skyhorsepublishing.com.

Skyhorse® and Skyhorse Publishing® are registered trademarks of Skyhorse Publishing, Inc.®, a Delaware corporation.

Visit our website at www.skyhorsepublishing.com.

10 9 8 7 6 5 4 3 2 1

Library of Congress Cataloging-in-Publication Data is available on file.

Cover design by Michael Short
Cover illustration by iStock

Print ISBN: 978-1-63158-219-6
Ebook ISBN: 978-1-51073-549-1

Printed in the United States of America

CONTENT

INTRODUCTION: SHARING MY STORY   XIII

Coming Home: A Journey from Virginia to New York   xiii

CHAPTER 1: STARTING YOUR FAMILY HISTORY   1

Planting the Seeds of Your Family History   2

Interview Family Members   3

Family Documents   4

Organizing Your Research   5

Cite Your Sources!   5

CHAPTER 2: UNITED STATES RECORDS RESEARCH   6

Census Records Research   6

     Search United States Census Records   9

     Search State Census Records   20

     Nonpopulation Schedules   22

Vital Records Research   23

United States Court System and Court Records   78

     Tax Records   79

     Probate Records   81

     Finding Your Ancestors in Probate Records   83

     Criminal Court Proceedings   84

Property Records   *86*

     The Homestead Act of 1862   90

     State Land States   92

CHAPTER 3: OTHER RECORDS   96

City Directories   *96*

Cemetery Research   *97*

Church Records   *99*

Newspapers   *101*

Voter Records   *104*

CHAPTER 4: IMMIGRATION AND NATURALIZATION RECORDS   107

Immigration   *107*

     Finding Ancestors Who Arrived in the United States
before 1820   109

     Immigration to the United States from 1820 to 1857   112

Naturalization   *124*

     Naturalization prior to 1906   126

     Naturalization after 1906   128

     Passport Applications   135

Special Cases   *138*

     Chinese Immigration   138

     Women and Citizenship   140

     World War I Naturalizations   140

CHAPTER 5: US MILITARY RESEARCH   141

The Revolutionary War (1775–1783)   *141*

     Revolutionary War Service Records   143

     Pension and Bounty Land Warrant Applications   144

     Revolutionary War Final Payment Vouchers   145

The War of 1812, "Second War of American Independence"   *145*

  Compiled Military Service Records for War of 1812   147

  Prisoner of War Records for 1812   147

  War of 1812 Pension Files   148

The Indian Wars (1784–1858)   *149*

  Pension and Bounty Warrant Land Applications   150

Mexican War (1846–1848)   *151*

  Index, Service, and Pension Records   151

Civil War (1861–1865)   *151*

  United States Army and Navy (Union)   152

  Confederate States of America   152

  United States Colored Troops (USCT)   153

  Compiled Military Service Records   155

  Prisoner of War Records   156

  Civil War Pension Records   156

  Confederate Pension and Soldiers' Home Records   157

  Other Civil War Records   174

Spanish-American War   *176*

World War I   *177*

  African American Troops in World War I   178

  Native Americans in World War I   178

  Records Related to World War I   178

  Veterans Homes   181

World War II   *181*

  Finding Your World War II Ancestor   182

  Japanese American Internment   184

Other Conflicts   *186*

  Korean War (1950–1953)   186

  Vietnam War (1954–1975)   186

CHAPTER 6: ETHNIC ANCESTRY 188

African American Family History 188

Transatlantic Slave Trade 190

Domestic Slave Trade 190

Plantation System 191

Reconstruction (1863–1877) 192

Freedmen's Bureau 191

1870 Brick Wall 197

Researching Free People of Color 200

Emancipation and Freedom 200

Caribbean 202

Native American Ancestry 205

Identifying the Tribe 206

Five Civilized Tribes, Dawes Commission, and Rolls 206

Slavery among the Five Civilized Tribes 210

CHAPTER 7: EUROPEAN RESEARCH 215

English, Welsh, and Scotish 216

Birth, Marriage, and Death Records 216

Census Resources 217

Irish 218

Irish Civil Registrations 219

Irish Census Resources 219

Italian 219

Italian Civil Registrations 220

German 221

German Records 221

Jewish Genealogy 222

Holocaust research 222

CHAPTER 8: ADOPTION RESEARCH   223

Useful Documents When Researching Adoptees   *225*

Organizations to Help You with Your Research   *226*

CHAPTER 9: DNA   229

DNA Basics   *230*

DNA Companies   *230*

My DNA Results   *231*
    AncestryDNA Results   232
    23andMe Results   233

ACKNOWLEDGMENTS   235

APPENDIX   237

United States Quick Reference Guide to Census and Vital Records by State   *237*

NATIONAL ARCHIVES AND RECORDS ADMINISTRATION FACILITIES   245

STATE ARCHIVES AND HISTORICAL SOCIETIES   249

VITAL RECORDS OFFICES   251

ADDITIONAL RESEARCH RESOURCES   259

THE
FAMILY TREE
TOOLKIT

INTRODUCTION
SHARING MY STORY

COMING HOME: A JOURNEY FROM VIRGINIA TO NEW YORK

I believe we all have a desire to understand our heritage. Genealogy is a thriving area of study for enthusiasts and hobbyists. It's actually the second most popular hobby in the United States after gardening. Since the introduction of the Internet, there has been a tremendous growth in the genealogy industry. Using a variety of websites such as Familysearch.org, Fold3.com, Newspapers.com, Myheritage.com, Findmypast.com, and Ancestry.com, genealogists are able to access federal census records, vital records, newspapers, and more. African American genealogy is especially challenging because many records of African Americans are listed by their first name without a surname or by the name of the enslaved individuals. However, with some work and dedication, an African American genealogist can reconstruct the past and understand their ancestors' lives, even as enslaved individuals. Using court documents, tax lists, federal and state census records, as well as plantation documents and church records, African American genealogists can paint a picture of their genealogical past.

This quest has been attempted by many and has resulted in some useful teaching tools such as *Roots* by Alex Haley and *Slaves in the Family* by Edward Ball. By using a variety of techniques and after investing years of research, these authors,

African American and white respectively, have been able to tell the stories of their ancestors. About eight years into researching my family, I was able to identify the last enslaver of my fourth great-grandfather, visit the location where my family was enslaved, and see and photograph a building where some of my family once lived and worked. I have since learned so much more about my ancestors and connected with cousins around the world.

THE DISCOVERY

In 1996, while in law school in Lansing, Michigan, I wrote to the town historian in Le Roy, New York, requesting information on my great-grandmother, Esther Lewis Kendrick, and her grandmother, Emily Carter Sellers. The Le Roy historian at the time put me in touch with my first cousin three times removed, Marion Sellers Phillips. During a conversation with her, I learned that Emily Carter Sellers had migrated to Livingston County from Culpeper, Virginia.

After graduating from law school, I moved to Arlington, Virginia. I never lost interest in my family roots in Livingston and Genesee counties. During those three years of school, I began to weave a story of their lives as slaves in Madison and Culpeper counties. I discovered Culpeper by accident while traveling to a golf tournament in Gainesville, Virginia. When I saw a sign that read CULPEPER 38 MILES, my heart jumped and my mind began to race. *Was I really just thirty-eight miles away from my family's ancestral home in Virginia?* The next day I drove to Culpeper and walked the downtown streets, wondering if my ancestors had roamed them, too. After discovering Culpeper, I began to make biweekly trips there and to neighboring Madison County to research and photograph the area where my family had once lived and worked.

WALKING IN THE FOOTSTEPS

While in Madison County, I discovered that Lewis Carter and Martha Payne—my fourth great-grandparents—were enslaved there and were the proud parents of seven children, all born there. At that time, I knew very little about the lives of Lewis and Martha while they were enslaved. Evidence suggests that he was an "agent" during Reconstruction and worked on the farm of J. W. Taylor. Fannie Belle Carter, the third child of Lewis and Martha, was also known as "Fair Belle."

She was twice married, once to a man thirty years her junior, and she outlived both of her husbands. Fannie had eight children by her first husband. When she married for the second time, her eldest son was older than his stepfather. When Lewis Carter died, Fannie sued Emily and their sister Mary Carter Price for their inheritance. At that time, Emily and Mary were both residing in upstate New York. The crux of the dispute was land located in Culpeper County that was purchased by Lewis and his son Marcelleus Carter. Unfortunately, I have not been able to learn the outcome of the chancery case. During one of my visits, the records were being restored by Culpeper County and were not available for public viewing.

Of all my ancestors, Fannie intrigues me the most because I know the least about her life in Culpeper County. I am confident that she has descendants in the Culpeper area, and I intend to find those descendants and to expand my family's connection to that area. The descendants of Lewis and Martha in Virginia include the surnames Green, Murray, Perry, and Price in Culpeper County, and Mallory in Madison County.

According to the 1870 census, Lewis and Martha lived next door to a prestigious boys' school, Locust Dale Academy. This school was founded in 1858 by Andrew James Gordon, a native of Vermont, and was adjacent to the property of Gordon's father-in-law, Larkin Willis. Willis lived with his wife, Lelia, and children in a white home with green trim at the corner of Routes 634 and 15 in Madison County, Virginia. Upon obtaining a map of Madison County, I ventured to locate the Willis home.

When I arrived at their home, I was stunned at the condition: it was abandoned but in perfect shape. I drove up to the house and stared in astonishment. As I explored the grounds, I looked out to the neighboring property and realized that I was walking in the footsteps of my ancestors. More than 130 years ago, they had stood where I was standing, and as I closed my eyes, I could almost hear their voices in the distance. As I drove away, I decided to head to Culpeper County to find Cedar Grove Baptist Church. During my research, I had discovered that one of my ancestors was a founding trustee of Cedar Grove.

I drove along a tree-lined road to Culpeper County, and with every twist and turn I took in the scenery. Railroad tracks lined the road, and as the sun crept down in the distance, I realized I was home. I had crossed the county line to

Culpeper County, and within a few minutes, I arrived at Cedar Grove Baptist Church, which was established in 1883. In 1887, J. P. Sellers, Robert Murray, and Richard Taylor purchased the half-acre of land where the church now stands.

Emily Ann Carter, the daughter of Lewis and Martha, married J. P. on March 7, 1867, in Madison County, Virginia. James Garnett II, the well-known pastor of Crooked Run Baptist Church in Culpeper, Virginia, performed the ceremony. J. P., the son of Phillip Sellers and Delia Green, was born in 1847 in Albemarle County, Virginia. J. P. and Emily migrated from Culpeper County to Livingston County, New York, with their eight children between 1887 and 1890.

J. P. and Emily would establish the Sellers family in upstate New York, which today includes descendants in Erie, Genesee, Livingston, and Monroe counties. Upon arriving in Fowlerville, J. P. and his sons, James, William, and Phillip, began farming the land, while the women took care of the home. On September 22, 1893, on the Rose farm in Livingston County, Martha Marie Sellers, the eldest child of J. P. and Emily, married John Lewis. John Lewis came to New York around 1884, where he worked as a farm laborer. John and Martha had three daughters: Esther, Emily, and Martha Lewis. When Emily Sellers died on June 29, 1938, she was survived by two daughters, three sons, one sister, sixteen grandchildren, and twenty-one great-grandchildren.

Upon arriving at Cedar Grove Baptist Church, I parked on the dirt road beside the church. The church was green and white with a chapel in the front and an addition in the back. A small cemetery was located to the right of the church, and upon cursory review of the cemetery, I was not able to locate any relatives. I took several photographs of the church. In my mind's eye, I could see J. P. and his family walking up its steps.

COMING HOME

Six years passed before I got in touch again with Marion Sellers Phillips. During the summer of 2003, I began planning my vacation to my ancestral home of Livingston County, New York. I decided to visit in October when the leaves were turning—it would be a beautiful time in upstate New York. Two weeks prior to my trip, I contacted town clerks, historians, relatives, church members, and whomever I could find to let them know that I was coming.

I arrived to warm and welcoming receptions from those I met in the tri-county area (Monroe, Livingston, and Genesee counties). With the aid of town clerks in Livingston County, I discovered additional information about the Bundy family and their connection to J. P. and Emily Sellers. On August 17, 1892, Delilah Sellers, the second child of J. P. and Emily, married Charles Pope Bundy. Charles was born in 1863 in Middlesex County, Virginia, the son of free blacks Samuel and Mary Bundy. In 1881, Charles came to New York to join his brother, Thomas H. Bundy, in the trade of barbering. There is confusion about Thomas's service during the Civil War, since he was born a free man of color. Some accounts affiliate him with the 47th Virginia Infantry of the Confederate Army as a cook. According to *A Complete Military History and Record of the 108th Regiment N. Y. Vols, from 1862–1894* by George H. Washburn (1894), Thomas was captured by the 108th New York Infantry and was then made a prisoner of war. Charles learned barbering from his brother, Thomas. Upon his brother's death in 1885, he opened his own barbershop. He managed it until his death on the day after Christmas in 1896, after enduring interstitial hepatitis for many years. His funeral was held at the United Presbyterian Church in Caledonia, where he is interred in the cemetery there. When Charles died, he was survived by his wife and their two young children, three-year-old James Samuel Bundy and nine-month-old Benjamin Franklin Bundy.

Delilah and her children moved in with her sister and brother in-law, Martha and John Lewis. Martha died unexpectedly on March 23, 1899, leaving John to raise their small children. On November 21, 1901, John married his deceased wife's sister, Delilah. John died on September 22, 1929, leaving behind his wife, Delilah, three daughters, one stepson, and six grandchildren. Delilah died on December 18, 1972, at the age of 102. At the time of her death, Delilah was survived by three stepdaughters, twelve grandchildren, and thirty-two great-grandchildren. Delilah died when I was just six months old: how wonderful it would have been to have known her. I continue to learn more and more about her every day.

My ancestral journey is remarkable and overwhelming at the same time. I have uncovered a tremendous amount of history about African Americans in Livingston County from descendants who still reside in Caledonia and the surrounding areas. Most of the African Americans who reside in Livingston and Genesee counties have ancestors from Culpeper County, Virginia. Like J.P. and Emily Sellers, their ancestors migrated north, leaving behind family and friends. It is my duty and calling to continue this journey. My goal is to establish a connection between those left behind in Culpeper County and those who left to build new lives in upstate New York. I will continue to walk in the footsteps of my ancestors as I search and discover my ancestral heritage.

The story of my ancestral journey from Culpeper to New York illustrates some of the techniques I used to find my family history. I share some of the beliefs I had about African American research and methodology when I was just starting out in genealogy. We all come on this journey with preconceived notions and myths about family history research. Since that time, I have learned how to prove or disprove a family story or an assumption.

I want to share my own story to let you know you are not alone! So, whatever narrative you have created for your ancestor will probably be completely different by the time you finish this book!

CHAPTER 1
STARTING YOUR FAMILY HISTORY

Welcome to the first step of discovering your family history! Together we will embark on a journey to learn more about you and your ancestors. You may have a burning question about your identity, a family story you want to prove or disprove, or just an innate curiosity about family history. As one of the hosts of *Genealogy Roadshow*, I hear from guests on the show who have unanswered questions about their family history or a family story they want to confirm. In each episode, we attempt to answer those questions with documents leading to sometimes surprising and satisfying results. Gathering your family history is like putting pieces of a puzzle together—except you have no idea what the picture will look like at the end!

Some relatives will evade you at all costs and at every turn. They seem to have disappeared or just fallen out of the sky. Those are the most challenging relatives and we all have them! To combat those elusive ancestors, we have, what I refer to as, "our family history angels." Family history angels lead you down the right path and become your guiding light on this journey. They are a gift that keeps on giving by helping you discover more ancestors. Discovering your family history can be a life-changing event that alters your sense of identity and purpose. Everyone has a story, and those stories are waiting to be discovered.

PLANTING THE SEEDS OF YOUR FAMILY HISTORY

How do you begin? Start with yourself and work backward by creating a biographical sketch about your life and your family. A host of tools are available that can help you on your journey as you begin to document your family history. You can use Evernote, Google Docs, Pages, One Note, or any application that allows you to quickly enter and organize notes. Below is a list of questions to help get you started on your biographical sketch. You may not have answers to all of these questions, and that's okay.

- What are your parents' names?[1]
- When and where were your parents born?
- When did your parents meet and where?
- Is your mother still alive? If not, when and where did she die? Where is your mother buried? Do you know her maiden name and her parents' names?
- Is your father still alive? If not, when and where did he die? Where is your father buried? Do you know his parents' names?
- What do you remember most about your childhood?
- Do you have siblings? If so, what do you remember about your childhood with your siblings?
- Do you have any funny stories about growing up?
- What was your favorite toy?
- Is there a particular sight or smell that reminds you of your childhood?
- Did you have a favorite nursery rhyme or song?
- What do you remember about your family home?
- What do you remember about your hometown? Is there anything that made it famous or infamous?
- What were your favorite and least favorite subjects in school?
- Did you have anything happen in your childhood that changed your perspective?
- What did you want to be when you grew up?

---

1 This applies to stepparents and adoptive parents.

- If you went to college, where did you go and why?
- How did you choose your major in college?
- Did you change your major in college? If so, how many times?
- If you started a family out of high school, how did that change you?
- Did you go straight to work after high school? If so, where did you work?
- What was your first job?
- What was your favorite job and why?
- Did you serve in the military? If so, what branch of the military?
- Do you have a spouse or partner? If so, how did you meet and where did you meet?
- If you are married, when and where did you get married?
- What was your favorite moment from the ceremony?
- How long have you been with your spouse or partner?
- Do you have children? If so, how many children? When and where were they born?
- What are some of your favorite memories with your children?

Answering these questions will help get your creative juices flowing and give you an idea of the information you can collect on your spouse, parents, and grandparents. The point of this exercise is to help you craft a story. Family history is more than a collection of names, dates, and locations—it's about providing historical context to document and share your ancestors' lives.

INTERVIEW FAMILY MEMBERS

To fill the gaps in your family history, start by interviewing family members including your parents, grandparents, siblings, aunts, uncles, and cousins. Record these interviews using audio and/or video on your smartphone.

A FAMILY HISTORY GEM

When I started doing genealogy, one of the first resources I used was *Notable Black American Women, Book II* edited by Jesse Carney Smith.[1] This volume had a biographical sketch of Georgia R. Dwelle that was extremely useful in discovering her family history. It included information about her father, who was enslaved, and his father, a white man from Massachusetts.

1 Smith, J. *Notable Black American Women, Book II*. New York: Gale Research, 1996.

There are several interviewing and storytelling apps available for the iPhone and Android. Try to get as much information as possible from each interview with follow-up questions. For any family members who immigrated to the United States, ask the following questions:

- What was their country of origin? Did their family live in that area for a long time?
- When and where did they arrive in the United States? Is that location different from where they live now or where you grew up?
- Did other relatives come to the United States at the same time or prior to their arrival?

Here are a few online resources to help with questions when you are interviewing relatives:

- www.thoughtco.com/fifty-questions-for-family-history-interviews -1420705
- www.deseretnews.com/article/865595932/Genealogy-150-questions-to -ask-family-members-about-their-lives.html
- oralhistory.library.ucla.edu/familyHistory.html

FAMILY DOCUMENTS

Make sure you ask about documents such as family Bibles, marriage or death certificates, obituaries, school information, old family letters, diaries, journals, and photographs. These documents help fill in the gaps of your family tree. When you locate a family document, make a physical copy if the condition allows or a digital copy for your records. This could be as simple as taking a picture with your own smartphone or digital camera. Remember to write down who gave you the document, the date, and the location. Most recently, I went to the Rochester area to celebrate the 125th anniversary of Second Baptist Church in Mumford, New York. My family has been attending Second Baptist Church since its founding in 1891. During the visit, my second cousin two-times-removed pulled out a shoebox of obituaries and funeral programs her mother kept of family members and neighbors. While she thought it was morbid, I was super excited to learn new information about my family tree!

ORGANIZING YOUR RESEARCH

Use Evernote, Google Docs, Pages, or OneNote to organize notes on individual family members, locations, historical events, and other information about your family history. You can also create a family tree online using tools provided by major genealogy websites. As you build out your family tree, you will amass digital and physical documents. It's important to create a digital strategy upfront. I use Dropbox to organize and share documents and photos of my family history research. I have created separate folders for my maternal ancestors and my paternal ancestors. Each subfolder represents a different maternal and paternal branch in my family tree. It's very similar to the structure on the ancestral chart but more extensive. You can use other file-sharing sites such as Box.com or Google Drive to share and access information while you're at an archive or repository.

CITE YOUR SOURCES!

During the excitement of researching one's family history, it is common to forget to write down where, when, and how you got your family's information. Although there are a number of records available online that can be easily attached to your family tree, it's still important to cite your sources. Not every document is online, and most are in state archives, libraries, courthouses, and historical and genealogical societies. I made the mistake of not citing my sources when I started doing my family history research, and I am still paying for it today. For guidance on how to cite your sources, visit the website Evidence Explained (www.evidenceexplained.com) created by Elizabeth Shown Mills.

Are you ready to discover your family history? Good luck!

CHAPTER 2

UNITED STATES RECORDS RESEARCH

———

Researching your family history has become easier over the past decade because of access to records online through websites such as Ancestry.com, Familysearch.org, Findmypast.com, and Myheritage.com. While not all records have been digitized, some of the most commonly used in family history research are available online. These include census, court, land, military, and vital records. As you search these records for your ancestors, think about their FAN club. Not a FAN club in the traditional sense, but Friends, Associates, and Neighbors (FAN). This is a phrase that was coined by Elizabeth Shown Mills. When you broaden your search to include documents related to the FAN club in your ancestor's community, you uncover additional information about your ancestor.

CENSUS RECORDS RESEARCH

Census records are a great starting point for family history research. Depending on the year of enumeration, they provide a wealth of information about a household and its individuals. Census records, like other documents, will contain errors for a variety of reasons. Nicknames were given as first names, names were spelled phonetically, and ages were off by five, ten, or even twenty years.

TIP

The Soundex is a phonetic algorithm for indexing names and was used in the federal population census records. The code uses the first letter of the last name and three numerical digits. The Soundex is based on the way the surname sounds and not how it is spelled. Soundex is beneficial because it helps you locate your ancestors in the census. You can generate an example from http://www.eogn.com/soundex/.

During your research, it is useful to create a census profile to track the first and subsequent census years for your ancestors. It's easy to create a census profile in Microsoft Excel: create columns for Name, Federal Census Year, Special Schedules (Federal), State Census Year, and Notes.

TIP

Add the spelling of your ancestor's name and their age for each census year to their census profile. This can be added to the Federal Census Year and State Census Year columns. You might get a good laugh out of the variety of spellings and their ages over the years.

The first US census enumeration began on Monday, August 2, 1790, and the responsibility for conducting the 1790 census was assigned to the marshals of the US judicial districts by Congress. The law required a visit to every household and posting of completed schedules in "two of the most public places" in each jurisdiction.[1] Article I, Section 2 of the US Constitution states that representatives and direct taxes shall be apportioned among the several states according to their respective numbers. Marshals continued to take the federal census until 1840. In 1849, a bill was enacted that established a census board whose membership

---

1 United States Census Bureau, 2016.

consisted of the secretary of state, attorney general, and postmaster general.[2] The federal census from 1790 to 1840 only listed the head of household.

TIP

Looking for a Revolutionary War ancestor? The 1840 census asked for the names of pensioners of the Revolutionary War or lists of people who served in the military, including veterans and widows. These individuals were named within the household on the census.

From 1850 to 1870, the United States Federal Census listed members of the household, including each person's age, sex, birthplace, and occupation. The 1870 census was the first federal census to enumerate formerly enslaved African Americans. The 1880 census was the first census to list relationships to the head of household. It also included information on parents' birthplace, birth month within the year, marriage within the year, and months unemployed. Most of the 1890 census population schedules were badly damaged by a fire where they were stored in the Commerce Building in January 1921. There is a special schedule for Union army surviving soldiers, sailors, marines, and widows, known as the 1890 veterans schedule. According to the Bureau of the Census: "The US Pension Office requested this special enumeration to help Union veterans locate comrades to testify in pension claims and to determine the number of survivors and widows for pension legislation."

The US federal census records are released to the public seventy-two years after the date of enumeration. The Bureau of the Census will release the 1950 census records in 2022.

---

2 US Census Bureau, Census History Staff, 2017.

SEARCH UNITED STATES CENSUS RECORDS

Start with the 1940 Census: search for ancestors born prior to 1940 online at one of the following websites:

- familysearch.org/1940census
- www.ancestry.com/1940-census
- www.archives.gov/research/census/1940/start-research.html

Search the 1930 census and earlier US census records at these websites: Ancestry.com, FamilySearch.org, Findmypast.com, and MyHeritage.com.

TIP

If you are researching an immigrant ancestor, make sure you track their immigration and naturalization information. The 1900 census recorded the year of immigration, number of years in the United States, and naturalization. In 1910, individuals were asked whether they were able to speak English and if not, what language they spoke. In 1930, foreign-born people were asked which language was spoken in the home before coming to the United States.

Bureau of the Census: US Federal Census 1790–1940
Information Collected About Inhabitants

This is a quick reference guide to help the reader understand the information captured in each US census. Each census should contain information about your ancestor's location including state, territory, county, parish, town, township, or city. This information is somewhat sparse in the earlier years but becomes abundant in 1880 and beyond. This information was compiled using printed and online resources from the United States Census Bureau.

UNITED STATES FEDERAL CENSUS, 1790–1940

CENSUS YEAR: 1790

INFORMATION COLLECTED: Name of each head of household, free white males under sixteen, free white males of sixteen years and up, free white females, number of slaves, number of other free persons

NONPOPULATION SCHEDULES: N/A

ADDITIONAL INFORMATION: Records were lost for Delaware, Georgia, Kentucky, New Jersey, North Carolina, and Virginia. Some of this information has been reconstructed using tax records.

CENSUS YEAR: 1800

INFORMATION COLLECTED: Names of each head of household; for free white males' and females' age: under ten, ten but under sixteen, sixteen but under twenty-six, twenty-six but under forty-five, and over forty-five; number of all other free persons; number of slaves

NONPOPULATION SCHEDULES: N/A

ADDITIONAL INFORMATION: Records were lost for Georgia, Indiana Territory, Tennessee, Kentucky, Mississippi Territory, New Jersey, Northwest Territory, and Virginia.

CENSUS YEAR: 1810

INFORMATION COLLECTED: Names of each head of household; for free white males' and females' age: under ten, ten but under sixteen, sixteen but under twenty-six, twenty-six to forty-five, and over forty-five; number of all other free persons; number of slaves

NONPOPULATION SCHEDULES: Manufacturing Schedule

ADDITIONAL INFORMATION: Records were lost for the District of Columbia, Georgia, Indiana Territory, Louisiana Territory (Missouri), Mississippi Territory, New Jersey, and Tennessee. Partial Losses for the Illinois Territory and Ohio.[3]

---

3 Ancestry.com.

CENSUS YEAR: 1820

INFORMATION COLLECTED: Names of each head of household; number of free white males and females aged: under ten years, ten years but under sixteen years, sixteen years but under eighteen (males only), sixteen but under twenty-six, twenty-six but under forty-five, forty-five and upward; number of male and female slaves aged: under fourteen, fourteen but under twenty-six years, twenty-six but under forty-five, forty-five and upward; number of free colored males and females aged: under fourteen, fourteen but under twenty-six, twenty-six but under forty-five, forty-five and upward; number of free colored males and females aged: under fourteen, fourteen but under twenty-six, twenty-six but under forty-five, and over 45; number of foreigners not naturalized; number of persons including slaves engaged in agriculture, commerce, and manufactures; number of other free persons not taxed.

NONPOPULATION SCHEDULES: Manufacturing Schedule

ADDITIONAL INFORMATION: Records have been lost or destroyed for Arkansas Territory, Missouri Territory, and New Jersey, as were half of the records for half of the counties in Alabama and counties in Eastern Tennessee.

CENSUS YEAR: 1830

INFORMATION COLLECTED: Names of each head of household; number of free white males and females aged: under five to over one hundred years asked in intervals of ten years; aliens not naturalized; number of slaves and free people of color aged: under ten, ten to twenty-four, twenty-four to thirty-six, thirty-six to fifty-five, fifty-five to one hundred, and over one hundred; number of white persons and slaves or colored people who were deaf and dumb aged: under fourteen, fourteen and under twenty-five, twenty-five and over; white persons, slaves, or colored persons who were blind

NONPOPULATION SCHEDULES: N/A

ADDITIONAL INFORMATION: Printed forms were used to collect the census data. Records were lost for counties in Maryland, Massachusetts, and Mississippi.

UNITED STATES FEDERAL CENSUS, 1790–1940

CENSUS YEAR: 1840

INFORMATION COLLECTED: Name of family head; free white males and females aged: under five to over one hundred asked in intervals of ten years; slaves and free people of color aged: under ten, ten to twenty-four, twenty-four to thirty-six, thirty-six to fifty-five, fifty-five to one hundred, and over one hundred; number of persons in each family employed in mining, agriculture, commerce, manufactures and trade, navigation of the ocean, navigation of canals, lakes, and rivers, and learned professional engineers; pensioners for revolutionary or military service and age; deaf and dumb, blind, and insane white persons aged: under fourteen, fourteen and under twenty-five, twenty-five and over; white persons insane and idiots at public and private charge; deaf, dumb, blind, or insane colored persons; colored persons insane and idiots at public and private charge

NONPOPULATION SCHEDULES: N/A

ADDITIONAL INFORMATION: The 1840 census added categories of "insane and idiotic." In 1844, Dr. Edward Jarvis finds glaring errors in the compilations of the "insane and idiotic," such as listings of insane blacks in many northern towns where no blacks had been tabulated, or, in other towns, greater numbers listed as insane than were actually listed as residents.

Jarvis and other members of the American Statistical Association submitted a memorial to Congress enumerating the errors in the 1840 census and declared the new enumeration of diseases to be "a bearer of falsehood to confuse and mislead." The House of Representatives directed Secretary of State John C. Calhoun to investigate and report on the "gross errors" in the 1840 census. After a brief investigation, the results of the census stood.[4]

CENSUS YEAR: 1850

INFORMATION COLLECTED: Dwelling—houses in order of visitation; families numbered in the order of visitation; name of every person whose usual place of abode on the first day of June 1850 was in this family; age; sex; color (white, black, or mulatto); profession, occupation, or trade of each male person over fifteen; value of real estate owned; place of birth, naming the state, territory, or country; married within the year; attended school within the year; persons over twenty who cannot read and write; whether deaf and dumb, blind, insane, idiotic, pauper, or convict

---

4 Nobles, Melissa, *Shades of Citizenship: Race and Census in Modern Politics* (Stanford: Stanford University Press, 2000), 32–33.

UNITED STATES FEDERAL CENSUS, 1790–1940

NONPOPULATION SCHEDULES: Agriculture, Manufacturing, Mortality, and Social Statistics

ADDITIONAL INFORMATION: For those born in the United States, enumerators were instructed to list the state in which the person was born. For those not born in the United States, enumerators were told to enter the person's native country.

CENSUS YEAR: 1850 Slave Schedule

INFORMATION COLLECTED: Name of owner; number of slaves; age; sex; color; fugitive from the state; number manumitted; and deaf, dumb, or idiotic

NONPOPULATION SCHEDULES: N/A

ADDITIONAL INFORMATION: The Delaware Slave Schedule is included at the end of the Sussex County returns. The District of Columbia Slave Schedule is included after the free population.

CENSUS YEAR: 1860

INFORMATION COLLECTED: Dwelling—houses in order of visitation; families numbered in the order of visitation; name of every person whose usual place of abode on the first day of June 1860 was in this family; age; sex; color (white, black, or mulatto); profession, occupation, or trade of each male person over fifteen; value of real estate; value of personal estate; place of birth, naming the state, territory, or country; married within the year; attended school within the year; persons over twenty who cannot read and write; deaf, dumb, blind, insane, idiotic, pauper, or convict

NONPOPULATION SCHEDULES: Agriculture, Manufacturing, Mortality, and Social Statistics

ADDITIONAL INFORMATION: N/A

CENSUS YEAR: 1860 Slave Schedule

INFORMATION COLLECTED: Name of owner; number of slaves; age; sex; color; fugitive from the state; number manumitted; deaf, dumb, or idiotic and number of slave houses

NONPOPULATION SCHEDULES: N/A

ADDITIONAL INFORMATION: N/A

UNITED STATES FEDERAL CENSUS, 1790–1940

CENSUS YEAR: 1870

INFORMATION COLLECTED: Dwelling—houses in order of visitation; families numbered in the order of visitation; name of every person whose usual place of abode on the first day of June 1870 was in this family; age; sex; color (white, black, mulatto, Chinese, or American Indian); profession, occupation, or trade of each person, male or female; value of real estate; value of personal estate; place of birth, naming state or territory or the country, if of foreign birth; parentage, father of foreign birth, mother of foreign birth; if born this year, state month; education, attended school within the year; cannot read; cannot write; deaf, dumb, blind, insane, or idiotic; constitutional relations: male citizens twenty-one and older; male citizens twenty-one and older, where right to vote is denied or abridged on other grounds than rebellion or other crime

NONPOPULATION SCHEDULES: Agriculture, Manufacturing, Mortality, and Social Statistics

ADDITIONAL INFORMATION: This was the first federal census to enumerate formerly enslaved African Americans. "C" was used for Chinese and "I" for American Indians.

After complaints that some regions were not fully counted, the bureau ordered a recount in several places including Indianapolis, Philadelphia, and New York.[5]

CENSUS YEAR: 1880

INFORMATION COLLECTED: Name of street; house number; dwelling house numbered in order of visitation; families numbered in order of visitation; name of every person whose usual place of abode on the first day of June 1880 was in this family; color: white (W), black (B), mulatto (M), Chinese (C), Indian (I); sex; age at last birthday prior to June 1880: if under one, give months in fraction, if born within the census year, give the month; relationship of each person to the head of household; single, married, divorced, widowed; married during the census year; profession, occupation, or trade of each person, male or female; number of months this person has been unemployed during the census year; blind; deaf or dumb; idiotic; insane; marred, crippled, bedridden, or otherwise disabled; attended school within the census year; cannot read; cannot write; place of birth, naming state or territory, or the country, if of foreign birth; place of birth of father, naming state or territory or country if foreign born; place of birth of mother, naming state or territory or country if foreign born

---

5 Anderson, Margo J. *The American Census: A Social History* – Second Edition. (New Haven: Yale University Press, 2015), 91.

NONPOPULATION SCHEDULES: Agriculture, Manufacturers, Mortality, Social Statistics, Defective, Dependent, and Delinquent

ADDITIONAL INFORMATION: Defective, dependent, and delinquent supplemental schedules collected information on the insane, idiots, deaf-mutes, blind, homeless children, people in prison, paupers, and indigents.

CENSUS YEAR: 1890

INFORMATION COLLECTED: Number of dwelling house in order of visitation; number of families in the dwelling house; number of persons in the dwelling house; number of this family in order of visitation; number of persons in this family; full name including initial of middle name; soldier, sailor, or marine during the American Civil War (Union or Confederate); widow of a soldier; relationship to head of family; race; sex; age; marital status; married within the last year; mother of how many children and how many were living; place of birth; birthplace of father; birthplace of mother; how many years in the United States; is this person naturalized? has the person taken naturalization papers out?; profession, trade, or occupation; number of months unemployed in the past year; months attended school in the past year; can read or write; speaks English and if not, what language?; suffering from an acute chronic disease and if so, what is the name of that disease and the length of time affected?; is the person defective of mind, sight, hearing, or speech or is the person crippled, maimed, or deformed? If yes, what was the name of his defect?; Is the person a prisoner, convict, homeless child, or pauper?; whether the home or farm was rented or owned; whether the home or farm was free from mortgage.

NONPOPULATION SCHEDULES: N/A

ADDITIONAL INFORMATION: This was the first census to distinguish between East Asian races. Races were white, black, mulatto, Quadroon, Octoroon, Chinese, Japanese, or Indian. Quadroons have one-quarter black ancestry and Octoroons have one-eighth black ancestry.

The US Census Bureau has bulletins available online of the Five Civilized Tribes, Six Nations of New York, Cherokees of Eastern North Carolina, Moqui Pueblo Indians of Arizona, and Pueblo Indians of New Mexico from the 1890 census. Go to census.gov and search for the "1890 Overview," click "Reports and statistics from the 1890 Census."

UNITED STATES FEDERAL CENSUS, 1790–1940

CENSUS YEAR: 1890 Veteran's Schedule

INFORMATION COLLECTED: House number; family number; name of surviving soldiers, sailors, marines, and widows; rank; company; names of regiment or vessel; date of enlistment; date of discharge; length of service; post office address; disability incurred; remarks

NONPOPULATION SCHEDULES: N/A

ADDITIONAL INFORMATION: N/A

CENSUS YEAR: 1900

INFORMATION COLLECTED: Name of street; house number; number of dwelling house in order of visitation; number of this family in order of visitation; name of every person whose usual place of abode on the first day of June 1, 1900; relationship to family head; sex; color or race; age; date of birth, month and year; age at last birthday; marital status; number of years married; number of children born and number now living; birthplace of person and parents; if foreign born, year of immigration, number of years in the United States, and whether naturalized; occupation, trade, or profession of each person ten years of age and older; months not employed; attended school in months; can read and write; speaks English; owned or rented; owned free or mortgaged; farm or house; number on farm schedule

NONPOPULATION SCHEDULES: Agriculture (destroyed)

ADDITIONAL INFORMATION: Information in the American Indian census: Indian name; tribe of this person; tribe of this person's father; tribe of this person's mother; fraction of person's lineage that is white; is this person living in polygamy?; is this person taxed?; if this person has acquired US citizenship, what year?; did this person acquire citizenship by receiving an allotment of land from the federal government?; is this person's house "movable" or "fixed"?

Notes on Taxation: An American Indian was "taxed" if detached from their tribe and living in the white community. These American Indians were subject to general taxation or acquired citizenship through a land allotment by the federal government.

Notes on Movable or Fixed: A person was "movable" if living in a temporary structure and "fixed" if living in a permanent dwelling of any kind.

CENSUS YEAR: 1910

INFORMATION COLLECTED:
Name of street; house number in cities and towns; dwelling number in order of visitation; number of this family in order of visitation; name of every person whose usual place of abode on April 15, 1910, was in this family; relationship to family head; sex; color or race; age at last birthday; marital status; number of years of present marriage; mother of how many children: number born and number now living; birthplace; birthplace of parents; year of US immigration; whether naturalized or alien; whether able to speak English or if not, language spoken; trade, profession, or occupation; general nature of industry, business, or establishment; employer, employee, or working on own account; if an employee, whether out of work on April 15, 1910; number of weeks out of work in 1909; can read or write; school attendance since September 1909; owned or rented; owned free or mortgaged; farm or house; number of farm schedule; whether a survivor of Union or Confederate army or navy; whether blind (both eyes); whether deaf or dumb

NONPOPULATION SCHEDULES: Agriculture (destroyed)

ADDITIONAL INFORMATION: Information collected on American Indians: tribe of this person; tribe of this person's father; tribe of this person's mother; proportion of this person's lineage that is American Indian; proportion of this person's lineage that is white; proportion of this person's lineage that is black; number of times married; is this person living in polygamy?; if yes, are his wives sisters?; name of educational institution where graduated; is this person taxed?; did this person receive an allotment of land from the federal government?, if so what year?; are they residing on his or her own land?; is this person living in a "civilized" or "aboriginal" dwelling?

A person was "civilized" if living in a log frame, brick, or stone house, etc. A person was "aboriginal" if living in a tent, tepee, cliff dwelling, etc.

A "taxed" person is defined the same as in 1900.

UNITED STATES FEDERAL CENSUS, 1790–1940

CENSUS YEAR: 1920

INFORMATION COLLECTED: Name of street; house number or farm; dwelling number in order of visitation; number of this family in order of visitation; name of every person whose usual place of abode on January 1, 1920, was in this family; relationship to family head; home owned or rented; if owned, free, or mortgaged; sex; color or race; age at last birthday; marital status; year of immigration; naturalized or alien; year of naturalization; attended school since Sept 1, 1919; can read or write; place of birth and mother tongue; father's place of birth and mother tongue; mother's place of birth and mother tongue; whether able to speak English; trade, profession, or occupation; business, industry, or establishment; employer, employee, or working on own account; number of farm schedule

NONPOPULATION SCHEDULES: Agriculture

CENSUS YEAR: 1930

INFORMATION COLLECTED: Name of street; house number or farm; dwelling number in order of visitation; number of this family in order of visitation; name of every person whose place of abode on April 1, 1930, was in this family; relationship to family head; home owned or rented; value or monthly rental; radio set; whether on a farm; sex; race; age at last birthday; marital status; age at first marriage; attended school or college since Sept. 1, 1929; can read or write; birthplace of person and parents; if foreign born, language spoken in home before coming to United States; year of immigration; naturalization; able to speak English; trade, profession, or occupation; business, industry, or establishment; class of worker; whether out of work; number on unemployment schedule; veteran; what war or expedition; number on farm schedule.

NONPOPULATION SCHEDULES: Agriculture, Unemployment Schedule (destroyed)

ADDITIONAL INFORMATION: According to the National Archives and Records Administration (NARA), the Unemployment Schedules and Supplemental Schedule have not been located. Enumerators were instructed to no longer use the "mulatto" classification. Persons with White and Black ancestry or American Indian and Black ancestry were reported as Black. A person with White and American Indian ancestry was reported as American Indian.
Mexican was used for people who were born in Mexico, whose parents were born in Mexico, and who did not fall into another racial category.

For foreign born, enumerators were instructed to distinguish Canada-French from Canada-English and Irish Free State from Northern Ireland.

Information on Supplemental Schedule for Indian population: Sheet number; line number; Name; Sex; Age; full American Indian or mixed lineage; tribe; person's post office; agency where enrolled.

CENSUS YEAR: 1940

INFORMATION COLLECTED: Name of street; house number in cities and towns; number of household in order of visitation; home owned or rented; value of home or monthly rental; does this household live on a farm?; name of every person whose usual place of residence on April 1, 1940, was in this household; relationship to family head; sex; race; age at last birthday; marital status; attended school or college since March 1, 1940; highest grade of school completed; birthplace, if foreign born, give country where birthplace was situated on January 1, 1937; citizenship of foreign born; residence on April 1, 1935: City, town, or village having more than 2,500 or more habitants; county; state or foreign territory; on a farm; for persons 14 years old and over: employed for pay during the week of March 24–30; employed in public emergency work (WPA, CCC); seeking work; has a job; engaged in housework, school, unable to work, or other; number of hours worked during the week of March 24–30; duration of unemployment up to March 30, 1940; trade, profession or kind of work; industry or business; class of worker; weeks worked in 1939; wages or salary; income of more than $50 from other sources; number on corresponding farm schedule

NONPOPULATION SCHEDULES: N/A

ADDITIONAL INFORMATION: Supplemental questions for persons listed on lines 14 and 29: name; place of birth for father and mother; mother tongue; veteran of the US military, wife, widow, or child under eighteen of veteran; war or military service; if child, is the veteran father dead?; for persons 14 years and older: federal social security number; deductions for federal old-age insurance or railroad retirement in 1939; amount of deductions from wage or salary; usual occupation; usual industry; class of worker; for women who are or have been married—has this person been married more than once?; age at first marriage; number of children ever born

Use state census records to supplement the US federal census and build a complete census profile for your ancestor. To find indexes and images online, search the catalogs on Ancestry.com, Familysearch.org, and Myheritage.com.

US Census Bureau: State Census Years[6]

This is a quick reference guide to the State and Territorial census records. They are a great resource to fill in the ten-year gap between the US Federal Censuses. These census records may contain information not captured in the US Federal Census.

STATE	CENSUS YEARS
Alabama	1820, 1821, 1823, 1850, 1855, 1866, 1907; 1907 & 1921 census of Confederate veterans
Alaska	1870, 1878, 1879, 1881, 1885, 1887, 1890–95, 1904–07, 1914, 1917
Arizona	1866, 1867, 1869, 1872, 1874, 1876, 1880, 1882
Arkansas	1823, 1829, 1865, 1911 census of Confederate veterans
California	1816, 1836, 1844, 1852—some earlier census records were taken in the late eighteenth century
Colorado	1861, 1866, 1885
Connecticut	1917 military census
Delaware	1782
District of Columbia	1803, 1867, 1878
Florida	1825, 1855, 1866, 1867, 1868, 1875, 1885, 1895, 1935, 1945
Georgia	1798, 1800, 1810, 1827, 1834, 1838, 1845, 1852, 1853, 1859, 1865, 1879
Hawaii	1866 (mostly Maui), 1878 (Hawaii, Maui, and Oahu), 1890, 1896
Idaho	No records exist
Illinois	1810, 1818, 1820, 1825, 1830, 1835, 1840, 1845, 1855, 1865
Indiana	1807, 1853, 1857, 1871, 1877, 1883, 1889, 1901, 1913, 1919, 1931
Iowa	1836, 1838, 1844, 1846, 1847, 1849, 1851, 1852, 1854, 1856, 1885, 1895, 1905, 1915, 1925
Kansas	1855, 1865, 1875, 1885, 1895, 1905, 1915, 1925
Kentucky	No records exist
Louisiana	1853,1858

---

6 "State Censuses," United States Census Bureau, https://www.census.gov/history/www/genealogy/other_resources/state_censuses.html.

STATE	CENSUS YEARS
Maine	1837
Maryland	1776, 1778
Massachusetts	1855, 1865
Michigan	1837, 1845, 1854, 1864, 1874, 1884, 1888, 1894, 1904
Minnesota	1849, 1853, 1855, 1857, 1865, 1875, 1885, 1895, 1905
Mississippi	1801, 1805, 1808, 1810, 1816, 1818, 1820, 1822, 1823, 1824, 1825, 1830, 1833, 1837, 1840, 1841, 1845, 1850, 1853, 1860, 1866
Missouri	1797, 1803, 1817, 1819, 1840, 1844, 1852, 1856, 1860, 1864, 1876, 1880
Montana	1862–1863 Census of miners
Nebraska	1854, 1855, 1856, 1865, 1869, 1885
Nevada	1862, 1863, 1875
New Hampshire	No records exist
New Jersey	1855, 1865, 1875, 1885, 1895, 1905, 1915
New Mexico	1790, 1823, 1845, 1885
New York	1790, 1825, 1835, 1845, 1855, 1865, 1875, 1892, 1905, 1915, 1925
North Carolina	1786
North Dakota	1885, 1915, 1925
Ohio	No records exist
Oklahoma	1890, 1907
Oregon	1842, 1843, 1845, 1849, 1850, 1853, 1854, 1855, 1856, 1857, 1858, 1859, 1865, 1870, 1875, 1885, 1895, 1905
Pennsylvania	No records exist
Rhode Island	1774, 1777, 1782, 1865, 1875, 1885, 1905, 1915, 1925, 1935
South Carolina	1825, 1839, 1869, 1875
South Dakota	1885, 1895, 1905, 1915, 1925, 1935, 1945
Tennessee	1891
Texas	1829–1836
Utah	1856
Vermont	No records exist
Virginia	1782, 1783, 1784, 1785, 1786
Washington	1856, 1857, 1858, 1860, 1871, 1874, 1877, 1878, 1879, 1880, 1881, 1883, 1885, 1887, 1889, 1891, 1892, 1898
West Virginia	No records exist
Wisconsin	1836, 1838, 1842, 1846, 1847, 1855, 1865, 1875, 1885, 1895, 1905
Wyoming	1875, 1878

```
┌─────────────────────────────────────────────────────────────┐
│                                                               │
│                         TIP                                   │
│   ═══════════════════════════════════════════════════════    │
│                                                               │
│   Voter registrations, which will be discussed later, can be  │
│   helpful in determining your ancestor's location during the  │
│   off years of federal and state census records.             │
│                                                               │
└─────────────────────────────────────────────────────────────┘
```

NONPOPULATION SCHEDULES

The nonpopulation schedules for the US census were used to identify resources and trends within the population. These schedules include Agriculture; Defective, Dependent, and Delinquent; Products of Industry; Manufacturing; Mortality; Social Statistics; and Veterans Schedule. Mortality Schedules taken in 1850, 1860, 1870, and 1880 enumerate persons who had died within a year of the enumeration date.[7]

Search for "US Federal Census Mortality Schedules, 1850–1885" on Ancestry .com.

Mortality Schedules should contain the following information:[8]

- Name
- Age at last birthday
- Sex
- Race
- Marital status
- Profession, occupation, or trade
- State, territory, or country of birth of person and parents
- Length of residence in county
- Month in which person died
- Disease or cause of death
- Place where disease contracted (if not at place of death)
- Name of attending physician

---

7 Hinckley, Kathy W. *Your Guide to The Federal Census for Genealogists, Researchers and Family Historians.* Cincinnati, OH: Betterway Books, 2002.

8 "Mortality Schedules," United States Census Bureau https://www.census.gov/history/www/genealogy/other _resources/mortality_schedules.html.

VITAL RECORDS RESEARCH

Now that you have interviewed family members and built a census profile for your ancestors, you should have a good idea where your ancestors lived. Get to know the county, city, and state where they resided, including resources available for family history research. This will help you when looking for vital records for your ancestors and understanding the privacy laws governing access to these records.

Vital records (birth, marriage, divorce, and death) are considered primary sources because they are typically created at the time of the event with the exception of delayed birth certificates. Standardization of vital records reporting varies from state to state. Even if there was a law requiring statewide registration, there was no guarantee of immediate compliance. Some states did not require birth certificates until the 1910s. Anyone born before that date may not have a birth certificate or record. In those cases, the delayed birth certificate becomes the official record of birth and can be useful. For example, in Virginia, it provides:

- Name
- Sex
- Number of child in order of birth
- If a twin, first or second
- Were parents married?
- Names of parents, race, birthplace, and age at time of this birth
- Occupation
- Witness and relationship
- Evidence submitted to the bureau

In the absence of vital records, you can use newspapers, journals, census records, and family Bibles. Birth records are useful to determine the exact birth date and location, parents' names, parents' birth locations, parents' occupations, and other information. Access to copies of vital records may be restricted to immediate family members or legal representatives due to privacy. Because birth records are created at the time of the event, presumably, the information is accurate. However, I have seen cases where a father's name is not recorded on the birth record or the name of another man is recorded instead of the biological father. If the father is unknown, DNA can help resolve this mystery.

Marriage records include marriage licenses and marriage certificates. Depending on the state and county requirements, the information in these documents varies. Marriage records are available at the county level in probate records, in the records of the town clerk, or at the vital records office. Marriage records will typically provide the name of the bride and groom; their ages, birth locations, and current residence; witnesses; date of marriage license; date of marriage; names of the bride's and groom's parents; previous marriages; and whether either party was single, divorced, or widowed prior to the marriage.

Divorce records are generated at the dissolution of a marriage and are typically found in the county courthouse. These records include the names of the husband and wife, date of marriage, date of divorce, marriage location, cause for divorce, number of children, occupation, and other information.

TIP

Some vital records at the county level may have been destroyed due to burning of the courthouse during the American Civil War or natural disasters such as a fire, hurricane, or other weather-related damage. Check the local historical societies and archives to learn what records are available for research.

Death record availability can vary state-by-state due to privacy restrictions. I always say a death certificate is only as good as the informant. The informant on a death record provides information about the decedent such as birth date, birth location, spouse, age, and parents' names and birth locations. If the person acting as the informant has limited knowledge about the decedent, the death certificate will not have as much information as is needed to establish relationships, go back further, or make a connection with a possible relative. This point is critical when looking at death certificates for those who were formerly enslaved or immigrants.

Death certificates contain a variety of information. Typically, the following items are included:

- Name of deceased
- Birth date and location
- Death date and location
- Age
- Sex
- Color
- Marital status
- Name of wife or husband
- Occupation
- Cause of death
- Contributing factors to death
- Informant
- Burial, cremation, or removal
- Undertaker

Some earlier death records were kept by towns, cities, and counties depending on the year the settlements were founded. In New England, some records were kept in the mid-1800s or earlier. These records are available in printed publications, on microfilm, or have been transcribed online.

> ## TIP
>
> Sometimes the relationship of the informant to the decedent is recorded on the death certificate. If the informant's name is not familiar to you, then do some research to determine what the informant's relationship was to the decedent. They could be part of the FAN club.

To find the records, search the Familysearch.org wiki for the town or county of interest. Click on "Vital Records," and you'll see the wiki page has links to online records for Ancestry.com, Familysearch.org, Findmypast.com, Myheritage.com, and other websites. The wiki might include some printed resources, as well. Other sources of death information include cemetery records, church records, newspapers, and the Social Security Death Index (SSDI).

For more vital records online, in addition to the "US Vital Records at a Glance" table below, search the collections at Ancestry.com, Findmypast.com, and Myheritage.com. Don't forget to search local resources for vital records that have been digitized and indexed by state archives, state vital records offices, local libraries, and historical societies. Information in the following table has been pulled from multiple sources based on a state-by-state comparison.

Alabama

YEAR	ONLINE AVAILABILITY	ORDERING COPIES OF RECORDS AND RESTRICTIONS
1908: Statewide Registration	**BIRTH RECORDS** *Familysearch.org:* Alabama Births, 1881–1930 Index **MARRIAGE RECORDS** *Ancestry.com:* Alabama, County Marriages, 1805–1967; Alabama, Select Marriages, 1816–1942; Alabama, Marriage Index, 1800–1969; Alabama, Marriage Indexes, 1814–1935; Alabama, Compiled Marriages from Selected Counties, 1809–1920 *Familysearch.org:* Alabama County Marriages, 1809–1950; Alabama Marriages, 1816–1957; Alabama County Marriages, 1818–1936 *Findmypast.com:* Alabama Marriages, 1816–1957 **DIVORCE RECORDS** Alabama Divorce Index, 1950–1959 **DEATH RECORDS** *Ancestry.com:* Alabama, Death Index, 1908–1959; Alabama, Deaths and Burials Index, 1881–1974 *Familysearch.org:* Alabama Deaths and Burials, 1881–1952 Index *Findmypast.com:* Alabama Deaths, 1908–1974	Birth, Marriage, Divorce, and Death Records are available from the Alabama Center for Health Statistics, Alabama Public Health Department, for a fee. **BIRTH RECORDS:** 1908 **MARRIAGE:** 1936 **DIVORCE:** 1950 **DEATH RECORDS:** 1908 **BIRTH RECORDS:** Alabama required individual counties to register births starting in 1881. **MARRIAGE RECORDS PRIOR TO AUGUST 1936:** Available at the probate court for each county. **DIVORCE RECORDS PRIOR TO 1950:** Contact the circuit court in the county where the divorce was granted. **RESTRICTIONS:** Birth certificates are restricted for those born within the last 125 years. Marriage and Divorce certificates are not restricted. Death Records are restricted for access for 25 years from the date of death.

Alaska

YEAR	ONLINE AVAILABILITY	ORDERING COPIES OF RECORDS AND RESTRICTIONS
1913: Statewide Registration	*Ancestry.com:* Alaska Vital Records, 1818–1963 *Familysearch.org:* Alaska Vital Records, 1816–1959	Birth, Marriage, Divorce, and Death Records are available from Health Analytics and Vital Records, for a fee. **BIRTH, MARRIAGE, & DEATH RECORDS:** 1913 **RESTRICTIONS:** Birth Records are strictly confidential for 100 years and 50 years for all other records.

YEAR	ONLINE AVAILABILITY	ORDERING COPIES OF RECORDS AND RESTRICTIONS
1909: Statewide Registration	**BIRTH RECORDS** *Arizona Department of Health Services:* Public Birth Certificates, 1855–1941 *Ancestry.com:* Arizona Birth Records, 1881–1948; Arizona Birth Records, 1880–1935; Arizona Births & Christenings, 1909–1917 *Familysearch.org and Findmypast.com:* Arizona Births & Christenings, 1909–1917	Copies of the Birth and Death Certificates can be ordered from the county health department or Arizona Department of Health Services: **BIRTH CERTIFICATES:** 1909 **DEATH CERTIFICATES:** 1909
	MARRIAGE RECORDS *Ancestry.com:* Arizona, County Marriage Records, 1865–1972; Arizona Marriage Collection, 1864–1982; Arizona Select Marriages, 1888–1908 *Familysearch.org:* Arizona County Marriage, 1871–1964 *Familysearch.org and Findmypast.com:* Arizona Marriages, 1865–1949	**RESTRICTIONS:** Birth and Death Certificates are available on the Arizona Department of Health Services website. Birth Certificates are released 75 years after the individual's birth, and death certificates are 50 years after the person's death.
	DIVORCE RECORDS In the district court of each county until 1912. After 1912, the records are at the superior court.	Arizona is a closed records state restricting access to Birth and Death Records to immediate family members and selected others.
	DEATH RECORDS *Arizona Department of Health Services:* Public Death Certificates, 1870–1966 *Ancestry.com:* Arizona Death Records, 1887–1960; Arizona Select Deaths and Burials, 1910–1911, 1933–1994. Arizona County Coroner and Death Records, 1881–1971 *Familysearch.org:* Arizona Deaths, 1870–1951 *Findmypast.com:* Arizona Deaths and Burials, 1881–1917	

YEAR	ONLINE AVAILABILITY	ORDERING COPIES OF RECORDS AND RESTRICTIONS
1914: Statewide Registration	**BIRTH RECORDS** *Familysearch.org:* Arkansas Births and Christenings, 1812–1965 **MARRIAGE RECORDS** *Ancestry.com:* Arkansas County Marriages Index, 1837–1957; Arkansas Marriage Index, 1933–1939; Arkansas Marriages, 1779–1992; Arkansas Compiled Marriages, 1851–1900; Arkansas Marriages, 1820–1949; Arkansas Compiled Marriages, 1779–1850 *Familysearch.org:* Arkansas County Marriages, 1837–1957; Arkansas Marriages, 1837–1944 **DIVORCE RECORDS** *Ancestry.com and Familysearch.org:* Arkansas Divorce Index, 1923–1939 **DEATH RECORDS** *Ancestry.com:* Arkansas Death Index, 1914–1950 *Arkansas Department of Health:* Death Certificates Search 1935–1961 *Familysearch.org:* Arkansas Death and Burials Index, 1882–1929, 1945–1963; Arkansas Death Index, 1914–1950	Copies are available from the County Health Department or Arkansas Department of Health: **BIRTH CERTIFICATES:** 1914 **MARRIAGE RECORDS:** January 1917 **DIVORCE RECORDS:** January 1923 **DEATH CERTIFICATES:** 1914 **BIRTH RECORDS:** Limited Birth Records from 1881 from Little Rock and Fort Smith **DEATH RECORDS:** Limited Death Records from 1881–1914 are available for Little Rock and Fort Smith. **RESTRICTIONS:** Copies of Birth Certificates are restricted for those born within the last 100 years. Death Records that are more than 50 years old can be released to the public. Marriage and Divorce Records are not available to the general public. They are available to relatives and designated representatives. Academic researchers have access to records.

California

YEAR	ONLINE AVAILABILITY	ORDERING COPIES OF RECORDS AND RESTRICTIONS
1905: Statewide Registration	**BIRTH RECORDS** *Ancestry.com & Familysearch.org:* California Birth Index, 1905–1995 *Familysearch.org & Findmypast.com:* California Births & Christenings, 1812–1988 **MARRIAGE RECORDS** *Ancestry.com:* California Marriage Index 1960–1985; California Marriage Index 1949–1959 *Familysearch.org & Findmypast.com:* California County Marriages 1850–1952; California Marriages, 1850–1945 *Familysearch.org:* California Marriage Index, 1960–1985 **DIVORCE RECORDS** *Ancestry.com:* California Divorce Index 1966–1984 **DEATH RECORDS** *Ancestry.com & Familysearch.org:* California Death Index, 1940–1997; California Death Index, 1905–1939	Order copies of records from California Department of Public Health, for a fee. **BIRTH RECORDS:** 1905 **MARRIAGE RECORDS:** 1949–1986, 1998–1999, 2009 to present **DIVORCE RECORDS:** 1962–1984 **DEATH RECORDS:** 1905 For Birth Records and Death Records prior to July 1905, contact the County Recorder. For Marriages contact the County Recorder where the Marriage License was issued, there might be fees associated with obtaining copies of these records. **RESTRICTIONS:** California provides a certified informational copy for any interested person.

YEAR	ONLINE AVAILABILITY	ORDERING COPIES OF RECORDS AND RESTRICTIONS
1907: Statewide Registration	**VITAL RECORDS** Colorado Department of Personnel & Administration, Historical Records Index Search, has birth, marriage, divorce, and death records. **MARRIAGE RECORDS** *Ancestry.com:* Colorado County Marriages and State Indexes, 1862 to 2006; Colorado Statewide Marriage Index, 1900 to 1939 *Familysearch.org:* Colorado County Marriages, 1864–1995; Colorado Statewide Marriage Index, 1853 to 2006 **DIVORCE RECORDS** *Ancestry.com:* Colorado Divorce Index, 1851–1985 *Myheritage.com:* Colorado Divorces, 1878–2004	Birth and Death Records are available from the Vital Record Section, Colorado Department of Public Health and Environment, for a fee. **BIRTH RECORDS:** 1910 **DEATH RECORDS:** 1900 Some Birth and Death Records prior to 1907 are available in the counties and towns. **RESTRICTIONS:** Copies of Birth Certificates are restricted to family members or genealogists with a notarized signed release from the immediate family members. Check the Colorado Department of Public Health for Eligibility Requirements.

YEAR	ONLINE AVAILABILITY	ORDERING COPIES OF RECORDS AND RESTRICTIONS
1897: Statewide Registration	**BIRTH RECORDS** *Ancestry.com:* Connecticut Town Birth Records, pre-1870 (Barbour Collection) *Familysearch.org:* Connecticut Births and Christenings, 1649–1906 **MARRIAGE RECORDS** *Ancestry.com:* Connecticut, Town Marriage Records, pre-1870 (Barbour Collection); Connecticut Marriage Index, 1959–2012; Connecticut Marriage Index, 1620–1926 *Familysearch.org:* Connecticut Marriage Index 1959–2001; Connecticut Marriages, 1630–1997 *Myheritage.com:* Connecticut Marriage Index, 1996–2002 **DIVORCE RECORDS** *Familysearch.org:* Connecticut Divorce Index, 1968–1997 *Findmypast.com:* Connecticut Divorces, 1960–2010 **DEATH RECORDS** *AmericanAncestors.org:* Connecticut Marriages and Deaths, 1790–1833; Connecticut Vital Records to 1870 *Ancestry.com:* Connecticut Death and Burial Index, 1650–1934; Connecticut Town Death Records, pre-1870 (Barbour Collection) *Familysearch.org:* Connecticut Death Index, 1949–2001; Connecticut Death and Burials, 1772–1934 *Findmypast.com:* Connecticut Deaths, 1949–2010	Copies of Birth, Marriage, and Death Certificates are available from the Connecticut Department of Health. **BIRTH:** 1897 **MARRIAGE:** 1897 **DEATH:** 1897 **VITAL RECORDS:** For records prior to 1897, contact the town clerk's office **DIVORCE RECORDS:** Copies of these records are available at the Superior Court where the divorce was granted. **RESTRICTIONS:** Copies of Birth Certificates are restricted to those born within the last 100 years.

YEAR	ONLINE AVAILABILITY	ORDERING COPIES OF RECORDS AND RESTRICTIONS
Statewide Registration: Births & Deaths (1881) Marriages (1847)	**BIRTH RECORDS** *Ancestry.com:* Delaware, Birth Records, 1800-1932 *Familysearch.org:* Delaware Vital Records, 1650-1974; Delaware Births and Christenings, 1710–1896; Delaware State Birth Records, 1861–1922 **MARRIAGE RECORDS** *Ancestry.com*: Delaware Marriage Records, 1750–1954; Delaware Marriage Records, 1806–1933; Delaware Marriage Records, 1744–1912 **DEATH RECORDS** *Ancestry.com:* Delaware Death Records, 1811–1933 *Family search.org:* Delaware Death and Burials,1815–1955; Delaware Death Records, 1855–1961; *Delaware Public Archives:* The collection Gateway has a searchable index for death registers.	Vital Records can be ordered from Delaware Department of Health and Social Services **BIRTH RECORDS:** 1913 **DEATH RECORDS:** 1913 **RESTRICTIONS:** Delaware Public Archives has birth records older than 72 years and marriages older than 40 years.

YEAR	ONLINE AVAILABILITY	ORDERING COPIES OF RECORDS AND RESTRICTIONS
Statewide Registration: Births and Deaths (1874) Marriages (1811)	**BIRTH RECORDS** *Ancestry.com & Findmypast.com:* District of Columbia, Select Births and Christenings, 1830–1955 *Familysearch.org:* District of Columbia, Birth Returns, 1874–1897 **MARRIAGE RECORDS** *Ancestry.com:* District of Columbia, Marriage Records, 1810–1953; District of Columbia, Compiled Marriage Index, 1830–1921. *Familysearch.org:* District of Columbia Marriages, 1811–1950 *Findmypast.com:* District of Columbia Marriages, 1830–1921 **DEATH RECORDS** *Ancestry.com:* District of Columbia, Select Deaths and Burials Index, 1769–1960 *Findmypast.com:* District of Columbia Deaths and Burials, 1840–1964 *FamilySearch.org:* District of Columbia Deaths and Burials, 1840–1864; District of Columbia Deaths, 1874–1961	Birth and Death Records can be ordered from the District of Columbia Department of Health Vital Records **BIRTH RECORDS:** 1874 **DEATH RECORDS:** 1874 **DIVORCE RECORDS:** The index of Divorce Records prior to Sept. 1956 are available at the Clerk of the US District Court **RESTRICTIONS:** Copies of Birth Certificates are restricted to those born within the last 100 years. Death Records are public 50 years after the date of death. Check the District of Columbia Department of Health website for eligibility requirements. Records from 1863 to Sept. 16, 1956, are housed at Washington National Records Center in Suitland, Maryland. You must know the Divorce Case Number and make an appointment at least 24 hours in advance. Records after Sept. 16, 1956, are at the Clerk of the Superior Court.

Florida

YEAR	ONLINE AVAILABILITY	ORDERING COPIES OF RECORDS AND RESTRICTIONS
Statewide Registration: Births & Deaths (1899) Marriages (1927)	**BIRTH RECORDS** *Familysearch.org:* Florida Births and Christenings, 1880–1935 **MARRIAGE RECORDS** *Ancestry.com:* Florida Marriage Collection, 1822–1875 and 1927–2001 *Familysearch.org:* Florida County, Marriages, 1830–1957 **DIVORCE RECORDS** *Ancestry.com & Familysearch.org:* Florida Divorce Index, 1927–2001 *Myheritage.com:* Florida Divorces, 1970–1999 **DEATH RECORDS** *Familysearch.org:* Florida Death Records Index, 1877–1939; Florida Death Index, 1877–1998	Order Birth and Death Certificates from Florida Department of Health, Office of Vital Statistics. Marriage and Divorce Records until June 1927 are kept by the Clerk of the Court where the marriage license was issued and the divorce was granted. The Florida Department of Health, Bureau of Vital Statistics, has records after June 1927. **RESTRICTIONS:** Copies of Birth Certificates are restricted to family members and legal representatives. For Death Records, anyone in Florida can order a Death Certificate without cause of death. "Cause of death" becomes public information 50 years following the death date.

Georgia

YEAR	ONLINE AVAILABILITY	ORDERING COPIES OF RECORDS AND RESTRICTIONS
Statewide Registration: Births & Deaths (1919)	**BIRTH RECORDS** *Ancestry.com, Familysearch.org:* Georgia Births and Christenings, 1754–1960 **MARRIAGE RECORDS** *Ancestry.com:* Georgia Compiled Marriages, 1754–1850; Georgia Marriages, 1699–1944; Georgia Marriages, 1851–1900 *Familysearch.org:* Georgia Marriages, 1808–1967 **DEATH RECORDS** *Familysearch.org:* Georgia Deaths, 1914–1927; Georgia Deaths, 1928–1940; Georgia Death Index, 1933–1998	Order copies of Birth Certificates from Georgia Department of Public Health. **RESTRICTIONS:** Copies of Birth Certificates are restricted to family members or legal representative. Georgia Marriage Records may be available at the county level and from the Georgia Department of Archives. Information on divorces prior to 1853 can be found at the Georgia Department of Archives and History. State Office of Vital Records can search and confirm divorces from June 1952 to August 1996. Before and after these dates, confirmation is available from the Clerk of Superior Court in the county where the divorce was granted. **DEATH RECORDS:** Available from 1919 to the present from Georgia Department of Health. Certified of Death Records are available to family members or legal representatives of the family.

YEAR	ONLINE AVAILABILITY	ORDERING COPIES OF RECORDS AND RESTRICTIONS
1842: Statewide Registration	**BIRTH RECORDS** *Familysearch.org:* Hawaii Births and Christenings, 1852–1933 **MARRIAGE RECORDS** *Familysearch.org:* Hawaii Marriages, 1826–1922; Hawaii Marriages, 1826–1954 **DEATH RECORDS** *Familysearch.org:* Hawaii, Deaths and Burials, 1862–1919	Ordering Birth Certificates: State of Hawaii, Department of Health Vital Records, available at Familysearch.org **RESTRICTIONS:** Copies of Birth Certificates are restricted to those born within the last 100 years. State registration of divorce did not start until 1950. These were usually recorded in the Circuit Court.

Idaho

YEAR	ONLINE AVAILABILITY	ORDERING COPIES OF RECORDS AND RESTRICTIONS
1911: Statewide Registration 1907-1911: Counties were required to record births	**BIRTH RECORDS** *Familysearch.org:* Idaho, Birth Index, 1861–1911; Idaho County Births and Deaths Records 1883–1929 *Findmypast.com:* Idaho Births & Baptisms, 1856–1965 **MARRIAGE RECORDS** *Ancestry.com:* Idaho Marriage Records, 1863–1967; Idaho County Marriage Records, 1863–1967 *Findmypast.com:* Idaho County Marriages, 1864–1950 **DIVORCE RECORDS:** *Ancestry.com*: Idaho Divorce Index, 1947–1967 **DEATH RECORDS** *Ancestry.com*: Idaho Death Index, 1890–1964 *BYU Special Collections:* Idaho Death Index, 1911–1951 *Familysearch.org*: Idaho Death Certificates, 1938–1961 *Findmypast.com:* Idaho Death Certificates, 1911–1937	Order copies of Vital Records from Idaho Bureau of Vital Statistics and Health. Birth and Death Records from July 1911. Marriage and Divorce Records from May 1947. Older records may be obtained from county files. **MARRIAGE RECORDS**: Registers and Original Marriage Applications may be found at the county recorders. **DIVORCE RECORDS:** Available at the clerk of the District Court were the divorce was granted. **RESTRICTIONS:** Copies of birth certificates are restricted to those born within the last 100 years. Death records are not restricted if they are more than 50 years after the death. If less than 50 years, records are only available to close family members.

YEAR	ONLINE AVAILABILITY	ORDERING COPIES OF RECORDS AND RESTRICTIONS
Statewide Registration: Births & Deaths (1916) Marriages (1962)	**BIRTH RECORDS** *Familysearch.org:* Illinois Statewide Birth Indexes, 1824–1940; Cook County Illinois Birth Certificates, 1878–1938 **MARRIAGE RECORDS** *Ancestry.com:* Illinois Marriages, 1851–1900; Illinois Compiled Marriages, 1791–1850; Illinois County Marriages, 1800–1940 *Familysearch.org*: Illinois Marriages, 1815–1935; Illinois State Archives: Statewide Marriage Index, 1763–1900 **DEATH RECORDS** *Ancestry & Familysearch.org*: Illinois, Deaths and Stillbirths, 1916–1947 *Illinois State Archives:* Illinois Statewide Death Index, Pre-1916; Illinois Death Certificate Database, 1916–1950	**BIRTH RECORDS:** County clerks recorded births before 1916 **MARRIAGE RECORDS:** The county clerk's office has Marriage Registers, Marriage Returns, Licenses, and Applications. **DIVORCE RECORDS:** Available from the County Clerk of the Circuit Court in the county where the divorce occurred. **DEATH RECORDS:** Available from the Illinois Department of Public Health, the Illinois State Genealogical Society, and the Illinois State Archive Reference Room. Check the websites of each for the latest fees and forms. **RESTRICTIONS:** Uncertified copies of Birth and Death Records are available for genealogical research if the birth was more than 75 years ago and the death more than 20 years ago.

Indiana

YEAR	ONLINE AVAILABILITY	ORDERING COPIES OF RECORDS AND RESTRICTIONS
Statewide Registration: Birth (1907) Marriages (1800) Deaths (1900)	**BIRTH RECORDS** *Ancestry.com:* Indiana Births, 1880–1920 *Familysearch.org and Findmypast.com:* Indiana Births and Christenings, 1773–1933 **MARRIAGE RECORDS** *Ancestry.com:* Indiana Marriages, 1810–2001; Indiana Marriage Collection, 1800–1941 *FamilySearch.org:* Indiana Marriages, 1811–2007 *Findmypast.com:* Indiana Marriages, 1811–1959; Indiana Marriages, 1790–1992 *Indiana State Library:* Indiana Marriages through 1850; Indiana Marriages 1958–2015 *Indiana Supreme Court, Division of State Court Administration:* 1993–Present, Marriage License Public Lookup **DEATH RECORDS** *Ancestry.com*: Indiana Deaths, 1882–1920 *Allen County Public Library:* Pre-1882 Indiana Deaths *Familysearch.org:* Indiana Death Index, 1882–1920	**BIRTH AND DEATH RECORDS:** Contact the Indiana State Department of Health and check the website for updates. **MARRIAGE RECORDS:** Usually in the county where the marriage took place and may date from the formation of the county. **DIVORCE RECORDS:** The laws regarding, and who had power to grant, them changed over the years. Check the court records for the county where your ancestors may have filed for divorce. **RESTRICTIONS:** Birth and Death records are limited to those with a direct interest.

YEAR	ONLINE AVAILABILITY	ORDERING COPIES OF RECORDS AND RESTRICTIONS
JULY 1, 1880: Statewide Registration	**BIRTH RECORDS** *Ancestry.com:* Iowa Births and Christenings Index, 1800–1999 *FamilySearch.org:* Iowa Births and Christenings, 1830–1950; Iowa, County Births, 1880–1935 **MARRIAGE RECORDS** *Familysearch.org, Findmypast.com,* **and** *Myheritage.com:* Iowa Marriages, 1809–1992 *Ancestry.com:* Iowa, Marriage Records, 1880–1940 *Familysearch.org:* Iowa, County Marriages, 1838–1934 **DEATH RECORDS** *Ancestry.com, Familysearch.org, Findmypast.com,* **and** *Myheritage.com:* Iowa Deaths and Burials, 1850–1990 *Familysearch.org:* Iowa County Death Records, 1880–1992; Iowa Death Records, 1921–1940	Birth, Marriage and Death Records can be ordered from Iowa Department of Public Health. Check their website for updates and details. Birth Records are available from the state beginning July 1, 1880; Marriage Records beginning July 1, 1916; and Death Records beginning July 1, 1904. Some early Divorce Records are available in the county District Court. Check the county website for updates including forms and fees. In 1906, County Clerks of the Court were required to report all divorces to the Iowa Department of Health. **RESTRICTIONS:** Entitled persons include the person named on the record, immediate family or legal representative, or guardian with proof of entitlement. Records of Vital Statistics recorded at the state level must be older than 75 years to be made public by the State Archives.

Kansas

YEAR	ONLINE AVAILABILITY	ORDERING COPIES OF RECORDS AND RESTRICTIONS
Statewide Registration: Births & Deaths (1911) Marriages (1913)	**BIRTH RECORDS** *Ancestry.com:* Kansas Births and Christenings, 1885–1911 *Familysesarch.org:* Kansas Births and Christenings, 1818–1936 **MARRIAGE RECORDS** *Ancestry.com:* Kansas Marriage Index from Select Counties, 1854–73 *Familysearch.org:* Kansas Compiled Marriage Index, 1811–1911; Kansas Marriages, 1840–1935 *Kansas Historical Society:* Kansas Marriage Index, 1854–1861 **DEATH RECORDS** *Ancestry.com & Familysearch.org:* Kansas Deaths and Burials Index, 1885–1930	**BIRTH & DEATH RECORDS:** Copies of records starting from July 1911 are available from the Office of Vital Statistics. **MARRIAGE RECORDS:** Copies of records starting from July 1913 are available from the Office of Vital Statistics. **DIVORCE RECORDS:** Check the Clerk of the Court in the county where the divorce was granted. Starting in July 1951, Divorce Certificates were filed with the Office of Vital Statistics. **RESTRICTIONS:** Only immediate family members can request records after 1940. For records prior to 1940, individuals must be related as at least a cousin.

YEAR	ONLINE AVAILABILITY	ORDERING COPIES OF RECORDS AND RESTRICTIONS
Births: 1852 in some counties and Statewide in 1911 Marriages: Some counties have records from the 1780s and Statewide in 1958 Deaths: 1852 in some counties and Statewide in 1911	***Kentucky Vital Records Index from the University of Kentucky:*** Kentucky Marriage Index, 1973–1993; Kentucky Divorce Index, 1973–1993; Kentucky Death Index, 1911–1986 & 1987–1992 **BIRTH RECORDS** *Ancestry.com:* Kentucky Birth Records, 1847–1911 *Findmypast.com:* Kentucky Birth Index, 1911–1999 **MARRIAGE RECORDS** *Ancestry.com:* Kentucky Marriages, 1851–1900; Kentucky County Marriages, 1783–1965 *Familysearch.org:* Kentucky Marriages Index, 1785–1979; Kentucky County Marriages, 1797–1954 *Findmypast.com*: Kentucky Marriages, 1973–1999 **DIVORCE RECORDS** *Ancestry.com:* Kentucky Divorce Records, 1962–2005 **DEATH RECORDS** *Ancestry.com:* Kentucky Death Records, 1852–1965 *Familysearch.org:* Kentucky Deaths and Burials, 1843–1970 *Findmypast.com:* Kentucky Deaths, 1911–1999	Birth, Marriage, and Death Records from 1911 can be ordered from the Kentucky Office of Vital Statistics. Check the website for forms and instructions on fees.

Louisiana

YEAR	ONLINE AVAILABILITY	ORDERING COPIES OF RECORDS AND RESTRICTIONS
Statewide Registration: Births and Deaths (1911)	**BIRTH RECORDS** *Familysearch.org:* Louisiana Births and Christenings, 1811–1830 and 1854–1934 *Louisiana Secretary of State*: Louisiana Birth Records (Includes Orleans Parish records as early as 1790), 1819–1917 **MARRIAGE RECORDS** *Familysearch.org:* Louisiana Parish Marriages, 1837–1957 *Louisiana Secretary of State:* Orleans Parish Records, 1831–1966 **DEATH RECORDS** *Familysearch.org:* Jefferson Parish Deaths, 1850–1875; Statewide Index, 1894–1954 *Louisiana Secretary of State:* Louisiana Death Records, 1911–1967	**BIRTH RECORDS:** Some records prior to 1918 are available at the Louisiana State Archives. Check the website for more details. **MARRIAGE RECORDS:** Contact the Clerk of Court for all parishes except Orleans. The Louisiana State Archives has records for Orleans Parish. **DIVORCE RECORDS:** Clerks in the District Courts of the Parish where the divorce occurred. **DEATH RECORDS:** Prior to 1911 to 1967, records are available at the Louisiana State Archives. Some earlier Death Records are available, so check website for more details. **RESTRICTIONS:** Copies of Birth Records are restricted to those born within the last 100 years. Death records are not restricted if it is more than 50 years after the death.

YEAR	ONLINE AVAILABILITY	ORDERING COPIES OF RECORDS AND RESTRICTIONS
1892: Statewide Registration	**VITAL RECORDS** *Familysearch.org:* Maine Vital Records, 1670–1921 **BIRTH RECORDS:** See above **MARRIAGE RECORDS** *Familysearch.org:* Maine Marriage Records, 1771–1907; *Maine State Archives:* Marriage Index, 1862–1967 and 1977–1996 **DIVORCE RECORDS** *Ancestry.com:* Maine Divorce Records, 1798–1981 **DEATH RECORDS** *Ancestry.com:* Maine Death Records, 1761–1922 *Familysearch.org:* Maine Deaths and Burials, 1841–1910	Births, Marriages, and Deaths Records before 1892 are available at the town level; after 1892, contact the Vital Records Office. Divorce Records prior to 1892 are housed in the clerk's office of the District Court where the divorce was granted.

Maryland

YEAR	ONLINE AVAILABILITY	ORDERING COPIES OF RECORDS AND RESTRICTIONS
Statewide Registration: Births & Deaths (1898) Marriage (1777)	**BIRTH RECORDS** *Familysearch.org:* Maryland Births and Christenings, 1639–1955 **MARRIAGE RECORDS** *Familysearch.org:* Maryland Marriages, 1666–1970; Maryland County Marriages, 1658–1940 **DEATH RECORDS** *Familysearch.org:* Maryland Deaths and Burials, 1877–1992 *Maryland State Archives:* Baltimore City Death Index, 1875–1972; Maryland Death Index, 1898–1944	**BIRTH RECORDS:** Records before 1924 are at the Maryland State Archives. Records after 1924 are available from the Maryland Division of Vital Records. **MARRIAGES RECORDS:** The Maryland State Archives has records from 1640 to 2013. **DIVORCE RECORDS:** Divorces were granted by the Maryland State Legislature starting in 1783 and until 1842. The Clerk of the Circuit Court in the county where the divorce was granted has records after 1854. Check with the Maryland State Archives for later records. **DEATH RECORDS:** For deaths prior to 1969, check the Maryland State Archives website for updated information. For deaths after 1969, contact the Maryland Division of Vital Records. **RESTRICTIONS:** Copies of Birth Records are restricted to those born within the last 125 years. Death Records are not restricted if they are more than 20 years after the death.

YEAR	ONLINE AVAILABILITY	ORDERING COPIES OF RECORDS AND RESTRICTIONS
1841: Statewide Registration	**VITAL RECORDS** *Familysearch.org:* Massachusetts, Delayed and Corrected Vital Records, 1753–1900 **BIRTH RECORDS** *Ancestry.com:* Massachusetts Town Birth Records, 1620–1850 *Familysearch.org:* Massachusetts Births, 1841–1915 **MARRIAGE RECORDS** *Ancestry.com:* Massachusetts Town Marriage Records, 1620–1850; Massachusetts Marriages, 1633–1850 *Familysearch.org & Findmypast.com:* Massachusetts Marriages, 1841–1915 **DEATH RECORDS** *Ancestry.com:* Massachusetts Town Death Record, 1620–1850; Massachusetts Death Index, 1901–1980; Death Index, 1970–2003 *Familysearch.org:* Massachusetts Death, 1841–1915	Massachusetts Archives have vital records that are available from 1841–1925. **DIVORCE RECORDS:** Since 1922, the Probate Court handled Divorce Records.Check the county where the couple lived or where the divorce was granted. The Registry of Vital Statistics has a statewide index that starts in 1952. For vital records after 1925, contact the Massachusetts Registry of Vital Records and Statistics.

Michigan

YEAR	ONLINE AVAILABILITY	ORDERING COPIES OF RECORDS AND RESTRICTIONS
Statewide Registration: Births & Deaths (1867) Marriages (1805)	**BIRTH RECORDS** *Familysearch.org:* Michigan Births, 1867–1902; Michigan Births and Christenings, 1775–1995 **MARRIAGE RECORDS** *Ancestry.com:* Michigan Marriages to 1850; Michigan Marriages, 1851–1875; Michigan County Marriages, 1822–1940 *Familysearch.org:* Michigan, County Marriages, 1820–1935; Michigan Marriages, 1822–1995 **DIVORCE RECORDS** *Ancestry.com:* Michigan Divorce Records 1897–1952 **DEATH RECORDS** *Ancestry.com:* Michigan Deaths, 1971–1996 *Familysearch.org*: Michigan, 1921–1952 *Death Certificates Index:* Michigan Department of Health: Michigan Death Index, 1867–1897	Birth, Marriage, and Death Records starting in 1867 are available from the State of Michigan Vital Records Office. **MARRIAGE RECORDS** For earlier records, contact the county clerk. **DIVORCE RECORDS** State of Michigan Vital Records Office has Divorce Records as early as 1897. Check the courts in the county where your ancestor lived for earlier records. **DEATH RECORDS** The Detroit Department of Health has Detroit records since 1897. **RESTRICTIONS:** Copies of Birth Records are restricted to those born within the last 100 years. Birth, Marriage, Divorce, and Death Records over 100 years are not restricted.

YEAR	ONLINE AVAILABILITY	ORDERING COPIES OF RECORDS AND RESTRICTIONS
Statewide Registration: Birth (1900) Marriage (1958) Death (1908)	**BIRTH RECORDS** *Ancestry.com & Familysearch.org:* Minnesota Births and Christenings Index, 1840–1980; Minnesota Birth Index, 1935–2002 *Familysearch.org:* Minnesota County Birth Records, 1863–1983 *Minnesota Historical Society:* Minnesota Birth Certificates Index, 1900–1934 **MARRIAGE RECORDS** *Familysearch.org:* Minnesota Marriages, 1849–1950; Minnesota County Marriages, 1860–1949; Minnesota Marriage Index, 1958–2001 **DIVORCE RECORDS** *Ancestry.com & Familysearch.org:* Minnesota Divorce Index, 1970–1995 **DEATH RECORDS** *Familysearch.org:* Minnesota Deaths and Burials, 1835–1900; Minnesota Death Records, 1866–1916; Minnesota Death Index, 1908–2002	**BIRTH & DEATH RECORDS:** Minnesota Department of Health Office of Vital Records has copies of births from January 1900 and deaths from January 1908. Noncertified copies are available to anyone for informational purposes only. For Birth Records prior to 1900, contact the Minnesota Historical Society. For Death Records before 1908, contact the County Vital Records office. **MARRIAGE RECORDS & DIVORCE RECORDS:** Located in the District Courts in the county where the event occurred. **RESTRICTIONS:** All Minnesota Death Records and most Minnesota Birth Records are public. Minnesota Statutes, section 144.225, subdivision 7, limits who can get a birth or death certificate to a person who has tangible interest. Review the Minnesota Department of Health for definitions.

Mississippi

YEAR	ONLINE AVAILABILITY	ORDERING COPIES OF RECORDS AND RESTRICTIONS
Statewide Registration: Births & Deaths (1912) Marriages (1926)	**MARRIAGE RECORDS** *Familysearch.org*: Mississippi Marriages, 1800–1911; Mississippi Tippah County Marriages, 1858–1979 **DEATH RECORDS** Statewide Index to Mississippi Death Records, 1912–1943	**BIRTH & DEATH RECORDS:** Records prior to November 1912 may be at the county archives. Records after this date are at the Mississippi State Vital Records. **MARRIAGE RECORDS:** January 1, 1926, to January 30, 1938; January 1, 1942, to present are at the Mississippi State Vital Records. Check their website for the forms and an update on fees. **DIVORCE RECORDS:** The Mississippi Board of Health has an index (male only) of divorces from the 1920s. Records were typically kept by the Chancery Court in the county.

Missouri

YEAR	ONLINE AVAILABILITY	ORDERING COPIES OF RECORDS AND RESTRICTIONS
Statewide Registration: Birth & Death Records (1883–1893 & 1910) Marriage Records (1881)	**BIRTH RECORDS** *Ancestry.com:* Missouri Birth Records, 1851–1910 *Familysearch.org:* Missouri, Births and Christenings, 1827–1935 **MARRIAGE RECORDS** *Ancestry.com:* Missouri Marriages to 1850; Missouri Marriage Records, 1851–1900; Missouri Marriage Records, 1805–2002 *Familysearch.org:* Missouri Marriages, 1750–1920; Missouri Civil Marriages, 1820–1874 **DEATH RECORDS** *Ancestry.com:* Missouri Death Records, 1834–1910 *Familysearch.org:* Missouri Deaths and Burials, 1867–1976 *Missouri Digital Heritage:* Missouri Birth & Death Records, Pre-1910; Missouri Death Certificates, 1910–1967; Coroner's Inquest Database	**BIRTH & DEATH RECORDS:** Download the application from Missouri Department of Health & Senior Services Bureau of Vital Records. You can submit the application to your local health department. Check their website for an update on fees. **MARRIAGE AND DIVORCE RECORDS:** Missouri Department of Health & Senior Services Bureau of Vital Records has records from 1948 to the present. Check Recorder of Deeds in the county where the marriage occurred for a copy of the marriage license. Divorce Decrees are available at the Circuit Court in the county.

Montana

YEAR	ONLINE AVAILABILITY	ORDERING COPIES OF RECORDS AND RESTRICTIONS
Statewide Registration: Birth & Death (1907) Marriages: Kept at county level, Statewide in 1943	**BIRTH & DEATH RECORDS** *Ancestry.com:* Montana County Births and Deaths, 1830–2011 *Familysearch.org:* Montana County Births and Deaths, 1840–2004 **MARRIAGE RECORDS** *Ancestry.com & Findmypast.com:* Montana Marriages, 1863–1900 *Familysearch.org:* Montana Marriages, 1889–1947 *Findmypast.com:* Montana County Marriages, 1865–1950 **DIVORCE RECORDS** *Ancestry.com:* County Divorce Records, 1865–1950 **DEATH RECORDS** *Ancestry.com:* Montana Death Index, 1907–2015 *Familysearch.org:* Montana Death Index, 1860–2007 *Findmypast.com:* Montana Deaths, 1954–2011 *Montana Genealogical Society:* Montana State Death Registry Pre-1954 and 1954–2002	**BIRTH & DEATH RECORDS:** Records from 1907 are available from the Montana Office of Vital Statistics. **MARRIAGE & DIVORCE:** Indexes to Marriage Licenses and Divorce Decrees since July 1943 are held at the Montana Office of Vital Statistics.

YEAR	ONLINE AVAILABILITY	ORDERING COPIES OF RECORDS AND RESTRICTIONS
Statewide Registration: Birth & Death (1904) Marriage: Kept at county level, Statewide registration, in 1909	**MARRIAGE RECORDS** *Ancestry.com*: Nebraska Marriages, 1856–1898 *Familysearch.org:* Nebraska Marriages, 1855–1995 **DEATH RECORDS** *Familysearch.org:* US Social Security Death Index	**BIRTH RECORDS:** City of Omaha has records since 1869 and Lincoln since 1889; contact the county clerks for copies. Birth Records start in 1904, and up until 1911, they were filed under the father's name in the register. Birth Certificates were started in 1912 and can be ordered from the Nebraska Department of Health & Human Services Vital Records. **MARRIAGE & DIVORCE RECORDS:** These records start in 1909 and are available from the Nebraska Department of Health & Human Services Vital Records. Before 1909, check the county or the Nebraska State Historical Society for Marriage Licenses. For divorces before 1909, check the Clerk of the District Court where the divorce was granted. **DEATH RECORDS:** The City of Omaha has records since 1873, and Lincoln since 1889; contact the county clerks for copies. Death Records start in 1904; you can order copies from the Nebraska Department of Health & Human Services Vital Records. **RESTRICTIONS:** Copies of Birth, Marriage, Divorce, and Death Records are restricted to those born within the last 50 years.

Nevada

YEAR	ONLINE AVAILABILITY	ORDERING COPIES OF RECORDS AND RESTRICTIONS
Statewide Registration: Births & Deaths (1911) Marriage: Kept at county level and Statewide in 1968	**BIRTH RECORDS** *Ancestry.com:* Nevada Birth Index, 1975–2012 *Familysearch.org:* Nevada County, Births and Deaths, 1871–1992 **MARRIAGE RECORDS** *Ancestry.com & Familysearch.org:* Nevada Marriage Index Database, 1956–2005 **DIVORCE RECORDS** *Ancestry.com:* Nevada Divorce Index, 1968–2015 **DEATH RECORDS** *Familysearch.org:* Nevada County, Births and Deaths, 1871–1992	**BIRTH & DEATH RECORDS:** The Office of Vital Statistics has Birth and Death Records since 1911 from July 1, 1911. Prior to 1911, contact the County Recorder's office. **MARRIAGE & DIVORCE RECORDS:** The Office of Vital Statistics will search for and verify this information between 1968 and September 2005. You will need to provide the full name(s), approximate date of events, and the city/county where marriage or divorce occurred. Check the website of the Nevada Division of Public and Behavioral Health (DPBH) for updates. **RESTRICTIONS:** Birth and Death Records are confidential and will only be released to a qualified applicant. Check the Nevada Division of Public and Behavioral Health for more information.

YEAR	ONLINE AVAILABILITY	ORDERING COPIES OF RECORDS AND RESTRICTIONS
Records are available from the early 1600s	**VITAL RECORDS** *Familysearch.org:* New Hampshire, Vital and Town Records Index, 1656–1938 **BIRTH RECORDS** *Ancestry.com:* New Hampshire Birth Records, 1659–1900 *Familysearch.org:* New Hampshire Births and Christenings, 1714–1904; New Hampshire Birth Records, Early to 1900; New Hampshire Birth Certificates, 1901–1915 **MARRIAGE RECORDS** *Ancestry.com:* New Hampshire Marriage and Divorce Records, 1659–1947 *Familysearch.org:* New Hampshire Marriage Records, 1637–1947; New Hampshire Marriages, 1720–1920; New Hampshire Marriage Certificates, 1948–1959 **DIVORCE RECORDS** *Ancestry.com:* New Hampshire Marriage and Divorce Records, 1659–1947 **DEATH RECORDS** *Familysearch.org:* New Hampshire Death Records, 1654–1947; New Hampshire Death Certificates, 1938–1959; New Hampshire Deaths and Burial Records Index, 1784–1949	Birth, Marriage, and Death Records since 1640 are located in the town clerk's office. The Bureau of Vital Records has Birth, Marriage, and Death Records since 1883. Divorce Records since 1808 are available from the Clerk of Superior Court in the county where the divorce was granted. **RESTRICTIONS:** Vital Records are private and restricted to individuals with a direct and tangible interest. Check the Secretary of State, Vital Records Access Policies.

YEAR	ONLINE AVAILABILITY	ORDERING COPIES OF RECORDS AND RESTRICTIONS
Statewide Registration: Birth & Death (1848) Marriage: Early records around 1725 and statewide registration in 1848	**BIRTH RECORDS** *Ancestry.com:* New Jersey, Births and Christenings, 1660–1931 *Familysearch.org:* New Jersey, Births and Christenings, 1660–1980 **MARRIAGE RECORDS** *Ancestry.com:* New Jersey Marriage Records, 1683–1802; New Jersey, Compiled Marriage Records, 1684–1895; New Jersey Marriage Records, 1670–1965 *Familysearch.org:* New Jersey County Marriages, 1678–1985; New Jersey County Marriages, 1682–1956 *New Jersey State Archives:* Colonial Marriage Bonds, 1666–1799; Marriage Records, May 1848–May 1878 **DEATH RECORDS** *Ancestry.com:* New Jersey Death Index, 1901–1903 *Familysearch.org:* New Jersey Deaths, 1670–1988 *New Jersey State Archives:* June 1878–June 1895	**BIRTH, MARRIAGE & DEATH RECORDS:** For copies of records from May 1848 to Dec. 1917, contact the New Jersey State Archives. After this date, the New Jersey State Health has copies of records. The New Jersey State Archives has microfilm copies of these records; check their website for availability. **MARRIAGE RECORDS:** Filed with the county clerk in 1795 or the year the county was formed. **DIVORCE RECORDS, KNOWN AS "DISSOLUTION RECORDS":** Records between 1743 to 1886 are held at the New Jersey State Archives. Divorces were granted by Decree of the Chancery Court or a legislative act. For records after 1886, contact the Superior Court Records Information Center. **RESTRICTIONS:** Records for Family History research are available if the birth occurred more than 80 years ago, if the marriage occurred more than 50 years ago, and if the death occurred more than 40 years ago. **NOTE:** Records of the Birth of Slave Children were filed with county clerk beginning in 1804 and are available at the New Jersey State Archives.

YEAR	ONLINE AVAILABILITY	ORDERING COPIES OF RECORDS AND RESTRICTIONS
Statewide Registration: Births & Deaths (1920, 1907 at the county level) Marriages: County formation	**BIRTH RECORDS** *Familysearch.org:* New Mexico Births & Christenings, 1726–1918 **MARRIAGE RECORDS** *Familysearch.org:* New Mexico Marriages, 1751–1918 **DEATH RECORDS** *Familysearch.org:* New Mexico Deaths, 1889–1945; New Mexico Deaths & Burials, 1788–1798 and 1838–1955	**BIRTH & DEATH RECORDS:** Only immediate family is eligible to obtain a Vital Record. Nonimmediate family must provide tangible proof of legal interest for requested record. **MARRIAGE RECORDS:** Licenses are available from the county clerk of the county where the Marriage License was issued. **DIVORCE RECORDS:** Decrees are available from the district court where the court order was filed. Check the New Mexico Department of Health website for updates. **RESTRICTIONS:** Vital records that are less than 100 years old may not be accessible. Check the New Mexico Department of Health Vital Records website.

YEAR	ONLINE AVAILABILITY	ORDERING COPIES OF RECORDS AND RESTRICTIONS
1880: Statewide Registration	**BIRTH RECORDS** *Ancestry.com:* New York, New York, Birth Index, 1878–1909 *Familysearch.org:* New York, Births and Christenings, 1640–1962 **MARRIAGE RECORDS** *Ancestry.com:* New York, New York Marriage Index, 1866–1937; New York City Marriage Indexes, 1907–1995 *Ancestry.com:* New York County Marriage Records, 1847–1849, 1907–1936 *Familysearch.org:* New York, County Marriages, 1908–1935 **DEATH RECORDS** *Ancestry.com*: New York, New York Death Index, 1862–1948 *Familysearch.org:* New York Deaths and Burials, 1795–1952; New York, State Health Department, Genealogical Research Death Index, 1957–1963	**BIRTH, MARRIAGE & DEATH RECORDS:** Contact the New York State Department of Health to obtain records since 1880 except for New York City. They do have birth records for the Boroughs of Queens and Richmond from 1881 to 1897. If your ancestor lived in New York City, contact the New York City Municipal Archives for a list of their holdings. If your ancestor lived in Albany, Buffalo, or Yonkers prior to 1914, Birth and Death Records are held at Local Registers and Marriage Records at the City Clerk in the respective city. **DIVORCE RECORDS:** The New York State Archives has Chancery Court Records from 1787 to 1847. The Supreme Court in each county has Divorce Proceedings. Contact the Supreme Court in the county where the divorce was granted. Divorce Proceedings less than 100 years old require a court order. **RESTRICTIONS:** Copies of Birth Records are available 75 years after filing and if the person is deceased. Marriage Records are available 50 years after filing and if both spouses are deceased. Death Records are available 50 years after the date of death. These are waived for direct line descendants with proof. Check the New York Department of Health website for updates.

YEAR	ONLINE AVAILABILITY	ORDERING COPIES OF RECORDS AND RESTRICTIONS
Statewide Registration: Births & Deaths (1913) Marriage (1868)	**BIRTH RECORDS** *Ancestry.com & Familysearch.org:* North Carolina Birth Index, 1800–2000 *Familysearch.org:* North Carolina Births and Christenings, 1866–1964 **MARRIAGE RECORDS** *Ancestry.com:* North Carolina, Marriage Index, 1741–2004; North Carolina, Marriage Records, 1741–2011 *Familysearch.org:* North Carolina Marriages, 1759–1979; North Carolina, County Marriages, 1762–1979 **DIVORCE RECORDS** *Ancestry.com:* North Carolina, Divorce Index, 1958–2004 **DEATH RECORDS** *Ancestry.com:* North Carolina, Death Certificates, 1909–1976; North Carolina, Death Indexes, 1908-2004 *Familysearch.org:* North Carolina Deaths and Burials, 1898–1994 *Findmypast.com:* North Carolina Deaths, 1906–1930; North Carolina Deaths, 1931–1994	**BIRTH RECORDS** For records before 1913, contact the Register of Deeds Office in the county where the birth occurred. Starting in 1913, records are available from North Carolina Vital Records. **MARRIAGE RECORDS** Prior to 1962, contact the County Register of Deeds. For 1962 to the present, contact North Carolina Vital Records. **DIVORCE RECORDS** Prior to 1958, contact the Clerk of the Court where the divorce was filed. For 1958 to the present, contact North Carolina Vital Records. **DEATH RECORDS** For Death Certificates prior to 1930, contact the North Carolina State Archives.

North Dakota

YEAR	ONLINE AVAILABILITY	ORDERING COPIES OF RECORDS AND RESTRICTIONS
Statewide Registration: Births & Deaths (1923) Marriages (1925)	**MARRIAGE RECORDS** *Ancestry.com:* North Dakota, Marriage Records, 1872–2017 *Familysearch.org:* North Dakota, County Marriages, 1882–1925 **DIVORCE RECORDS** *Ancestry.com:* Cass County, North Dakota, Divorce Index, 1878–1943 **DEATH RECORDS** *North Dakota Department of Health:* Public Death Index, 1892 to present	**BIRTH RECORDS & DEATH RECORDS:** For information on ordering certified copies, check the Vital Records Office at the North Dakota Department of Health. **MARRIAGE RECORDS & DIVORCE RECORDS:** Contact the County Recorders or Clerks where the marriage occurred or the divorce was granted.

YEAR	ONLINE AVAILABILITY	ORDERING COPIES OF RECORDS AND RESTRICTIONS
Statewide Registration: Births & Deaths (1908) Marriages (1949)	**BIRTH RECORDS** *Ancestry.com:* Ohio, Births and Christenings Index, 1774–1973; Ohio Birth Index, 1908-1964 *Familysearch.org:* Ohio Births & Christenings, 1821–1962; Ohio County Births, 1841–2003 **MARRIAGE RECORDS** *Ancestry.com:* Ohio Marriages, 1789–1898; Ohio Marriages, 1803–1900 *Familysearch.org*: Ohio County Marriages, 1789–2013; Ohio Marriages, 1800–1958 *Findmypast.com:* Ohio Marriages, 1970, 1972–2011 **DIVORCE RECORDS** *Ancestry.com:* Ohio Divorce Abstracts, 1962–1963, 1967–1971, and 1973–2007 *Findmypast.com:* Ohio Divorces, 1962–2011 **DEATH RECORDS** *Ancestry.com:* Ohio Death Records Index, 1908–1932, 1938–2007 *Familysearch.org:* Ohio County Death Records, 1840–2001; Ohio Deaths and Burials, 1854–1997; Ohio Deaths, 1908–1953 *Findmypast.com:* Ohio Deaths, 1959–2012 *Myheritage.com:* Ohio Deaths, 1908–1966; *Ohio History Connection:* Ohio Public Records Index	**BIRTH RECORDS:** Between 1867 and 1908, Birth Records were recorded in county probate courts. The Ohio History Connection has Probate Records from this time period. For records after December 20, 1908, contact the Office of Vital Statistics. **DEATH RECORDS:** The Ohio History Connection has Ohio Death Records from December 20, 1908, to December 31, 1963. The Office of Vital Statistics has Death Records from January 1, 1964, to the present. Check their website for an update on fees. **MARRIAGE AND DIVORCE RECORDS:** For Records, contact the County Probate Court for marriages and the Clerk of the Court for Divorce Records. The Office of Vital Statistics has an index of Marriages from January 1, 1950, and Divorce Records from January 1, 1954, to the present. **RESTRICTIONS:** Ohio is an "open records" state, meaning vital records are considered public records. Review the fees, process, and forms at the Ohio Office of Vital Statistics.

Oklahoma

YEAR	ONLINE AVAILABILITY	ORDERING COPIES OF RECORDS AND RESTRICTIONS
Statewide Registration: Births & Deaths (1908) Marriages: 1890 or county formation	**BIRTH RECORDS** *Oklahoma Department of Health:* State Vital Records Index **MARRIAGE RECORDS** *Ancestry.com & Familysearch.org:* Oklahoma, County Marriages, 1890–1995 *Familysearch.org:* Oklahoma Select Marriages, 1870–1930 *Ancestry.com, Familysearch.org & Myheritage.com:* Oklahoma Marriages, 1870–1930 *Findmypast.com:* Oklahoma Marriages 1842–1912 *Oklahoma Historical Society:* Oklahoma County Marriage Records, 1889–1951 **DIVORCE RECORDS** *Ancestry.com & Oklahoma Historical Society:* Oklahoma County Divorce Records, 1923–1944 **DEATH RECORDS** *Oklahoma State Department of Health:* Death Index	**BIRTH & DEATH RECORDS:** The Oklahoma Vital Records Service has records since October 1908. **MARRIAGE & DIVORCE RECORDS:** These records are available in the county court where the marriage license was issued and the divorce was granted. **RESTRICTIONS:** Births occurring less than 125 years ago are closed records. Deaths occurring less than 50 years are closed records.

YEAR	ONLINE AVAILABILITY	ORDERING COPIES OF RECORDS AND RESTRICTIONS
Statewide Registration: Births & Deaths (July 1903) Marriages (1906)	**VITAL RECORDS** *Ancestry.com:* Early Oregonians Index, 1800–1860 *Oregon State Archives:* Oregon Historical Records Index **BIRTH RECORDS** *Ancestry.com, Familysearch.org, Findmypast.com & MyHeritage.com:* Oregon Births & Baptisms, 1868–1929 *Familysearch.org:* Oregon Births, 1860–1952 **MARRIAGE RECORDS** *Ancestry.com:* Oregon, Marriage Indexes, 1906–2009; Oregon County Marriages, 1851–1975 *Familysearch.org:* Oregon Marriages, 1853–1935; Oregon Marriage Records, 1849–1952 **DIVORCE RECORDS** *Oregon State Archives:* Oregon Historical Records Index, select Divorce **DEATH RECORDS** *Ancestry.com:* Oregon Death Index, 1898–2008 *Familysearch.org:* Oregon Deaths 1877–1952; Oregon Death Index, 1903–1998 *Myheritage.com:* Oregon Deaths, 1903–1930	**VITAL RECORDS:** To order certified copies, contact the Center for Health Statistics at the Oregon Health Authority.Restrictions will apply. **DIVORCE RECORDS:** Prior to 1853, contact the Oregon State Archives. For 1853–1925, contact the Circuit Court of the county where the divorce was granted; and for 1925 to the present, contact the Oregon State Health Division. **RESTRICTIONS:** Birth records less than 100 years from the date are restricted. Death Certificates have a 50-year access restriction for the date of death.

Pennsylvania

YEAR	ONLINE AVAILABILITY	ORDERING COPIES OF RECORDS AND RESTRICTIONS
Statewide Registration: Births & Deaths (Jan. 1906) Marriages: County Level Philadelphia County: Birth & Death in 1893 and Marriage in 1885	**BIRTH RECORDS** *Ancestry.com:* Pennsylvania Births, 1852–1854; Pennsylvania Birth Records, 1906–1910 *Familysearch.org:* Pennsylvania Births and Christenings, 1709–1950 ***Pennsylvania State Archives:*** Birth Indices 1906–1912 **MARRIAGE RECORDS** *Ancestry.com:* Pennsylvania Compiled Marriages, 1700–1821; Pennsylvania Marriages, 1852–1854; Pennsylvania County Marriages, 1845–1963 *Familysearch.org:* Pennsylvania Marriages, 1709–1940; Pennsylvania County Marriages, 1885–1950; Pennsylvania Civil Marriages, 1677–1950 **DEATH RECORDS** *Ancestry.com:* Pennsylvania Death Certificates, 1906–1966 *Findmypast.com:* Pennsylvania Burials, 1816–1849 ***Pennsylvania State Archives:*** Death Indices 1906–1967	**BIRTH & DEATH RECORDS:** For prior to 1906, contact the Clerk of the Orphans Court where the event occurred. **MARRIAGE & DIVORCE RECORDS:** Contact the courthouse where the marriage license was issued or divorce decree was granted. **DIVORCE RECORDS:** Contact the Office of the Prothonotary or Office of Judicial Records in the county where the divorce was granted.

Rhode Island

YEAR	ONLINE AVAILABILITY	ORDERING COPIES OF RECORDS AND RESTRICTIONS
1853: Statewide Registration	**VITAL RECORDS** *American Ancestors.org:* Rhode Island Vital Records, 1636–1850 *Familysearch.org:* Rhode Island Town Clerk Vital and Town Records, 1630–1945; Rhode Island Vital Records, 1846–1898, 1901–1953 **BIRTH RECORDS** *Ancestry.com:* Rhode Island Births, 1636–1930 *Familysearch.org:* Rhode Island Births and Christenings, 1600–1914 **MARRIAGE RECORDS** *Ancestry.com:* Rhode Island Marriages, 1851–1920 *Familysearch.org:* Rhode Island Marriages, 1724–1916 **DEATH RECORDS** *Ancestry.com:* Rhode Island Deaths, 1630-1930 *Familysearch.org:* Rhode Island Deaths and Burials, 1802–1950	You can obtain vital records considered public records in two ways: contact the town or city where the event occurred, or through the Rhode Island State archives. **RESTRICTIONS:** Birth and Marriage Records over 100 years are considered public record. Death Records over 50 years are considered public record. Records that are not public are only available to individuals with a direct and tangible interest. Check with the State of Rhode Island Department of Health.

South Carolina

YEAR	ONLINE AVAILABILITY	ORDERING COPIES OF RECORDS AND RESTRICTIONS
Statewide Registration: Births & Deaths (1915) Marriages (1911)	**BIRTH RECORDS** *Ancestry.com:* South Carolina, Delayed Birth Records, 1766–1900; City of Charleston, South Carolina, Birth Records, 1877–1901 *Familysearch.org:* South Carolina, Delayed Birth Records, 1766–1900; South Carolina Births & Christenings, 1681–1935 **MARRIAGE RECORDS** *Ancestry.com:* South Carolina Marriage Index, 1641–1965 *Familysearch.org:* South Carolina Marriages, 1709–1913 **DEATH RECORDS** *Ancestry.com:* South Carolina Death Records, 1821–1965; South Carolina Death Index, 1950–1952 *Familysearch.org:* South Carolina Deaths, 1915–1965 *Findmypast.com:* South Carolina Deaths, 1915–1943 *South Carolina Department of Health:* South Carolina Death Indexes, 1915–1962	**BIRTH RECORDS:** Certificates since 1915 are available from South Carolina Department of Health & Environmental Control (DHEC), State Vital Records Office. A birth record becomes public 100 years after date of birth. **MARRIAGE RECORDS:** Records from July 1950 to December 2014 are available from South Carolina DHEC, State Vital Records Office. For records prior to this date, contact the Probate Court that issued the marriage license. **DEATH RECORDS:** After 50 years, these are considered public records and are available at the South Carolina Department of History and Archives. **DIVORCE RECORDS:** Divorce reports from July 1962 to December 2014 are available from South Carolina DHEC, State Vital Records Office. Earlier records were kept at the county level and might be restricted. Check with the clerk of the court where the divorce was granted.

YEAR	ONLINE AVAILABILITY	ORDERING COPIES OF RECORDS AND RESTRICTIONS
1905: Statewide Registration	**BIRTH RECORDS** *Ancestry.com:* South Dakota Birth Index, 1856–1917 *Familysearch.org:* South Dakota, Department of Health, Index to Births and Marriages, 1843–1914 and 1950–2016 *South Dakota Department of Health:* Birth Record Search Site with birth dates over 100 years **MARRIAGE RECORDS** *Ancestry.com:* South Dakota Marriages, 1905–2016 **DEATH RECORDS** *Ancestry.com:* South Dakota Death Index, 1879-1955	The Department of Health has Vital records from 1905, and these records are not open to the public. You can order an informational or certified copy from the Department of Health. Check their website for requirements on who can order a certified copy. Some Vital Records might be available from the counties prior to 1905. For Divorce Records before 1905, contact the Clerk of the Court in the county where the divorce was granted.

Tennessee

YEAR	ONLINE AVAILABILITY	ORDERING COPIES OF RECORDS AND RESTRICTIONS
Statewide Registration: Births & Deaths (1914) Marriages (1945)	**BIRTH RECORDS** *Familysearch.org:* Tennessee Birth & Christenings 1828–1939; Tennessee Birth Records, 1908–1912 **MARRIAGE RECORDS** *Ancestry.com & Familysearch.org:* Tennessee State Marriage Index, 1780–2002 *Ancestry.com:* Tennessee Compiled Marriages, 1851–1900 *Familysearch.org:* Tennessee County Marriages, 1790–1950 **DIVORCE RECORDS** *Ancestry.com:* Tennessee Divorce and Other Records, 1800–1965 **DEATH RECORDS** *Ancestry.com:* Tennessee Death Records, 1908–1958 *Ancestry.com & Familysearch.org:* Tennessee Deaths and Burials Index, 1874–1955 *Tennessee State Library & Archives:* Index to Tennessee Death Records, 1908–1912, 1914–1933	To learn more about ordering Birth, Marriage, and Death Records, review the Tennessee State Library and Archives (TSLA) website. For earlier records, check the county where the event occurred. The TSLA has extensive guides to help you locate Vital Records in counties and the archives. Check their website for updates. **RESTRICTIONS:** The Vital Records Office keeps Birth Records for 100 years and Marriage, Death, and Divorce Records for 50 years. They are then transferred to TSLA and open to the public.

YEAR	ONLINE AVAILABILITY	ORDERING COPIES OF RECORDS AND RESTRICTIONS
Statewide Registration: Birth & Death (1903) Marriage (1836)	**BIRTH RECORDS** *Ancestry.com & Familysearch.org:* Texas Birth Index, 1903–1997 *Familysearch.org:* Texas, Births and Christenings, 1840–1981; Texas Birth Certificates, 1903–1935 **MARRIAGE RECORDS** *Ancestry.com:* Texas County Marriages, 1817–1965; Texas Select County Marriage Records, 1837–2015 *Familysearch.org:* Texas Marriages, 1966–2010; Texas County Marriage Index, 1837–1977 *Findmypast.com:* Texas Marriages, 1968–2010 *Myheritage.com:* Texas Marriages, 1966–2007 and Divorces, 1968–2008 **DIVORCE RECORDS** *Familysearch.org:* Texas Divorce Index, 1968–2010. *Findmypast.com:* Texas Divorces, 1968–2010 **DEATH RECORDS** *Ancestry.com:* Texas Death Certificates, 1903–1982 *Familysearch.org:* Texas Death Records, 1890–1976; Texas Death Index, 1903–2000	**BIRTH RECORDS:** County clerks should have early records up to 1903. **VITAL RECORDS:** Contact the Texas Department of Health, Bureau of Vital Statistics, for copies of Birth, Marriage, and Death Records since 1903. **MARRIAGE AND DIVORCE RECORDS:** Obtain copies from the Clerk's Office where the event occurred. **RESTRICTIONS ON ACCESS:** For births within the past 75 years and deaths within the past 25 years, only immediate family members have access. Check the Texas Vital Statistics website for the definition of an immediate family member.

Utah

YEAR	ONLINE AVAILABILITY	ORDERING COPIES OF RECORDS AND RESTRICTIONS
Statewide Registration: Births & Deaths (1905) Earliest Birth Records (1890) Statewide Registration: Marriages (1978) Earliest Marriages (1887)	**BIRTH RECORDS** *Ancestry.com:* Utah Birth Registers, 1892–1944; Utah Birth Certificates, 1903–1911 *Familysearch.org & Findmypast.com:* Utah Births and Christenings, 1892–1941 *Familysearch.org:* Utah Birth Certificates, 1903–1914 *Myheritage.com:* Utah Salt Lake City Birth Records, 1890–1915 *Utah Division of Archives & Records Service:* Utah Birth Certificate Index, 1903–1909 **MARRIAGE RECORDS** *Ancestry.com:* Utah Select Marriages, 1887–1966 *Familysearch.org:* Utah Marriages, 1887–1935; Utah County Marriages, 1887–1940 *Findmypast.com:* Utah Marriages, 1845–1935 **DIVORCE RECORDS** *Familysearch.org:* Utah State Archives Records, 1848–2001 **DEATH RECORDS** *Familysearch.org* & Utah Division of Archives & Records Service: Utah Death Certificate Index, 1904–1964	**BIRTH RECORDS:** For births after 1905 and more than 100 years ago, contact the Utah State Archives. For births that occurred less than 100 years ago, contact the Utah State Department of Health. **MARRIAGE RECORDS:** Some Marriage Records are in the probate office and some maybe with the county clerks. They can be found at the Utah State Archives. The Family History Library has copies for most counties until about 1960. **DIVORCE RECORDS:** Check the State Archives for records after 1867 and the scope of their collection. For records after 1978, check the Utah State Department of Health. **DEATH RECORDS:** Contact the Utah State Department of Health for records less than 50 years old and for certified copies. **RESTRICTION ON ACCESS:** Birth Records are public 100 years after the date of birth. Death Records are public 50 years after the date of death. Marriage and Divorce Records are public 75 years after the date of the event.

YEAR	ONLINE AVAILABILITY	ORDERING COPIES OF RECORDS AND RESTRICTIONS
1857: Statewide Registration	**VITAL RECORDS COLLECTIONS** *Ancestry.com:* Vermont Vital Records, 1720–1908 *Familysearch.org:* Vermont Vital Records, 1760–1954; Vermont Vital Records, 1760–2008 **BIRTH RECORDS** *Ancestry.com:* Vermont Birth Records, 1909–2008; Vermont Birth Index, 1981–2001 *Familysearch.org:* Virginia Births and Christenings, 1765–1908 **MARRIAGE RECORDS** *Ancestry.com:* Vermont Marriage Records, 1909–2008 *Familysearch.org:* Vermont Marriages, 1791–1974 **DIVORCE RECORDS** *Ancestry.com:* Vermont Divorce Index, 1925–2003 **DEATH RECORDS** *Ancestry.com:* Vermont Death Records, 1909–2008; Vermont Death Index, 1925–2003 *Familysearch.org:* Vermont Deaths and Burials, 1871–1965	Birth, Death, Marriage, Civil Union, Divorce, and Dissolution Records are available from the Vermont Department of Health & Vital Statistics from 2012 to the present. For earlier records, check with the town clerk and contact Vermont State Archives and Records Administration. **RESTRICTIONS:** New requirements for the safety and security of birth and death certificates goes into effect on July 1, 2019. Check the Vermont Department of Health website for updates.

Virginia

YEAR	ONLINE AVAILABILITY	ORDERING COPIES OF RECORDS AND RESTRICTIONS
Statewide Registration: Births & Deaths (1912); Births & Death Records: 1853–1896 Statewide Registration (1853); Marriage (1853–1896)	**BIRTH RECORDS** *Ancestry.com:* Virginia Birth Records, 1912–2014; Delayed Birth Records, 1854–1911 *Familysearch.org:* Virginia Births & Christenings, 1853–1917 **MARRIAGE RECORDS** *Ancestry.com:* Virginia, Compiled Marriages, 1660–1800; Virginia Marriage Records, 1700–1850; Virginia Compiled Marriages, 1851–1929 *Familysearch.org & Findmypast.com:* Virginia Marriages, 1785–1940 **DIVORCE RECORDS** *Ancestry.com:* Virginia Divorce Records, 1918–2014 **DEATH RECORDS** *Ancestry.com:* Virginia, Deaths and Burials Index, 1853–1917; Virginia Death Records, 1912–2014 *Familysearch.org:* Virginia Deaths and Burials, 1853–1912 *Library of Virginia:* Virginia Death Records Indexing (DIVA), 1853–1896	In 1853, a law was passed requiring statewide registration of vital statistics. These records are housed in the court-house of the county or independent city. Births & deaths of enslaved individuals in Virginia are recorded as first name only or under the enslaver's name. **BIRTH & DEATH RECORDS:** Between 1896 and 1912, births and deaths were not recorded statewide except for a few metropolitan areas. Records after June 1912 can be ordered from the Virginia Department of Health, Division of Vital Records. **MARRIAGE RECORDS:** For records prior to 1853, contact the County Court Clerk. Records after 1853 are available from the Virginia Department of Health, Division of Vital Records. **DIVORCE RECORDS:** Records since 1918 are available from the Virginia Department of Health, Division of Vital Records. **RESTRICTIONS:** Birth Records are public after 100 years; Death, Divorce, and Marriage Records are public 25 years after the event.

YEAR	ONLINE AVAILABILITY	ORDERING COPIES OF RECORDS AND RESTRICTIONS
Statewide Registration: Births & Deaths(1907) Marriages (1968) At the county level prior to statewide registration.	**VITAL RECORDS COLLECTIONS** ***Familysearch.org:*** Washington County Records, 1803–2010 ***Washington State Archives:*** Digital Archives Birth, Marriage & Death records from various counties **BIRTH RECORDS** *Ancestry.com*: Washington Birth Index, 1907–1919; Washington Births, 1870–1935 ***Familysearch.org:*** Washington Birth Records, 1869–1950 **MARRIAGE RECORDS** *Ancestry.com:* Washington Marriages, 1854–2013; Washington State Marriage Indexes, 1969–2014 ***Familysearch.org & Findmypast.com:*** Washington County Marriages, 1855–2008 **DIVORCE RECORDS** *Ancestry.com:* Washington County, Divorce Records, 1852–1950 ***Washington State Archives:*** Department of Health Divorce Index, 1969–2014 **DEATH RECORDS** *Ancestry.com:* Washington Deaths, 1883–1960; Washington Death Index, 1940–2014 ***Familysearch.org:*** Washington County Deaths, 1891–1907 ***Washington State Archives:*** Washington Death Certificates, 1907–1960 and 1965–2014	**BIRTH RECORDS:** For births prior to July 1, 1907, contact the county auditor unless the birth was in King, Pierce, Snohomish, and Spokane counties, in which cases contact the local health department. **DEATH RECORDS:** For deaths that occurred prior to July 1, 1907, contact the Washington State Archives. For births and deaths after July 1, 1907, contact the Washington State Department of Health, Center for Health Statistics. Check the website for an update on fees, forms, and process. **MARRIAGE RECORDS:** Contact the State Archives regional branch for records prior to 1968. For records from 1968, contact the Washington State Department of Health, Center for Health Statistics. **DIVORCE RECORDS:** Contact the State Archives regional branch prior to 1968. For records from 1968 forward, contact the Washington State Department of Health, Center for Health Statistics.

West Virginia

YEAR	ONLINE AVAILABILITY	ORDERING COPIES OF RECORDS AND RESTRICTIONS
Statewide Registration: Births & Deaths (1917) Statewide Registration: Marriages (1853)	**VITAL RECORDS COLLECTIONS** ***West Virginia Archives & History:*** Vital Research Records Search **BIRTH RECORDS** *Ancestry.com:* West Virginia, Births Index, 1804–1938 *Familysearch.org:* West Virginia, Births and Christenings, 1853–1928; West Virginia Births, 1853–1930 **MARRIAGE RECORDS** *Ancestry.com:* West Virginia Marriages Index, 1931–1970; West Virginia Compiled Marriage Records, 1863–1900 *Familysearch.org:* West Virginia Marriages, 1780–1970 **DEATH RECORDS** *Ancestry.com:* West Virginia Death Index, 1853–1973 *Familysearch.org:* West Virginia, Deaths and Burials Index, 1854–1932; West Virginia Deaths, 1804–1999	**BIRTH & DEATH RECORDS:** Records from 1917 to the present are available from the West Virginia Vital Registration office. **MARRIAGE RECORDS:** Some counties have records as early as 1780. A Marriage Index from 1924 to 1963 is available from West Virginia Vital Registration Office. **DIVORCE RECORDS:** Available from the clerk of the Circuit Court in the county where the divorce was granted. **RESTRICTIONS:** Copies of Birth Records are available after 100 years. Marriage and Death Records are available after 50 years. A fire destroyed the state copies of Birth and Death Records from 1917 to 1921. The county clerk should have copies of records prior to 1921.

YEAR	ONLINE AVAILABILITY	ORDERING COPIES OF RECORDS AND RESTRICTIONS
1907: Statewide Registration	**BIRTH RECORDS** *Ancestry.com & Familysearch.org:* Wisconsin Birth Index, 1820–1907 *Familysearch.org*: Wisconsin Births and Christenings, 1826–1926 **MARRIAGE RECORDS** *Ancestry.com:* Wisconsin, Marriages, 1820–1907 *Familysearch.org:* Wisconsin, Marriages, 1836–1930 *Fond du Lac Public Library:* Wisconsin, Marriage Applications, 1899–1930 *Ancestry.com & Familysearch.org:* Wisconsin Marriages, 1973–1997 **DIVORCE RECORDS** *Ancestry.com:* Wisconsin Divorce Index, 1965–1984 **DEATH RECORDS** *Ancestry.com:* Wisconsin Death Index & Death Records, 1820–1907 *Familysearch.org:* Wisconsin Death Records, 1867–1907; Wisconsin, Deaths and Burials, 1835–1968 *Ancestry.com & Familysearch.org:* Wisconsin Death Records, 1959–1997	**BIRTH, MARRIAGE & DEATH RECORDS:** Any records before October 1, 1907, were kept at the county level but are available at the Wisconsin Historical Society. Birth, Marriage & Death records after 1907 are available at the Wisconsin Department of Health, Vital Records Office. Check the "Genealogy" section for more information. **DIVORCE RECORDS:** Wisconsin Department of Health Services, Vital Records Division, has records from October 1907 to 1967. Check the website for more information.

Wyoming

YEAR	ONLINE AVAILABILITY	ORDERING COPIES OF RECORDS AND RESTRICTIONS
Statewide registration: Births & Deaths (July 1909) Marriages & Divorces (May 1941)	**MARRIAGE RECORDS** *Findmypast.com:* Wyoming Marriages, 1867–1941 *Familysearch.org:* Wyoming Marriages, 1869–1923 *Familysearch.org & Myheritage.com:* Wyoming Marriages, 1877–1920 **DEATH RECORDS** *Wyoming State Archives:* Death Certificate Database http: //wyoarchives.state.wy.us/DCD /Index.aspx	**BIRTH CERTIFICATES:** Wyoming State Archives has Birth Certificates over 100 years old. For Birth Certificates less than 100 years old, contact the Wyoming Department of Health, Vital Statistics Service. **MARRIAGE RECORDS:** Certificates over 50 years old are available at the Wyoming State Archives. For records less than 50 years old, contact the Wyoming Department of Health, Vital Statistics Service. **DIVORCE RECORDS:** Wyoming State Archives does not have an index of divorces prior to 1941. Contact the county clerk of the District Court to get the docket number for the case. **DEATH RECORDS:** Certificates over 50 years old are available at the Wyoming State Archives. For certificates less than 50 years old, contact the Wyoming Department of Health, Vital Statistics Service. **RESTRICTIONS:** Copies of Birth Certificates are restricted to those born within the last 100 years. Death Records are not restricted if it is more than 50 years after the death. Marriage Records and Divorce Certificates are public 50 years after the date.

UNITED STATES COURT SYSTEM AND COURT RECORDS

To understand court records and how they fit into your family history research, you need to understand the structure of the United States Court System. The Federal Court System was established in 1789; it includes the United States Supreme Court, the highest court in the United States; twelve Regional Circuit Courts of Appeals; the United States Court of Appeals for the Federal Circuit; and over ninety judicial district courts.

For more information on understanding the federal courts, see http://www .uscourts.gov/sites/default/files/understanding-federal-courts.pdf.

The State Court systems include a Supreme Court, Court of Appeals, and Trial Courts. The court system in each state is organized differently, with some states having Family Courts and Orphans Courts. State courts have jurisdiction over matters involving family law, real property, private contract disputes, probate, and inheritance.

> ### TIP
>
> Once you know the state and county where your ancestor resided, review The Court Statistics Project, "State Court Structure Charts," at http://www.courtstatistics.org/ Other-Pages/State_Court_Structure_Charts.aspx before you start researching court records.

The County Courthouse was the center of the community and where the business of city, town, or county was handled, whether it was a dispute over property, purchasing of property, administering an estate, or some criminal action. When I started doing research on my Madison County and Culpeper County ancestors, I would drive to the county courthouse on a whim. This was at the beginning of the Internet's popularity, but before digitization of records. During my frequent trips, I found family history gems in both Culpeper and Madison counties. Some of the gems included cohabitation records for my enslaved ancestors, real property deeds, and property disputes between relatives.

TAX RECORDS

Tax records are a great resource to establish residence and property values for both real and personal property. The Clerk of Court will have information on the tax records that are available for research in your ancestor's county. Prior to visiting the courthouse, search their website for more information. Earlier tax records may be available at the state archives, libraries, or historical societies, online or in microfilm. Ancestry.com and Familysearch.org have tax records online—search their catalogs for the state or county of interest.

Early Tax Records Available Online and Microfilm

- **CONNECTICUT:** Tax records were kept at the town level. Once you identify the town where your ancestor lived, you can contact the town clerks.
- **DELAWARE:** The Family History Library (FHL) has tax lists taken from 1726 to 1850 on microfilm for Kent, New Castle, and Sussex Counties. Search the FHL catalog to determine if they are available for interlibrary loan at your local FHL center.
- **GEORGIA:** Free white men over the age of twenty-one and slaves age twenty-one to sixty were taxed. *The Georgia Tax Index, 1789–1799* and *Georgia Property Tax Digests, 1793–1893* are available on Ancestry.com. The Georgia Property Tax Digests contain information on white taxpayers and free blacks. Information on white taxpayers includes land ownership, profession, polls, and investments, including stock and securities and personal possessions. For free people of color, the digests include land ownership, polls, employer, and personal property. The *Savannah,*

Georgia Land Tax and Property Records, 1809–1938 is a register of city lots and is available on Ancestry.com.

- **KENTUCKY:** The *Kentucky Tax Lists, 1799–1801* is a list of thirty-two thousand taxpayers available on Ancestry.com based on the original tax lists at the Kentucky Historical Society. You can learn more about Kentucky tax lists in "An Overlooked Resource for Kentucky History & Land Title" by Kandie Anderson, Land Office, Kentucky Secretary of State.[9]

- **MASSACHUSETTS:** Tax documents are available from town clerks. FHL has microfilm records for *Property valuations and taxes, 1760–1771 and Valuations, 1780–1792, 1810–1811*. Check the FHL catalog for more information on this collection.

- **MARYLAND:** Rent rolls or quit rent lists were used prior to the Revolutionary War. Maryland assessed a tax in 1783 to pay for the Revolutionary War, and a name index is available online at the Maryland State Archives. Remember to find out when the county was formed to determine the availability of records. Located at the Maryland Historical Society, *The Calvert Papers* has tax lists for some counties in 1658, 1659, 1700–1724, and 1753–1762.

- **NEW YORK:** *Tax Assessment Rolls of Real and Personal Estates 1799–1804* is available on microfilm at the New York State Archives.

- **NEW JERSEY:** The tax rateables for 1773 to 1822 are available at the New Jersey State Archives and microfilm copies are available at the New Jersey Historical Society and the FHL. The rateables include single men, widows, and married couples, including whether they owned land.

- **NORTH CAROLINA:** Tax lists for North Carolina are published online at State Library of North Carolina Digital Collections. Ancestry.com has digitized the *North Carolina Taxpayers, 1701–1786 Vol. 1 & 2* by Clarence E. Ratcliff. This database consists of about 28,000 names from half of the counties in North Carolina formed before 1786.

- **OHIO:** *Ohio Tax Records 1800–1850* is available online at Ancestry.com and Familysearch.org, and they are records from the County Auditors. A majority of the records are from 1816 to 1838.

---

9 https://www.sos.ky.gov/admin/land/resources/articles/Documents/Tax%20Lists%201792-1840%20(rev).pdf.

- **PENNSYLVANIA:** Tax records are available online at Ancestry.com, and the *Rent Rolls, 1703–1744* from the Secretary of Land Office are available from the FHL.
- **RHODE ISLAND:** Tax lists were recorded at the town level and are available at the Rhode Island State Archives.
- **SOUTH CAROLINA:** Males from the age of twenty-one were taxed, and the records include description of some personal property, number of school children, and slaves. The South Carolina Department of Archives and History has taxation records, and some are available online.
- **TEXAS:** *Texas, County Tax Rolls* are available on Ancestry.com (1846–1910) and Familysearch.org (1837–1910).
- **VIRGINIA:** Starting in 1782, Virginia began statewide enumeration at the county level of land and personal property. Information recorded in the land and personal property tax records changed over the years. The following articles about Personal and Land Tax Records in Virginia provide information on the content of the tax records, use of tax records, and availability of records for research: *Using Land Tax Records in the Archives of Library of Virginia* http://www.lva.virginia.gov/public/guides/rn1_landtax.pdf and *Using Personal Property Tax Records in the Archives at the Library of Virginia* http://www.lva.virginia.gov/public/guides/rn3_persprop.pdf.

PROBATE RECORDS

Probate records are court records generated after someone's death, whether that person dies intestate or testate. To die intestate means the deceased did not have a will and their property was divided up among family members based on state law. When someone dies testate they have a will with an administrator or an executor. Wills and estate papers are useful for identifying family members and relationships; real and personal property values; and current residence of surviving family members. In the United States, most state laws are based on English Common Law, with the exception of Louisiana, which has a legal system based on Civil Code. In Louisiana, succession papers are generated in the process of settling a deceased person's estate and are the equivalent of probate records in other states. Below is a table of key terms that you will need to know when researching your family in wills and estates at the county courthouse.[10]

TERMS	DEFINITION
Administrator	A person granted administration of a will where no executors are named or the named executor is unable to act.
Accounts	A report of the transactions related to the distribution of the estate.
Appraiser	A third party who estimates the real and personal property value of estates. Appraisers were an important part of the Domestic Slave Trade in the United States.
Decedent	The deceased person who may own property both real and personal at the time of their death.
Division	Records describing how the property has been divided among the heirs of an estate. **TIP:** Divisions are important for tracking the migration of the enslaved prior to the Civil War.
Executor	Individual appointed by the decedent to distribute their estate. Executors can also be appointed by the court.
Heirs	Individuals who have the right to decedent's property under law.
Codicil	Changes to a will that is signed, dated, and witnessed like the original will.
Guardian/Guardianships	An individual appointed by the court to manage affairs for minors or incompetents.
Bonds	Typically required by the court to ensure that the administrator would complete their duties.

10 https://familysearch.org/wiki/en/Glossary_of_United_States_Probate_Terms.

TERMS	DEFINITION
Inventory	An assessment of the real and personal property of the decedent, part of a probate package.
Relinquishments	Waiving the right to property
Petitions	An application requesting the right to settle an estate. This is typically filed in the court where the decedent owned property.
Wills	A document created by the decedent appointing an executor, distributing real and personal property, and identifying heirs.

TIP

Probate Records are the foundation of Slave Ancestral Research. However, you must know the last enslaver to identify your enslaved ancestor, and most enslaved were identified by their first name only. Some probate records include bills of sales, deeds, or other documents related to the domestic slave trade. We will discuss finding the last enslaver in the chapter on African American Research.

FINDING YOUR ANCESTORS IN PROBATE RECORDS

Some of the early probate records have been published as abstracts of wills and inventories in book form and are available at historical societies, libraries, and the Family History Library. Many state libraries and archives have digitized and indexed early probate records. For example, the Library of Virginia has created an enhanced database based on *Virginia Wills and Administrations, 1632–1800: An Index of Wills Recorded in Local Courts of Virginia* by Clayton Torrence. Search the catalog of the state library and archives to find records available for the state, county, and city of former colonies. To find probate indexes online, search the catalogs at Ancestry.com, Findmypast.com, Familysearch.org, and MyHeritage .com. Ancestry.com and Familysearch.org have digitized probate records and made them available online. Some records are indexed, and others you can browse by county, record type, and other criteria.

To find your ancestor in probate records you will need the decedent's given name, date of death, or time period and the county where your ancestor died. The US Wills and Probate Records collection at Ancestry.com boasts more than 170 million documents from all fifty states. These records are only indexed by the name of the deceased. At Familysearch.org, search the catalog by state and keyword to browse probate records that have been digitized but not indexed. These records are organized by county, and within each county you can browse Bonds, Appraisements, Letters of Administration, Returns, and Vouchers and Wills.

CRIMINAL COURT PROCEEDINGS

Criminal proceedings are either for the prosecution of a crime or the prevention of a crime.[11] If your ancestor served time in prison, you might have discovered this fact while building their census profile. Yes, prisoners were enumerated in the Federal Census—that's how I discovered a distant relative in prison! Several prison record sets are available for research, such as criminal court records, execution, parole records, police files, and prison registers. Correctional facilities kept information on prisoners such as name, physical description, race, birthplace, conviction, sentence term, county of sentencing, county of residence, occupation, and mental health information.[12]

TIP

Newspapers can be useful in providing additional information about a criminal court proceeding.

---

11 Black, H., Nolan, J. and Nolan-Haley, J. *Black's Law Dictionary*. (St. Paul, MN: West. 1991.), 374.
12 Szucs, Loretto Dennis, and Sandra Hargreaves Luebking, eds. *The Source: A Guidebook Of American Genealogy*. 3rd edition. Provo, UT: Ancestry Publishing, 2006.

Online Resources for Criminal Records[13]

RECORD COLLECTION	INFORMATION	RECORDS ACCESS
US Penitentiary Records 1875–1963	Includes records from three prisoner indexes, jail records, and other information.	Ancestry.com
Black Sheep Ancestors	Prison Records arranged by State and divided into four categories: Court Records, Executions, Outlaws, Prisons & Convicts	Blacksheepancestors.com Prison Records
Alcatraz, California, US Penitentiary, Prisoner Index, 1934–1963.	Use this index to locate the inmate identification number.	Ancestry.com Case files are available at National Archives and Records Administration Pacific Regional Office.
Arizona Prison Records, 1875–1929	Convict registers, conduct records, description records, and commutations	Ancestry.com
Iowa Consecutive Registers of Convicts, 1867–1970	Convict registers from Iowa State Penitentiary, Anamosa State Penitentiary, and Iowa State Reformatory for Women	Ancestry.com
Leavenworth, Kansas, US Penitentiary, Name Index to Inmate Case Files, 1895–1936	Information about inmates includes a Record Sheet that gives details about the crime, court fines, sentence and other information.	Ancestry.com The original case files are located at the National Archives at Kansas City and arranged by inmate number.
Tulare County California Sheriff's Office and Jail Records, 1874–1963	Jail registers, registers of actions, descriptions of criminals, cash books, coroner's registers, and other records	Ancestry.com

---

13 Note: Collections change from time to time.

RECORD COLLECTION	INFORMATION	RECORDS ACCESS
Chester County, Pennsylvania, Criminal and Prison Record Indexes, 1681–1911	Prison Discharges, Prisoner Petitions, and Indictments	Ancestry.com Chester County, Pennsylvania—http://www.chesco.org/1394/Criminal-Prison-Records
Atlanta, Georgia, US Penitentiary Prisoner Index, 1880–1922	Index to Case Files of prisoners held at Atlanta US Federal Penitentiary from 1902–1922. Data include name, age, crime committed, race, inmate number, date of incarceration, and release.	Ancestry.com The original case files are located at the National Archives and Records Administration in Atlanta and are arranged by inmate number.
Louisiana State Penitentiary Records, 1866–1963		Ancestry.com, Familysearch.org These records are available for browsing.
McNeil Island, Washington, US Penitentiary, Photos, and Records of Prisoners Received, 1887–1939	Photographs and information on prisoners such as name, crime, when and where arrested, date and term of sentence, and physical description.	Ancestry.com
Pennsylvania Prison, Reformatory and Workhouse Records, 1829–1971	Records from the Allegheny County Workhouse, Eastern and Western State Penitentiary, and Pennsylvania Industrial Reformatory at Huntington	Ancestry.com

PROPERTY RECORDS

Starting in the colonial period, land in the United States was distributed slightly differently in each colony; some colonies used the headright system, a land grant system introduced to attract settlers to the colonies. The Virginia Company had the right to grant land on the colony of Virginia for a time before land distribution was reverted back to the Crown. For any ancestors who were early settlers in the United States, understanding how land was originally distributed to early settlers of the colonies will be beneficial when researching property records.

For example, the Calvert family obtained a grant from the Crown for Maryland and used the headright system to entice immigrants to Maryland. They issued land grants from 1633 to 1683 and established a land office in 1680. If your ancestor settled in Maryland, *The New Early Settlers of Maryland* by Dr. Carson Gibb is searchable online at the Maryland State Archives. A searchable index to *Settlers of Maryland, 1679–1783* by Peter Wilson Coldham is available at Ancestry.com. There are other searchable indexes available at the county and state level from historical societies and state archives in the former colonies.

Land Records are available at the federal, state, and county level across the United States depending on the year of statehood. These records include deeds, mortgages, patents, petitions, surveys, and other documentation related to the buying and selling of real and personal property. Some of the earlier land records have been digitized and indexed, making them easily available online. One of the most common property records used in family history research are deeds. They can help you uncover a wealth of information about your ancestors including:

- Current and previous residence
- Name of spouse
- Name of children and other relatives
- Neighbors living on adjoining property
- Migration patterns of your ancestors

TERM OR DOCUMENT	DEFINITION
Assignee	A person who has been assigned the rights or personal property of another individual
Chattel Mortgage	Used as security for personal property
Deed	A document transferring property from one party to another. There are various types of deeds: Deed of Trust, Partition Deed, Personal Property Deed, Quitclaim Deed, and Warranty Deed.
Deed of Trust	Land was deeded to a trustee to secure the property. Consists of three parties, the person mortgaging the property, the person lending the money, and the trustee holding the property until the mortgage is paid
Grantee	Recipient of property from the grantor who will be taking legal title
Grantor	The seller of the property such as a house typically passes legal title in a deed.
Land Patent	The transfer of land ownership from the government to an individual
Mortgage	A security instrument for the repayment of debt
Partition Deed	Divides land owned by two or more persons
Personal Property Deed	Conveyance of personal property such as enslaved human beings, household furniture, horses, and farm equipment
Quitclaim Deed	A deed releasing claim to property by one person to another
Survey	A third-party inspection of real property for the sale of property
Warranty Deed	The grantor warrants a good title to the property.

PUBLIC LAND V. STATE LAND STATES

The land within State Land States was controlled, distributed, and surveyed by colonial governments. They did not cede their unclaimed land to the United States when they became states.

STATE LAND STATES

Connecticut	New York
Delaware	North Carolina
Georgia	Pennsylvania
Hawaii	Rhode Island
Kentucky	South Carolina
Maine	Tennessee
Maryland	Texas
Massachusetts	Vermont
New Hampshire	Virginia
New Jersey	West Virginia

During your family history search, you might come across the term "public land" states. Public Land means land in which the federal government has title and these transfers are governed by the Bureau of Land Management (BLM). The BLM has divided the public land states into two regions: Eastern and Western. Most Federal Land records are available at the National Archives and Records Administration in Washington, DC, or at regional facilities.

EASTERN STATES	WESTERN STATES
Alabama	Alaska
Arkansas	Arizona
Florida	California
Illinois	Colorado
Indiana	Idaho
Iowa	Kansas
Louisiana	Montana
Michigan	Nebraska
Minnesota	Nevada
Mississippi	New Mexico
Missouri	North Dakota
Ohio	Oklahoma
Wisconsin	Oregon
	South Dakota
	Utah
	Washington
	Wyoming

THE HOMESTEAD ACT OF 1862

The Homestead Act was signed by President Abraham Lincoln on May 20, 1862. Homesteaders were given 160 acres of land if they maintained five years of continuous residence, improved the land, filed application papers, paid the filing fee, and filed for a deed of title.[14] The completed patent process generated a land entry case file providing detailed records of the dwellings, trees cleared, crops, fences, and family members who also resided on the land. Until 1908, the homesteader applications were kept in tract books, and all but Alaska and Missouri have survived. The tract books have been microfilmed and are available at the National Archives and Records Administration (NARA) and the Family History Library in Salt Lake City. The "United States Bureau of Land Management Tract Books, 1800–c.1955" are available for browsing at Familysearch.org. Tract books are grouped by state, land office, and legal description of the land.

---

14 https://familysearch.org/wiki/en/Homestead_Records#Researching_the_Records

If you do not have a legal description of the land, check the county records where the land was located. Search the BLM General Land Office https:// glorecords.blm.gov/search/default.aspx for a legal description of the land, date of entry, and patent information. To order a copy of the land entry case file from NARA, you will need to complete NATF Form 84 and provide the following information:

- Name
- State where the land was located
- Approximate date of entry

Pre-July 1908 general land entry files include:
- Legal description of the land
- Type of land entry
- Patent final certificate number
- Name of the land office

Post-July 1908 land entry files include:
- Serial patent number

To learn more about researching in the Land Entry Files of the General Land Office and Bureau of Land Management, review NARA Reference Information Paper #114 available at archives.gov.

LITTLE HOUSE ON THE PRAIRIE

During Season 2 of *Genealogy Roadshow*, I had the pleasure of walking through the Homestead application of a guest who was related to Laura Ingalls Wilder. As we reviewed the land entry case file, I was able to paint a picture of what life was like for their homesteading ancestor. This is another great resource to help you create historical context about your ancestor and their life.

When researching in states that are not public lands, the court clerk in the county will have copies of property records such as deeds, mortgages, petitions, and related documents. Be sure to check the website of the Clerk and Courthouse for information on hours, photocopy fees, and records availability. Some Court Clerks have started to digitize and index records, making them available online. The Family History Library in Utah has microfilm for various county courthouses in the United States. Search their catalog for lists of microfilm or online resources available for your county.

If the records are not online, once you arrive at the county courthouse, search the grantee and grantor indexes to find your ancestor. It's important to search both because you do not know if your ancestor was buying or selling property or both. Make sure you write down the deed book, pages, dates, and the parties' names. You can also use your phone or tablet to take photos of the pages.

TIP

Make friends with the clerks at the courthouse! If a deed book is missing or out for repair, they can help and provide you more information about the collection. They might be able to point you to other resources in the courthouse.

Searching for my relatives in Culpeper County, Virginia

During one of my many trips from Alexandria, Virginia, to Culpeper County, I stopped by the courthouse to search for information on my Sellers and Carter ancestors. I started by searching the Grantor and Grantee Indexes at the court-house, making notes of the names, deed book number, dates, and pages. Below are abstracts of the first deeds I found for the land my great-great-great-grandfather James Phillip Sellers purchased in Culpeper County, Virginia.

> *Wharton to Sellers, Warranty Deed*
> *Culpeper County, Va., Deed Book 19, pp. 224–225*
> *Drawn 29 May 1879; proved 14 June 1879*

JOHN S. WHARTON and his wife GABRIELLE D. of Culpeper County, Virginia and J. PHILLIP SELLERS of Culpeper County, Virginia in consideration of the sum of one hundred and fifty dollars in hand paid and secured by deed of Trust on the land below described to be paid, convey general warranty to J. PHILLIP SELLERS parcel of land adjoining the lot of Lee Brown, Preston and others and bounded for survey of A. G. Tutt dated April 7, 1879 as follows, "Beginning at a stake in TALLEY'S line, a corner to LEE BROWN'S lot; and running thence (1st) South 1 1/2 degrees, West 45 7/10 poles to a Stake in PRESTON's line, corner to PRESTON thence (2 degrees), South (87 5/8 degrees, West 69 4/10 poles to a stake in HUTCHINSON'S East line; corner to NEWMAN's lot; thence (3 degrees) North 3 degrees East 46 1/2 poles to a stake in TALLEY's line; thence (4 degrees) North 88 degrees east 69 4/10 poles to the beginning and containing twenty acres of land, be it the same more or less. Parcel of land and its appurtenances with the J. PHILLIP SELLERS his heirs and assigns forever.

J. S. Wharton (seal)

Ella D. Wharton (seal)

State of Virginia

County of Culpeper Court

W. C. Petty, a justice of the Peace for Culpeper County, Virginia, certifies this deed that John S. WHARTON signed to the writing on the 29th day of May 1879 and acknowledged on June 14, 1879.

W. C. Petty and Geo. E. Marshall, justices of the peace for Culpeper County, Virginia certify that Gabrielle D. WHARTON, wife of John S. WHARTON signed to the writing above, appeared in Court and being examined by us and apart from her husband having the writing freely explained to her, Gabrielle D. WHARTON acknowledged the said writing to be her act and declared that she has willingly executed and does not wish to retract it, this 14 day of June 1879.

W. C. Petty, JP

G. E. Marshall, JP

Culpeper County Court Clerk's office February 9, 1880 this deed was filed and admitted to record Delivered to J. P. Sellers on August 9th, 1886

What did we learn from this document?

Drawn up on May 29, 1879, and proved on June 14, 1879, this warranty deed from the Whartons granted twenty acres more or less of land to James P. Sellers for the sum of $150.00. James P. Sellers secured a Deed of Trust for the land that generated another deed to review:

Sellers, to Deed Trust, Halsey Trustee

Culpeper County, Va.; Deed Book 19, p.117–118

Drawn 29 May 1879; Proved July 21, 1879

J. PHILLIP SELLERS of Culpeper County, Virginia conveys to J. J. HALSEY, Orange County, Virginia land purchased by SELLERS of J. S. WHARTON and conveyed by deed of J. S. WHARTON and his wife, GABRIELLA D., which contains per A. G. TUTTS survey, April 7, 1879 twenty acres of land made, under the covenant of general warranty of title hereby made by said J. PHILLIP SELLERS to said J. J. HALSEY, his heirs, personal representatives and assigns in trust to secure the unpaid purchase money due on said lot as follows: first to BENJAMIN F. NALLE, assignee of WHARTON, the sum of forty dollars payable on or before January 1, 1880 with interest from the 17th day of May 1879 and the further sum of eighty dollars, payable on or before the first day of January 1, 1881 with interest from the 17th day of May 1879; and to John S. WHARTON or his assigns the sum of twenty-seven dollars payable on or before January 1st, 1881, with interest from the 17th day of May 1879 in default of payment of either or all the above sums, the said J. J. Halsey trustee, to close this deed and execute it as prescribed by statute of Virginia.

J. Phillip Sellers (seal)

Justice B. F. NALLE, notary public for Culpeper County, Virginia certifies that J. Phillip Sellers

signed to the writing on the 29th of May 1879 and acknowledged on the 18th of July 1879.

B. F. NALLE, NP

Culpeper County Court Clerk's office July 21st, 1879 this deed was filed and admitted to record.

C. B. Payne, Clerk

What did we learn from this document?

There are three parties in this Deed of Trust: James P. Sellers, the owner who is mortgaging the property; Benjamin F. Nalle, the assignee of Wharton; and J. J. Halsey, the trustee holding the property until the mortgage is paid. The payment terms of the deed of trust are James P. Sellers to pay Benjamin F. Nalle $40 with interest by January 1, 1880, and $80 with interest by January 1, 1881. A balance of $27 was due to J. J. Halsey with interest by January 1, 1881. In the margins of the deed book, it noted, "The debt for which this deed of trust was given to secure has been fully satisfied." More than fifteen years later, after James and his family moved to York, New York, he sold the land to Charles E. Taylor and Lucien A. Taylor for $240. This was presumably at a profit, depending on the interest he paid to Benjamin F. Nalle and J. J. Halsey.

Land Lotteries

When I started doing family history research over twenty years ago, I first encountered the Georgia Land Lotteries. I was researching the father of George Henry Dwelle, Clark J. Cook, who received land in the 1832 Cherokee Land Lottery in Georgia. Georgia held eight land lotteries between 1805 and 1833. The General Assembly passed an act for each authorizing the lottery, eligibility, and grant fees.[15] This was land primarily taken from the Cherokee and Creek tribes in Georgia. Andrew Jackson's victory over the Creeks during the War of 1812 effectively removed them from Georgia. The Indian removal made way for white settlers and was a keystone for President Andrew Jackson. The land lotteries of 1805, 1807, 1820, 1821, and 1827 involved Creek lands. While the land lottery in 1820 involved Creek and Cherokee lands, the 1832 and 1833 land lotteries involved Cherokee lands.[16] To find out if your ancestor participated in the Georgia Land Lotteries, search the catalog at Ancestry.com for resources. Once you find those resources, document the lottery year, district, acres, and any other information.

---

15 http://www.georgiaarchives.org/research/land_lottery.
16 http://www.georgiaencyclopedia.org/articles/history-archaeology/land-lottery-system.

CHAPTER 3
OTHER RECORDS

At this point in your family history journey, we have reviewed Census, Court, Property, and Vital Records—the typical starting points for researching your ancestors. Other records such as city directories, church records, newspapers, and voter registrations are useful in family history research. Most of these records are available online at Ancestry.com, Familysearch.org, Findmypast.com, Fold3.com, MyHeritage.com, and other websites.

CITY DIRECTORIES

Some city directories may only include the name of the male head of the household, while others include the wife's name in parentheses. If a woman was widowed, her husband's first name could also appear in parentheses on the same line within her household. The deceased husband would also be included in the online index. City directories are valuable in re-creating the migration of your ancestors. This is especially important for African Americans whose ancestors were part of the Great Migration from the rural South to urban areas for work. One of the most challenging parts of beginning a family history is the twenty-year gap between the 1880 and 1900 US federal censuses. While a number of city directories are online at Ancestry.com and Familysearch.org, don't forget to check local and regional repositories for directories that have been transcribed, digitized, or are on microfilm. Local libraries, state archives, and historical and genealogical societies in your area are great resources for these types of records. Below is a sampling of city directories and compiled public records available online including the location:

City Directories and Public Records Online

COLLECTION	LOCATION
US City Directories, 1822–1995	Ancestry.com
US Phone and Address Directories, 1993–2002	Ancestry.com
Online Historical Directories Website	https://sites.google.com/site/onlinedirectorysite/
United States Public Records, 1970–2009	Familysearch.org
US and UK City Directories, 1630–1830	Ancestry.com
Ohio and Florida City Directories, 1902–1960	Ancestry.com
US Public Records Index, 1950–1993, Volume 1	Ancestry.com
US Public Records Index, 1950–1993, Volume 2	Ancestry.com

CEMETERY RESEARCH

When I first started doing family history research, I reviewed funeral programs that my grandmother and other relatives had collected over the years. These programs can be minibiographical sketches of your relatives' lives. Funeral programs will include information about the funeral arrangement, the funeral home, and burial information including the cemetery. Obituaries and death notices in local and regional newspapers include cemetery information.

If you don't have access to newspapers, obituaries, or death certificates, Billion-Graves.com, Findagrave.com, and Interment.net can help you locate gravesites for your ancestors. Each site offers something different and relies on other family historians and locals to build their content, resulting in organic growth and almost daily updates. These volunteers upload pictures of tombstones, obituaries, newspaper articles, transcriptions of tombstones, and other information from the cemetery. Billiongraves.com advertises itself as the largest GPS site for cemeteries. Users can take photos, upload photos, transcribe photos of tombstones, and organize events for volunteers to take and upload photos at cemeteries around the world.

You can create a tree on Billion Graves using technology from Familysearch.org. Myheritage.com and Findmypast.com are working on offering this feature at a later date. By visiting a cemetery virtually or in person, you can find your ancestor's birth date, death date, military service, and relationships. I strongly encourage you to visit as many cemeteries as possible in person. In 2003, I walked through Machpelah Cemetery in Le Roy, New York, with the administrator and my mother looking for the graves of my ancestors. I was able to locate the unmarked graves of my third great-grandparents, James and Emily Sellers. There are a number of private cemeteries located on former plantations or farms in rural and southern areas of the United States that are documented in county histories. Some cities had separate cemeteries for different ethnicities such as African Americans. Information about these cemeteries can be found in county and town histories and family papers, and through local and historical societies. As always, it's important to know as much as possible about the county where your ancestors lived and died.

Findagrave.com, owned by Ancestry.com, has information on the gravesites of thousands of famous people and 160 million grave records from around the world. You can search by name, look up cemeteries, add burial records and virtual flowers to an ancestor's memorial. Findagrave.com does a great job linking family members who are also buried in the same cemetery. The National Gravesite Locator is a database of United States veterans and their families. The database includes veterans buried in Veterans Affairs National Cemeteries, State Veterans cemeteries, other military cemeteries, and private cemeteries. Search the database for ancestors who served in the military to find information on their burial and/or military service. Interment.net has transcriptions of graves from around the world and provides links to obituaries at Genealogybank.com.

CHURCH RECORDS

Church records include baptisms, christenings, confirmations, marriages, burial records, and sacramental records and vary based on the religious denomination, location, access to records, and whether or not the town or city was destroyed in a conflict. Baptisms and christenings give the child's name, gender, date of birth, place of birth, parents' names, and date and location of baptism or christening.

Growing up in Detroit, I attended church with my parents, grandparents, neighbors, and other extended family members. Church has always been essential to my community and culture. My first research subjects, George Henry Dwelle and his sons, Thomas H. Dwelle, and brother John H. F. Dwelle, were prominent pastors at churches in Georgia, North Carolina, and Pennsylvania. I wrote their former churches looking for information on their time as pastors. I received documents about the Ladies Club, the Mothers Club, Bible Study, and copies of their sermons. I was able to learn more about their church community, helping me build a more robust profile of the Dwelle men who have been subjects of articles and frequent lectures. These documents gave me a glimpse into the Friends, Associates, and Neighbors (FAN) network of George H. Dwelle, Thomas H. Dwelle, and John H. F. Dwelle.

How do you find the church your ancestor attended?

Interview family members asking the following questions:

- Did your family have a church home in the town, city, or county where your ancestors lived? A church home is a church where they were baptized or the family has been attending for generations!
- What religious denomination did your ancestors practice?
- Are there other religious denominations in the family tree?
- Did anyone convert to a religious denomination after immigration?
- What was their religious denomination back in the home country?
- Where did they get married?
- Is there a family Bible? If so, who has it and how can I get my hands on it?

Review the information you have compiled so far on your ancestors:

- Marriage records: were they all married at the same church or within the same religion?
- Immigration and naturalization: For immigrant ancestors, check the records you have compiled on their immigration and/or naturalization. Oftentimes religion was included in the passport application.
- Death certificates and obituaries: Does it include burial information? Are all your ancestors buried in one cemetery? Is it a church cemetery?

Check local resources for information about churches in the area:

- County histories: write down all the religious institutions in the area.
- Local newspapers: they may have information on the religious institutions in the area where your ancestor lived. If there isn't a local newspaper, expand your search to other areas, including neighboring towns and counties. Don't forget to check ethnic newspapers as well, because they often cover information in the state, not just in the city of publication.
- Local archives and societies: some of the archives, library, and historical and genealogical societies have information on religious institutions including records that might have been donated for preservation.

If the church is still around, connect with the church leadership and plan a visit. You would be surprised how excited and helpful they are once you tell them your ancestors were members. That has been my experience with Second Baptist Church in Mumford, New York, my family's church home. If there is a college or university in the area, check their library for information about the church and the community. Many records and manuscripts are donated to colleges and universities to preserve them for future generations. Reach out to the librarian in Special Collections or search the library's website to learn about the local collection and resources. Other great resources are professors and historians, who may have published papers, books, or articles on the area where your family lived. I have found all these avenues useful in providing historical context to add to my family's story.

NEWSPAPERS

Newspapers are an excellent resource for family history research since they document historical events. Newspapers were the social media of the day—they are a combination of Facebook, Instagram, and Twitter and are filled with photos, advertisements, legal notices, society columns, local happenings, birth and marriage announcements, obituaries, military information, visitors, family affairs, and international news. Newspapers.com, Genealogy Bank, and Chronicling America from the Library of Congress can help you with finding your ancestors in newspapers, both via subscription and for free. Search newspapers that span the United States, regionally, and locally for your ancestors.

I love the local happenings section of the newspaper because I love gossip! I have been lucky enough to find newspaper obituaries for ancestors who migrated multiple times providing details of their migration. These obituaries provide the location of their death, their age, date of birth, birth location, parents' names, spouse, children, siblings, church affiliation, occupation, and other information. For my family history research, the obituary has been a critical starting point in creating a biographical sketch of my ancestor. When searching newspapers, make sure you try numerous spelling variations, because most of the indexes use optional character recognition (OCR) scanning and they might interpret your ancestor's name incorrectly. For sites that span the United States or other countries, I put my ancestors' names in quotations and then add a plus sign for the location. This helps to narrow down the search results for very large collections or for an ancestor with a common name like Berry or Smith. For female ancestors, if you know their maiden name, do not forget to include it in the search. Some of the newspaper resources below are updated often with new collections:

TITLE	COLLECTION	LOCATION
Chronicling America	Historic newspaper pages from 1789 to 1924 and US Newspaper Directory	http://chroniclingamerica.loc.gov
LDS Genealogy	US Newspapers and Obituaries Directory organized by State	https://ldsgenealogy.com/newspapers-obituaries/
GenealogyBank	Over 7,000 US newspapers from 1690	Genealogybank.com
Newspaper Archive	Millions of newspaper pages from 1607 to present	Newspaperarchive.com
Newspapers.com	More than 5,000 newspapers from the early 1700s until the 2000s. The collection includes some African American newspapers.	A site owned by Ancestry.com, and members are provided a discount on subscription. Newspapers.com is also included in the Ancestry.com all-access subscription.
Alaska Newspapers Index	Newspapers from Fairbanks, Juneau, and Tanana	Alaska Newspapers Index https://education.alaska.gov/lam/newspapers.cfm
California Digital Newspaper Collection	Digitized California newspapers from 1846 to the present	https://cdnc.ucr.edu/cgi-bin/cdnc Partnership between Center for Bibliographical Studies and Research (CBSR) and University of California, Riverside
Washington Digital Newspapers	Historic newspapers in Washington and the National Digital Newspaper Program	https://www.sos.wa.gov/library/newspapers/newspapers.aspx
Colorado Historic Newspaper Collections	Over 200 Colorado newspapers published 1859 to 1923 with more than 920,000 digitized pages	https://www.coloradohistoricnewspapers.org

TITLE	COLLECTION	LOCATION
Newspapers of Connecticut	Newspapers from 1821 to 1929 from the Connecticut State Library	http://cslib.cdmhost.com/cdm/landingpage /collection/p15019coll9
Hoosier State Chronicle	Indiana's Digital Historic Newspaper program including papers from 1836 to 1922	https://newspapers.library.in.gov/
Old Fulton, NY, Post Cards	New York old newspapers and other documents from 1761 to 1989	http://fultonhistory.com/Fulton.html
Utah Digital Newspapers	Collection of historic Utah newspapers	https://digitalnewspapers.org
The Olden Times	Historic newspapers from US, England, Scotland, Ireland & Australia	http://theoldentimes.com
British Newspapers Archives	Regional and national newspapers from England, Wales, and Scotland	Findmypast.com
Wyoming Newspaper Project	Over 340 newspapers from 1849 forward	http://newspapers.wyo.gov

Just like with today's social media, you can't believe everything you read. And those who have been doing family history research for a while know this is true for newspapers and other records, so verifying the information from these sources is essential. While researching my maternal ancestors living in upstate New York, I discovered information about their social events, visitors, family affairs, church events, and even family reunions! It has changed my perspective of their lives. I thought they were just farmers in rural Rochester, New York, and being from the big city of Detroit, I could not relate. I now realize they were part of a vibrant

African American community in upstate New York. I have been able to reconstruct portions of their social activities through the *New York Age*. The *New York Age* was an African American newspaper published from 1887 to 1953. During this time period, someone in my family tree or who is part of the FAN network is included in the news or social columns about the communities in and around Rochester.

I have been able to verify the information I discovered about my ancestors in the *New York Age* with other documentation. For example, it was reported that my great-great-great-aunt Meta Sellers Lewis and her husband, Lewis Price, hosted Mordecai Wyatt Johnson and his wife for dinner. Mordecai W. Johnson was the first African American President of Howard University and studied at the Rochester Theological Seminary. The Seminary is located about twenty miles away from my ancestors' home in Caledonia. During my 2016 visit to Second Baptist Church for its 125th anniversary, I was able to verify that Mordecai Johnson was a guest preacher at Second Baptist Church in Mumford. So, it's likely, given their status and involvement in the community, that my ancestors did indeed host Mordecai W. Johnson for dinner.

VOTER RECORDS

No matter their political view, many of our ancestors were politically active for a variety of reasons. For those who were formerly enslaved, the right to participate in the electoral process and citizenship was a motivating factor. Voter registrations and lists will include your ancestor's name, race, occupation, political affiliation, residence, length of residence, date of registration, county of registration, and other information. Like other records, they are useful in adding to your ancestor's biographical narrative. To find out if your ancestor is in the voter registration records, search the state archives and local historical and genealogical societies to determine which records are available. Make sure you read any materials provided by the repository on what's included in the collection, what survived, and how to access the collection. Voter registrations might be included in the town and county records where your ancestor lived.

A FAMILY HISTORY GEM

The 15th amendment passed by Congress on February 26, 1869, ratified on February 3, 1870, granted African American men the right to vote.[1] My second great-grandfather Lewis Kendrick was formerly enslaved in Houston County, Georgia. On July 10, 1867, he was included in a voter registration list.[2] I had always believed that my Kendrick ancestors were from neighboring Macon County, Georgia, but this helped me establish Lewis's residency in Houston County.

---

1 https://ourdocuments.gov/doc.php?flash=false&doc=44

2 Kendrick, Louis. Precinct No. Henderson, Election District 23, *Georgia Returns of Qualified Voters and Reconstruction Oath Books*, 1867-1869, Provo, UT: Ancestry.com, 2012.

Sampling of Voter Registrations, Lists, and Oath Books Available Online

STATE	COLLECTION	LOCATION
Alabama	Voter Registration, 1867	Ancestry.com Alabama Department of Archives and History
Arizona	Voter Registrations, 1866–1955	Ancestry.com
California	Voter Registrations, 1866–1898; Voter Registrations, 1900–1968	Ancestry.com
Georgia	Returns of Qualified Voters, 1867–1869, and Reconstruction Oath Books, 1856–1896; 1901–1917 Savannah, Georgia Voter Records, 1856–1896; 1901–1917	Ancestry.com
Illinois	Chicago, Illinois Voter Registrations, 1888, 1890 & 1892	Ancestry.com

STATE	COLLECTION	LOCATION
Kansas	Kansas Registration Lists, 1854–1856; 1859, Leavenworth Kansas Voter Registration	Ancestry.com
Missouri	Jackson County Voter Registration Records, 1928–1956	Ancestry.com
North Carolina	County Records, 1833–1970	Familysearch.org
Texas	Voter Registration Lists, 1867–1869	Ancestry.com

CHAPTER 4
IMMIGRATION AND NATURALIZATION RECORDS

Most Americans have immigrant ancestors. In this chapter, we will explore records related to immigration and naturalization. One of the biggest myths in family history research is that your ancestor's name was changed at Ellis Island. Immigration officials did not change the names of the passengers when they arrived in the United States. Their names were recorded as they boarded the ships, and some families changed their names once they arrived in America to assimilate into American life and culture. For some families, this information has not been passed down through the generations.

IMMIGRATION

In this section, we review the immigration periods prior to 1820; between 1820 and 1957; and after 1957. Throughout history, the United States Congress has enacted laws to create a uniform process of immigration, restrict immigration using quotas, restrict certain ethnic groups from entering the United States, and create comprehensive reform. When researching immigrant ancestors, it's important to understand the US immigration laws.

LEGISLATION	IMPACT TO IMMIGRATION
Immigration Act of 1875	Forbade criminals and women brought to the United States for lewd and immoral purposes.
Immigration Act of 1882	Restricted certain immigrants including criminals, insane, or anyone unable to take care of themselves from coming to the United States and imposed a head tax on immigrants arriving in American ports.
Chinese Exclusion Act of 1882	The first major legislation implemented to prevent a specific ethnic group from immigrating to the United States. Excluded laborers both skilled and unskilled from entering the country.
Immigration Act of 1891	Established the Bureau of Immigration under the Treasury Department. In 1892, Ellis Island opened as a federal immigrant processing station, replacing Castle Garden.
Emergency Quota Act or the Immigration Restriction Act of 1921	Established numerical limits on immigration and established the National Origins Formula. Immigration was restricted to 3 percent of foreign-born persons from each nation that resided in the United States in 1910. The National Origins Formula is a system of immigration quotas.
Immigration Act of 1924 or the National Origins Act	Limited the annual number of immigrants admitted to the United States to 2 percent of the number of people from that country already living in the United States. This quota system was based on data from the 1890 Census.
Alien Registration Act of 1940 (Smith Act)	The act required noncitizens to register with the United States government. Aliens were required to complete a questionnaire and be fingerprinted.

LEGISLATION	IMPACT TO IMMIGRATION
Immigration and Naturalization Act of 1952 (McCarran-Walter Act)	Created a comprehensive statute for Immigration and naturalization. Immigrants with special skills or with relatives who were US citizens were exempt from quotas. Lowered the naturalization age requirement to eighteen years of age.
Immigration Act of 1965 (Hart-Celler Act)	The National Origins Formula was abolished, but numerical restrictions remained with country ceilings and a seven-category preference system.

On *Genealogy Roadshow*, immigration is a common family theme for those from Asia, the Caribbean, and Europe. How do you find information on your immigrant ancestor's homeland?

TIP

When searching for your immigrant ancestors, make sure you document their name, age, sex, religion, and country of origin. Gather this information in their US Federal Census profile and from vital records.

FINDING ANCESTORS WHO ARRIVED IN THE UNITED STATES BEFORE 1820

If your ancestor arrived prior to 1820, check the passenger records at the port of arrival. Some of the major ports were Boston, Baltimore, Philadelphia, and New Orleans. Boston was the leading port from 1630 to 1750. Philadelphia was founded in 1682, New Orleans was founded by the French in 1718, and Baltimore was founded in 1729.[1] The National Archives and Records Administration (NARA) has Philadelphia arrivals beginning in 1800 and New Orleans arrivals beginning in

---

1 https://familysearch.org/wiki/en/Beginning_Research_in_United_States_Immigration_and_Emigration _Records#What_are_United_States_immigration_and_emigration_records.3F.

1813.[2] About 500,000 Europeans immigrated to the United States prior to 1775, nd about 55,000 were involuntary prisoners. Of the 450,000 Europeans who came voluntarily, Christopher Tomlins estimates that 48 percent were indentured servants. The age of adulthood was twenty-four, and indentured servants over twenty-four usually served three years.[3] To find your immigrant ancestor, search the "US and Canada Passenger and Immigration Lists Index, 1500s–1900s" available on Ancestry.com. This database contains information on 4,712,000 individuals from the *Passenger and Immigration Lists Index* by William P. Filby and Mary K. Meyer, eds. http://search.ancestry.com/search/db.aspx?dbid=7486. Data collected on individuals:

- Name and age
- Place and year of arrival
- Records related to immigration or naturalization
- Source of the record
- Names of family members and their relationship to the primary individual

New England and the Great Migration

If your ancestor arrived in New England, a great resource is the Great Migration Project at the New England Historic and Genealogical Society (NEHGS). The Great Migration Study Project (https://www.greatmigration.org/) is a survey of immigration into New England from 1620 to 1640. The project profiles thousands of men, women, and children. An online index is available at https://www.greatmigration.org/pdf/index_names.pdf. Once you identify your ancestor's name in the index, write down the Great Migration database name, volume, and

2 Deeben, John Paul. *Genealogy Tool Kit : Getting Started on Your Family History at the National Archives.* Accessed June 15, 2017. http://www.torontopubliclibrary.ca/detail.jsp?Entt=RDM2905482&R=2905482.

3 Christopher Tomlins, "Reconsidering Indentured Servitude: European Migration and the Early American Labor Force, 1600–1775," *Labor History* (2001) 42#1 pp 5–43, at p. accessed on April 7, 2017 via https://en.wikipedia.org/wiki/Indentured_servitude.

page numbers. The Great Migration databases are available online at www
.americanancestors.org.

Was your ancestor sent to the United States as a prisoner prior to 1820?

English men, women, and children were deported to the United States for crimes. There may be information about their family history in the following resources:

- Bonded Passengers to America (Volumes I & II) 1615–1775 and 1617–1775 at http://search.ancestry.com/search/db.aspx?dbid=49089
- Emigrants in Bondage, 1614–1775; this collection provides names, parish of origin, occupation, sentencing court, offense, month and year of sentence, ship on which they were transported, and arrival in America. The database is available at http://search.ancestry.com/search/db.aspx?dbid=61074

Did your ancestor arrive as an indentured servant?

Indentured servants were men and women who agreed to work for seven years or other terms in exchange for transportation to British North America. The indentures received food, clothing, and shelter once they arrived. A few online databases document indenture contracts for Virginia and Pennsylvania. Virtual Jamestown has a database of over fifteen thousand indenture contracts created from the registers at Bristol, London, and Middlesex. These contracts include a wealth of information about the indenture and their family history including name, length of contract, parents' names, owner, home province and city, occupation, destination, and ship's name. You can access the database at http://www.virtual jamestown.org/indentures/about_indentures.html. For indentures in Philadelphia, search the following online resources:

- Philadelphia, Pennsylvania, Indentures, 1771–1773, are records compiled by Philadelphia's Mayor's Office. Information about indentures includes name, date of indenture, port of immigration, occupation, term of indenture, and notes: http://search.ancestry.com/search/db.aspx?dbid=4274.

- Philadelphia, (Pa.) Mayor. Record of indentures of individuals bound out as apprentices, servants, etc., and of German and other redemptioners in the office of the mayor of the city of Philadelphia, October 3, 1771, to October 5, 1773. Lancaster: Press of the New Era. 1907. https://archive.org/details/recordofindentur16phil.

IMMIGRATION TO THE UNITED STATES FROM 1820 TO 1957

In 1819, Congress passed legislation requiring captains arriving on ships from foreign ports to submit a list of all passengers to the Collector of Customs in the district where they arrived. The Collector of Customs was required to submit quarterly reports of those passenger lists to the Secretary of State who submitted that information to Congress. These passenger lists can be very useful in uncovering your ancestors who immigrated to the United States after 1820. To find the port of arrival, search the available passenger and immigration indexes available online:

- United States and Canada, Passenger and Immigration Lists Index, 1500s–1900s at http://search.ancestry.com/search/db.aspx?dbid=7486. Write down the name, place of arrival, and year. Once you know the arrival location, search for your ancestor in regional and local passenger arrival lists.
- United States Index to Passenger Arrivals, Atlantic and Gulf Ports, 1820–1874
- Name index for passenger arrivals in over seventy ports in the Atlantic and Gulf excluding New York City. Source: https://familysearch.org/search/collection/1921756
- United States, Atlantic Port Passenger Lists, 1920–1873 and 1893–1959. This collection contains records for ports in Alabama, Connecticut, Delaware, Florida, Georgia, Louisiana, Maine, Maryland, Massachusetts, Mississippi, New Hampshire, New Jersey, New York, North Carolina, Ohio, Pennsylvania, Rhode Island, South Carolina, Texas, Virginia, and Washington, DC. Source: http://search.ancestry.com/search/db.aspx?dbid=8758

Once you determine the port of arrival and the name of the ship, the next step is to review the passenger lists by region. Learn all that you can about the ship your ancestor arrived on in the United States. Some of the ships made several stops on their way to the United States. The following tables are organized by region and provide information on how to access crew and passenger lists online.

Selected Online Indexes of Crew and Passenger Lists for New England

RECORD TYPE	COLLECTION TITLE	PORT OF ARRIVAL	WEBSITE
Passenger List	Boston Passenger Lists, 1820–1891	Boston	Familysearch.org
Crew List	Massachusetts, Boston Crew Lists, 1811–1921	Boston	Familysearch.org
Crew and Passenger List	Massachusetts Passenger and Crew Lists, 1820–1963	Boston, New Bedford, Westover Air Force Base, Chicopee, and Woods Hole	Ancestry.com
Passenger List	Massachusetts, Boston Passenger Lists, 1891–1943	Boston	Familysearch.org
Passenger Lists	Massachusetts, Boston Passenger Lists Index, 1899–1940	Boston	Familysearch.org
Crew Lists	Massachusetts, Boston Crew Lists, 1917–1943	Boston	Familysearch.org

RECORD TYPE	COLLECTION TITLE	PORT OF ARRIVAL	WEBSITE
Crew and Passenger Lists	Massachusetts, Passenger and Crew Lists, 1949–1957	Boston and Fall River	Ancestry.com
Crew and Passenger Lists	New England Passenger and Crew Lists, 1911–1954	Various ports in Connecticut, Massachusetts, and Rhode Island	Familysearch.org
Crew Lists of US and Canadian citizens	Crew Lists Arriving at Robbinston, 1947–1954	Robbinston, Maine	Familysearch.org
Passenger Lists	Maine, Passenger Lists, 1894–1962	Various ports in Maine	Ancestry.com

Immigrants arriving in New York

For those researching ancestors who arrived in New York City, you have access to various indexes and databases for passenger information. The Access to Archival Database (AAD) available online has Passenger Lists records for about six million immigrants from Ireland, Germany, Italy, and Russia. To find these records, go to archives.gov and search for AAD. Go to the main page of the AAD and click "Passenger Lists" under Genealogy/Personal History. There are four record sets available for searching:

- The Records for Passengers Who Arrived at the Port of New York during the Irish Famine, created 1977–1989, documenting the period January 12, 1846, to December 31, 1851. These records contain name, age, sex, occupation, arrival date, port of embarkation, country of origin, and manifest identification number.
- Data Files Relating to the Immigration of Germans to the United States, created ca. 1977–2002, documenting the period 1850–1897.
- Data Files Relating to the Immigration of Italians to the United States, created ca. 1977–2002, documenting the period 1855–1900.
- Data Files Relating to the Immigration of Russians to the United States, created ca. 1977–2002, documenting the period 1834–1897.

More than 4.1 million Italians entered the United States between 1880 and 1920. In New York, the number of Italian immigrants was about 182,000 in 1900 and 629,000 in 1930.[4]

---

4 "People of New York—Italian," in New York Family History Research Guide and Gazetteer, prepared by New York Genealogical and Biographical Society. (New York: NYG&B, 2014), 185.

Castle Garden

Operated by the State of New York, Castle Garden opened in 1855 to process immigrants to New York City. During the time it was open until early 1890, when it closed, Castle Garden processed immigrants from a number of countries including England, Ireland, Italy, Germany, and Russia. Search the database at http://www.castlegarden.org/ to obtain information on eleven million immigrants from 1820 to 1892.

Ellis Island

After Castle Garden closed, the Federal Barge Office was operated until Ellis Island was opened in 1892. Ellis Island processed immigrants from 1892 until 1924. On June 15, 1897, a fire destroyed the immigration station and the passenger lists dating back to the 1840s. The Ellis Island archives has records for more than fifty-one million crew members, passengers, and immigrants from 1892 to 1957. These records are searchable online at http://www.libertyellisfoundation.org/.

Click "Passenger Search" and enter the name of your ancestor or the person you are researching. The search will return information about the individual, ship manifests, and ship photos. You can order a certificate commemorating arrival, copies of the ship manifests, and pictures of ships from the website for a fee. Another searchable index is the New York Passenger Arrival Lists (Ellis Island), 1892–1924, available on Familysearch.org.

> ## TIP
>
> When searching, remember to include wildcard searches, as sometimes less information is more to get a broader set of results. A wildcard is a character such as an asterisk that yields results with names spelled a variety of ways. For example, when searching for the surname Bundy using Bund*, I get results for Bundy, Bunday, Bundie, Bundey, and so on.

What information can you find at the Statute of Liberty–Ellis Island website?

CASE STUDY: I started my genealogy journey researching the Dwelle family from Augusta, Atlanta, Detroit, Raleigh, and Philadelphia. One of the ancestors was an immigrant, Eunice Mundell, who arrived on Ellis Island from Jamaica. She was born about 1903 and arrived in the United States a few months shy of her twentieth birthday. Eunice traveled on the *Princess May* from Kingston, Jamaica, arriving at Ellis Island on June 11, 1923. The ship manifest includes her occupation (a dressmaker) and the name and address of a friend or nearest relative in the country she left. Eunice left behind her mother, Eva Mundell, in Kingston. The ship she arrived on was built in England in 1888 and sold several times before it was bought in 1901 by the Canadian Pacific Steamships and renamed *Princess May*. The ship went to Jamaica and Cuba before heading to New York. It was later sold to the Standard Fruit Company.

When searching for immigration information, make sure you search multiple sites, because each site is indexed differently. The questions for passenger and customs lists changed over time, so it's important to map your ancestor's arrival with changes in the forms.

Online Resources for Passenger and Immigration Lists

RECORD TYPE	COLLECTION	INFORMATION	LOCATION
Passenger and Immigration Lists	New York, Passenger and Immigration Lists, 1820–1850—records of 1.6M individuals arriving in New York City	Name, age, birthplace, gender, occupation, country of origin, port of departure and arrival, date of arrival, destination, name of ship, family identification numbers, national archives series, microfilm and list numbers	Ancestry.com

RECORD TYPE	COLLECTION	INFORMATION	LOCATION
Passenger Lists	New York Passenger Lists, 1820–1891, for over 13 million immigrants	Name, age, sex, occupation, residence, date of residence, name of ship	Familysearch.org
Passenger Lists	New York, Passenger Lists, 1820–1957	Name, age, sex, arrival date, port of arrival, port of departure, ship's name	Ancestry.com
Crew and Passenger Lists	New York, New York, Passenger and Crew Lists, 1909, 1925–1957	Name, age, sex, marital status, birth date, birth place, naturalized (if naturalized, location and date), and address in the United States	Familysearch.org
Passenger and Crew Lists	Pennsylvania Passenger and Crew Lists, 1800–1962	Name, age, gender, ethnicity, nationality or last country of permanent residence, destination, arrival date, port of arrival, port of departure, ship name, microfilm roll, and page number	Ancestry.com
Passenger Lists	Pennsylvania, Philadelphia Passenger Lists, 1800–1882	Collection corresponds to NARA publication M425	Familysearch.org
Passenger Lists	Pennsylvania, Philadelphia Passenger Lists Index, 1800–1906	Collection corresponds to NARA publication M360	Familysearch.org
Passenger Lists	Pennsylvania, Philadelphia Passenger Lists, 1800–1948	First and last name, age, birth year, birth country, citizenship, arrival year, arrival city, and ship name	Findmypast.com

RECORD TYPE	COLLECTION	INFORMATION	LOCATION
Passenger Lists	Pennsylvania Passenger Lists, 1883–1945	Collection corresponds to NARA publication T840	Familysearch.org
Passenger Lists	Passenger Arrivals at the Port of Baltimore, 1820–1834	Name, age, sex, occupation, country of origin, country they intend to inhabit, ship and dates of arrival	Ancestry.com
Passenger Lists	Maryland, Baltimore Passenger Lists, 1820–1948	Collection contains records from three NARA publications: M255, M596 and T844.	Familysearch.org
Passenger Lists	Baltimore Passenger Lists, 1820–1948	Name, age, gender, ethnicity, nationality or last country of permanent residence, destination, arrival date, port of arrival, port of departure, ship name, microfilm roll, and page number	Familysearch.org
Crew and Passenger Lists	Maryland, Baltimore, Passenger and Crew Lists of Vessels and Airplanes, 1954–1957	Corresponds to NARA Publication M1477	Familysearch.org
Manifest of Arrivals	Detroit Manifest of Arrivals at the Port of Detroit, 1906–1954	Corresponds to NARA Publication M1478	Familysearch.org
Passenger Lists	Michigan, Detroit, Passenger Lists, 1900–1965	Name, age, birth year, birth location and arrival date	Findmypast.com
Crew Lists	Michigan Crew Lists for various ports, 1929–1966	Corresponds to NARA Publications A3432; A3413; A3418; A3421; A3430; A3443 & A3433	Familysearch.org

RECORD TYPE	COLLECTION	INFORMATION	LOCATION
Passenger Lists	New Orleans, Passenger Lists, 1813–1963	Passenger name, ship name, arrival date, and port of embarkation	Ancestry.com
Passenger Lists	Louisiana, Passenger Lists, 1820–1945	Corresponds to NARA Publications M259 and T905	Familysearch.org
Crew and Passenger Lists	California, Passenger and Crew Lists, 1882–1959	Name, age, birth date, birth place, gender, ethnicity/nationality, last residence, vessel or airline name, port of departure, port of arrival, date of arrival (or if unknown, date shore leave was granted or date of departure from the arrival port)	Ancestry.com
Passenger Lists	California, Los Angeles, Passenger Lists, 1907–1948	Corresponds to NARA Publication M1764	Familysearch.org
Aliens Arrivals	Texas and Arizona Arrivals, 1903–1910	Corresponds to NARA Publication A3365	Familysearch.org

New Orleans was the busiest port for Italian immigrants in the 1870s and 1880s. These immigrants migrated to other cities in Louisiana, Mississippi, and along the Mississippi River. By the 1890s, a majority of the Italian immigrants arrived in the Ports of Baltimore, Boston, New York, and Philadelphia. Within each of these communities, they created a Little Italy. Some Italian immigrants moved north to Buffalo and Pittsburgh.[5] Many immigrants traveling from the city of Palermo entered the United States at the port of New Orleans, Louisiana.

---

5 "La Famiglia Roots (1880–1910)." *The Italian Americans*, John Maggio: Executive Producer, Producer/Director, Writer; Muriel Soenens: Producer, Julia Marchesi: Producer & Gary Lionelli: Composer. PBS, 2015.

Transcribed from original passenger lists at the Louisiana State Library, Italian Passengers to Louisiana, 1905–1910, has information on seven thousand Italian immigrants from sixteen Italian passenger vessels arriving in New Orleans between May 1905 and February 1910. Data include names, ages, occupations, native countries or towns, and destinations.[6] Search the database on Ancestry .com: http://search.ancestry.com/search/db.aspx?dbid=4742.

Border Crossings from Canada and Mexico

Border Crossing Records include information on aliens and citizens crossing borders into the United States. In 1895, a joint inspection system was created between the United States and Canada. Passengers arriving in Canada heading to the United States were inspected by US officials at the Canadian port of arrival. This generated two record sets useful in researching your family history, immigration lists, and inspection cards.[7] For records available on individuals crossing the Mexican border between 1903 and 1955, review "Mexican Border Crossing Records" at https://www .archives.gov/research/immigration/border-mexico.html.

How do you find border crossing information for your ancestor?

To find border crossing information on your ancestor, search the available indexes listed in the table below. The information collected on each individual varies by database, but this should give you a general idea of the information available.

---

6 About Italian Passengers to Louisiana, 1905-10, http://search.ancestry.com/search/db.aspx?dbid=4742.

7 Smith, Marian L. "By Way of Canada: US Records of Immigration Across the US-Canadian Border, 1895-1954 (St. Albans Lists)" *Prologue*, Vol. 32, No. 3 (2000). https://www.archives.gov/publications/prologue/2000/fall/us-cana-da-immigration-records-1.html.

RECORD TYPE	COLLECTION	INFORMATION	LOCATION
Border Crossing Records for Aliens and Citizens	US Border Crossing from Canada to the US, 1895–1960	Name, age, gender, birth date and birth location, nationality, nearest friend or relative in former country or nearest relative/friend at destination	Ancestry.com
Border Crossing	From Mexico to US, 1895–1964	Name, age, birth date, birthplace, gender, ethnicity, port of arrival, and arrival dates	Ancestry.com
Index to Records of Aliens and Citizens	United States Border Crossings from Canada to the United States, 1895–1956	Name, age, gender, birth date, race, arrival date, port of arrival, departure and arrival contacts	Familysearch.org
Index to Records of Aliens and Citizens	United States Border Crossings from Mexico to the United States, 1903–1957	Name, age, gender, birth date, birth location, port of arrival, arrival date, destination	Familysearch.org
Card Manifests Of Aliens, Crew Lists, and Passenger Lists	Detroit Border Crossings and Passenger and Crew Lists, 1905–1963	Name, age, birth date, birthplace, gender, ethnicity/nationality, last residence, vessel or airline name, port of departure, port of arrival, and date of arrival	Ancestry.com

Once your immigrant ancestor arrived in the United States, they were typically on a path to naturalization. If you know the time period of naturalization for your ancestor, head to the section on Naturalization. If your ancestor was not a naturalized citizen, they may have registered as an alien with the United States Government.

In 1940, Congress passed the Alien Registration Act, also known as the Smith Act, as a national security measure. The Immigration and Naturalization Service (INS) was required to fingerprint and register every alien age fourteen or older living in the United States. Individuals were registered by filling out a questionnaire Form AR-2 and being fingerprinted at the local post office. Most of the registrants were born between 1875 and 1910. By the time the program ended on March 31, 1944, more than 5.6 million aliens had been registered. Each registrant was assigned an Alien Register Number and sent an Alien Registration Receipt Card. In 1944, the INS generated new A-files arranged by the numbers assigned in 1940. This file tracked interactions between the alien and the United States government. These files are available from the United States Citizenship and Immigration Services genealogy program (USCIS).[8] Search the United States Index to Alien Case Files, 1940–2003 for your ancestor's name:

Document the name, event type, event date, birth date, father's name, mother's name, and affiliate record identifier.

You can also request a name index search from the USCIS by completing Form G-1041 Index Search and paying the fee. Once you have identified the USCIS file number, you must complete Form G-1041-1A Record Copy Request and pay the fee.[9]

NATURALIZATION

Naturalization is the process that immigrants go through to become citizens of the United States. The first Naturalization Act was passed on March 26, 1790, to establish a uniform rule for naturalization: "Any alien being a free white person, who shall have resided within the limits and under the Jurisdiction of the United States for a term of two years, may be admitted to become a citizen thereof, on application to any common law court of record, in any one of the states wherein he shall have resided for the term of one year at least, and making proof to the satisfaction of such court, that he is a person of good character, and taking the oath of affirmation prescribed by law, to support the constitution of the United States, which oath or affirmation such court shall administer; and the clerk of the court shall record such application. . . ."[10]

"And the children of such persons so naturalized, dwelling within the United States, being under the age of 21 at the time of naturalization, shall also be considered citizens of the United States. And the children of the citizens of the United States, that may be born beyond sea, or out of the limits of the United States, shall be considered natural born citizens." One of the exceptions was

---

8 https://www.uscis.gov/history-and-genealogy/genealogy/alien-registration-forms-microfilm-1940-1944.

9 https://www.uscis.gov/sites/default/files/USCIS/History%20and%20Genealogy/Genealogy/genealogy_brochure.pdf.

10 *A Century of Lawmaking for a New Nation: US Congressional Documents and Debates, 1774-1875.* Statutes at Large, 1st Congress, 2nd Session, pg. 103, Library of Congress http://rs6.loc.gov/cgi-bin/ampage?collId=llsl&fileName=001/llsl001.db&recNum=226.

that the right of citizenship shall not descend to persons whose fathers have never been a resident in the United States.[11] In 1795, Congress repealed the Act of 1790 and changed the procedure. A free white person may be admitted to become a citizen of the United States, or any of them, on the following conditions:

- Resided in the United States for at least five years
- Declaring an oath of affirmation, resided at least two years within the jurisdiction of the court where they take the oath of allegiance
- Required declaration filed three years before admission as citizen[12]

Prior to 1906, Unites States citizenship could be granted by county, municipal, state, or federal courts. These records at the state, county, or municipal level are available at the state archives, while the federal records are available at the National Archives and Records Administration (NARA) regional facilities. On June 27, 1906, the Naturalization Act of 1906 passed and took effect on September 27, 1906. This established the federal government as the authority on naturalization policy and created the Bureau of naturalization and Immigration.

After 1906, copies of naturalizations were forwarded to the Immigration and Naturalization Service (INS). These records are available at NARA in Washington, DC, regional NARA facilities, and some may be available online. All naturalizations after September 26, 1906, that are more than fifty years old can be ordered online from the US Citizenship and Immigration Service (USCIS). The USCIS holds Certificate Files (C-Files) that document naturalizations after birth. These files contain records granting citizenship by US Courts between 1906 and 1956. C-Files are created from courts forwarding copies of Declaration of Intention, Petitions for Naturalization, and Certificates of Naturalization.[13] The USCIS has microfilmed C-Files dated from 1906 to 1944, while most of the records were

---

11 *A Century of Lawmaking for a New Nation: US Congressional Documents and Debates, 1774-1875.* Statutes at Large, 1st Congress, 2nd Session, pg. 104, Library of Congress http://rs6.loc.gov/cgi-bin/ampage?collId=llsl&fileName =001/llsl001.db&recNum=227.

12 Ibid.

13 https://www.uscis.gov/history-and-genealogy/genealogy/certificate-files-september-27-1906-march-31-1956,

destroyed in the 1950s. You will need to submit Form G-1041, Genealogy Index Search Request, and Form G-1041A, Genealogy Research Request and $65.00. Review the USCIS website for updates on forms and fees: https://www.uscis.gov /genealogy.

To determine when your ancestor was naturalized, search the US Naturalization Records Indexes, 1794–1995, and US Naturalization Records, 1840–1957, available on Ancestry.com. Naturalization records are also available on Familysearch.org and Fold3.com. Write down the name, birth date, state, and court of naturalization. Use the resources below to obtain additional information or copies of the naturalization papers.

TIP

Remember to review the profile you developed with information about your immigrant ancestor's birth date, location, census, and vital records information.

NATURALIZATION PRIOR TO 1906

To find information on your ancestors naturalized prior to 1906, search the following online indexes. Write down all information about their naturalization including the documents, witnesses, and any information about relatives. Please note that information varies for each individual depending on the records available.

RECORD TYPE	COLLECTION	INFORMATION	LOCATION
Naturalization Records	New York City Selected Naturalization Records, 1816–1845	Declarations of intent or affidavits of intention and reports of aliens	Ancestry.com
Naturalization Records	Naturalization Papers of Central and Western New York State, 1799–1847	Name, age, residence, place of origin, date of arrival, name of court record, and other information	Ancestry.com
Naturalization Records	Pennsylvania Naturalization Records, 1789–1880	Name, date, country, court, declaration of intention, oath of allegiance, and additional information	Ancestry.com
Naturalization Records	Pennsylvania Naturalizations, 1740–1773	Name, date, and location of naturalization	Ancestry.com
Naturalization Records	Persons Naturalized in the Province of Pennsylvania, 1740–1773	Name, location, and date of sacrament	Ancestry.com

TIP

If your ancestor lived in a large city, check the local libraries and historical societies for records. If they lived in a rural area, check the county courthouse for records. The websites for the libraries or societies should have information on their collections for immigration and naturalization.

NATURALIZATION AFTER 1906

PRE-1906 INFORMATION	POST-1906 INFORMATION
Name of immigrant	Name of immigrant
Port of arrival	Birth date and location
Date of arrival	Spouse, birth date, and location
Age	Children, birth date, and location
Residence	Marital status
Country of origin or allegiance	Port of arrival
	Vessel of arrival
	Occupation
	Physical description
	Marriage date
	Age
	Residence
	Last foreign address
	Marital status

NARA has published a list of online Naturalization Records by state.[14] I have included a list of online resources by state, and the list isn't comprehensive, but it's a good start:

Alabama
Naturalization Records, 1888–1991. http://search.ancestry.com/search/db.aspx?dbid=2512

Alaska
State Archives Naturalization Index. http://archives.alaska.gov/pdfs/collection _guides/naturalization_records.pdf

Arizona
Naturalization Records, 1909–1991. http://search.ancestry.com/search/db.aspx?dbid=60614

---

14 "Online Naturalization Records: 1790-1995," https://www.archives.g`ov/files/research/naturalization/419-online -naturalization-records.pdf.

Arizona

State Court Naturalization Records, 1869–1993. This collection contains images of records from Cochise, Coconino, Gila, Pima, and Yuma. http://search.ancestry .com/search/db.aspx?dbid=60877

Arkansas

Naturalization Records, 1907–1968. http://search.ancestry.com/search/db.aspx?dbid=2506

California

California State Naturalization Records, 1850–1986, from Amador, Butte, Colusa, El Dorado, Freson, Napa, Orange, Placer, Santa Barbara, Santa Clara, Sonoma, Stanisiaus, Sutter, Yolo, and Yuba. http://search.ancestry.com/search/db .aspx?dbid=8839

California Northern US District Court Naturalization Index 1852–1989, a card index to Naturalization Records in Northern California District and Circuit courts. https://familysearch.org/search/collection/1849982

California, San Diego Naturalization Index, 1868–1958. https://familysearch.org /search/collection/1840471

California Federal Naturalization Records, 1843–1999. http://search.ancestry.com /search/db.aspx?dbid=3998

Naturalization Index for San Diego, California, contains name, address, age, and petition number. https://www.fold3.com/title_97/naturalization_index_ca_san _diego#overview

Naturalization Records of the Superior Court of Los Angeles. https://www.fold3.com /title_108/naturalizations_ca_los_angeles#overview.

Naturalization Records for Southern California. https://www.fold3.com/title_110 /naturalizations_ca_southern#overview

Connecticut

District Court, Naturalization Indexes, 1851–1992. https://familysearch.org/search /collection/2141008

Delaware

Naturalization Records, 1796–1959. http://search.ancestry.com/search/db.aspx?dbid=1927

Florida

Naturalization Records, 1847–1995. http://search.ancestry.com/search/db.aspx?dbid=1850

Georgia

Georgia Naturalization Records, 1893–1991. http://search.ancestry.com/search/db.aspx?dbid=2500

Savannah Georgia Naturalization Records, 1790–1910. http://search.ancestry.com/search/db.aspx?dbid=2767

Idaho

Idaho State Archives Naturalization Index. https://history.idaho.gov/sites/default/files/uploads/Idaho_Naturalization_Records_Index.pdf

Idaho Naturalization Records, 1903–1982. http://search.ancestry.com/search/db.aspx?dbid=2032

Illinois

Northern District (Eastern Division), Naturalization Index, 1926–1979, is a card index to naturalization records. https://familysearch.org/search/collection/2040533

Northern District Naturalization Index, 1840–1950. https://familysearch.org/search/collection/1838804

Indiana

Naturalization Records and Indexes, 1848–1992. https://familysearch.org/search/collection/2137708

Kansas

Naturalization Abstracts, 1864–1972. http://search.ancestry.com/search/db.aspx?dbid=5175

Kentucky

Naturalization Records, 1906–1991. http://search.ancestry.com/search/db.aspx?dbid=2501

Louisiana

Naturalization Records, 1836–1998. http://search.ancestry.com/search/db.aspx?dbid=2507

Louisiana

Naturalization Records, 1831–1906. https://familysearch.org/search/collection/1459894

Maine

Federal Naturalization Records, 1787–1952. http://search.ancestry.com/search/db.aspx?dbid=2899

Maryland

Maryland Naturalization Indexes, 1797–1951. https://familysearch.org/search/collection/1838829

Maryland Naturalization Petitions, 1906–1931. https://familysearch.org/search/collection/1854313

Massachusetts

Massachusetts State and Federal Naturalization Records, 1798–1950. http://search.ancestry.com/search/db.aspx?dbid=2361

Massachusetts Naturalization Index, 1906–1996. https://familysearch.org/search/collection/1834334

Michigan

Index to Eastern District Naturalizations, 1837–1903. http://search.ancestry.com/search/db.aspx?dbid=6613

Michigan Federal Naturalization Records, 1887–1931. http://search.ancestry.com/search/db.aspx?dbid=61201

Minnesota

Naturalization Records Index, 1854–1957. http://search.ancestry.com/search/db.aspx?dbid=3826

Naturalization Card Index, 1930–1988. http://search.ancestry.com/search/db.aspx?dbid=60723

Minnesota Naturalization Card Index, 1930–1988. https://familysearch.org/search/collection/2120721

Mississippi

Naturalization Records, 1907–2008. http://search.ancestry.com/search/db.aspx?dbid=2502

Missouri

Missouri, County Marriage, Naturalization and Court Records, 1800–1991. https://familysearch.org/search/collection/2060668

Missouri, Western District Naturalization Index, 1848–1990. http://search.ancestry.com/search/db.aspx?dbid=2494

Missouri Naturalization Records, 1816–1955. https://s1.sos.mo.gov/records/archives/archivesdb/naturalization/

Name Index to Naturalizations for St. Louis (1840–1890). Records of the US Circuit and US District Courts, Eastern District of Missouri, Eastern Division (St. Louis), held at the National Archives at Kansas City. https://www.archives.gov/kansas-city/finding-aids/naturalization-st-louis.html

Saint Louis, Missouri, Naturalization Index—Some naturalizations prior to September 27, 1906, and naturalizations on or after September 27, 1906. https://www.slcl.org/content/saint-louis-missouri-naturalization-index

Nebraska

Naturalization Index: Chadron Records of US District Court, District of Nebraska, Chadron Division in the National Archives in Kansas City, Missouri. https://www.archives.gov/kansas-city/finding-aids/naturalization-chadron.html

Records of US District Court, District of Nebraska, McCook Division, in the National Archives in Kansas City, Missouri. https://www.archives.gov/kansas-city/finding-aids/naturalization-mccook.html

Nevada

Naturalization Petitions 1956–1991. http://search.ancestry.com/search/db.aspx?dbid=60615

New York

County Naturalization Records, 1791–1980. https://familysearch.org/search/collection/1999177

Denizations, Naturalizations, and Oaths of Allegiance in Colonial New York. http://search.ancestry.com/search/db.aspx?dbid=49120

Index to Petitions filed in New York City, 1792–1989. http://search.ancestry.com/search/db.aspx?dbid=7733

New York State and Federal Naturalization Records, 1790–1940. http://search.ancestry.com/search/db.aspx?dbid=2280

New York Naturalization Index (Soundex), 1792–1906. https://familysearch.org/search/collection/2043782

Index to Declarations of Intent, 1907–1924. http://search.ancestry.com/search/db.aspx?dbid=7509

New York, Western District, Naturalization Index, 1907–1996. https://familysearch.org/search/collection/1854307

New York, Southern District, Naturalization Index, 1917–1950. https://familysearch.org/search/collection/1840493

New York, County Supreme Court, Naturalization Petition Index, 1907–1924. http://
search.ancestry.com/search/db.aspx?dbid=4653

New York Southern District, Index to Petitions for Naturalization, 1824–1941. https://
familysearch.org/search/collection/1840501

New York Naturalization Records, 1882–1944. http://search.ancestry.com/search/db
.aspx?dbid=2499

North Carolina
Naturalization Records, 1872–1996. http://search.ancestry.com/search/db.aspx?dbid=2503

North Dakota
Name Index to North Dakota Naturalization Records. https://www.archives.gov
/kansas-city/finding-aids/naturalization-north-dakota.html

Name Index to Naturalization Records from Dakota Territory and South Dakota.
https://www.archives.gov/kansas-city/finding-aids/naturalization-south
-dakota.html

Ohio
Ohio, County Naturalization Records, 1800–1977. https://familysearch.org/search
/collection/1987615

Ohio Southern District Naturalization Index, 1852–1991. https://familysearch.org
/search/collection/2110749

Ohio, Naturalization Petition and Record Books, 1888–1946. http://search.ancestry
.com/search/db.aspx?dbid=2363 [end list]

Oklahoma
Naturalization Records, 1889–1991. http://search.ancestry.com/search/db.aspx?dbid=2508

Oregon
Naturalization Records, 1865–1991. http://search.ancestry.com/search/db.aspx?dbid=2530

Pennsylvania
Naturalization Records from Supreme and District Courts, 1794–1908. http://search
.ancestry.com/search/db.aspx?dbid=2393

Eastern District Naturalization Indexes, 1795–1952. https://familysearch.org/search
/collection/1937344

Eastern District Petitions for Naturalization, 1795–1931. https://familysearch.org
/search/collection/1913395

Federal Naturalization Records, 1795–1931. http://search.ancestry.com/search/db
.aspx?dbid=2717

Rhode Island
Indexes to Naturalization Records, 1890–1992. http://search.ancestry.com/search
/db.aspx?dbid=2897

South Carolina
Naturalizations, 1783–1850. http://search.ancestry.com/search/db.aspx?dbid=48272
Naturalization Records, 1868–1991. http://search.ancestry.com/search/db.aspx?dbid=2504

South Dakota
Naturalization Index—First Papers. http://history.sd.gov/Archives/Data/Naturalization
/FirstPapersSearch.aspx

Naturalization Index—Second Papers. http://history.sd.gov/Archives/Data
/Naturalization/SecondPapersSearch.aspx

County Naturalization Records, 1865–1972. https://familysearch.org/search/collection/2078640

Tennessee
Naturalization Records, 1888–1992. http://search.ancestry.com/search/db.aspx?dbid=2505

Texas
Texas Naturalization Records, 1865–1991. http://search.ancestry.com/search/db
.aspx?dbid=2509

Texas Naturalization Records, 1906–1989. https://familysearch.org/search
/collection/1389983

United States
New England Petitions for Naturalization Index, 1791–1906. https://familysearch.org
/search/collection/1840474

Utah
Utah Naturalization and Citizenship Records, 1858–1959. http://search.ancestry.com
/search/db.aspx?dbid=2235

Utah, Declarations of Intent for Naturalization, 1878–1895. http://search.ancestry
.com/search/db.aspx?dbid=6987

Washington

Petitions for Naturalization, 1860–1991. http://search.ancestry.com/search/db
.aspx?dbid=2531

Naturalizations 1853–1980. http://search.ancestry.com/search/db.aspx?dbid=2379

West Virginia

Naturalization Records, 1814–1991. https://familysearch.org/search/collection/1909003

Wisconsin

Milwaukee Naturalization Index, 1848–1990 https://familysearch.org/search/collection/2138589

PASSPORT APPLICATIONS

Did your ancestor travel abroad? Have you heard family stories about their international adventures? If the answer is yes, maybe your ancestor had a passport! Passports are issued to citizens for travel to another country and to reenter their home country. Passport applications are issued by the United States State Department. Passport applications between 1795 and March 1925 are available on microfilm at the NARA in Washington, DC, and online at Ancestry.com. Passport registers and indexes do not exist for passport applications before June 28, 1810. There are not any passport applications available for 1813 to 1829 and 1832.[15] US citizens were not required to have a passport for travel abroad until 1941 except during the Civil War and World War I.[16] Passport applications are a great resource for information about your ancestors including their name, date of birth, place of birth, physical description, occupation, foreign destination(s), and naturalization. Photographs have been required since December 21, 1914, so if your ancestor applied for a passport after this date, then a photo should be attached to their application.

---

15 Deeben, John Paul. *Genealogy Tool Kit: Getting Started on Your Family History at the National Archives.* Accessed June 15, 2017. pg. 41.

16 https://www.archives.gov/files/research/naturalization/400-passports.pdf.

COLLECTION TITLE	LOCATION
United States Passport Applications, 1795–1925	Ancestry.com and Familysearch.org
Registers and Indexes for Passport Applications, 1810–1906	National Archives: Microfilm Publication M1371
Index to Passport Applications, 1850–1852, 1860–1880, 1881, 1906–1923	National Archives: Microfilm Publication M1848
Passport Applications 1795–1905	Fold3.com

TIP

Passport applications can be multiple pages long, especially if they are related to military service. Remember to review all pages of the passport applications and document any family relationships, witnesses, residence, occupations, and other information.

Thomas Henry Dwelle was the son of a slave, Rev. George Henry Dwelle, and Eliza Dwelle. Born August 19, 1878, in Americus, Georgia, he applied for a passport on March 25, 1919, so he could travel to France as Young Men's Christian Association (YMCA) Secretary.

Thomas enlisted two witnesses for his application: Emmanuel M. Hewlett, a prominent African American attorney in Washington, DC, who knew him for twenty-five years and Sarah Belcher. Mrs. Belcher had known him since he was a child, and in her statement she identifies his parents, birth date, and birth location.

Mr. Dwelle was appointed a Security of the National War Work Council of the YMCA of the United States for one year, for service within the troops of the American Expeditionary Force in France. This information is documented in his passport application file of the YMCA and the War Department.

Source: "United States Passport Applications, 1795-1925," database with images, *FamilySearch* (https://familysearch.org/ark:/61903/1:1:QV5B-KKPZ : 4 September 2015), Thomas H Dwelle, 1919; citing Passport Application, District Of Columbia, United States, source certificate #78268, Passport Applications, January 2, 1906–March 31, 1925, 759, NARA microfilm publications M1490 and M1372 (Washington DC: National Archives and Records Administration, n.d.); FHL microfilm 1,605,806.

SPECIAL CASES

Chinese immigrants, women, and World War I veterans were impacted by immigration and naturalization policies in different ways. Below is an overview of each group, the immigration policies, and any records sets that might be available to help you find your ancestor.

CHINESE IMMIGRATION

The Chinese started immigrating to the United States during the California Gold Rush in the late 1840s. Starting in the 1850s, European attitudes toward Chinese immigrants began to focus on racial inferiority, religious practices, and economic competition. An information paper from the NARA, "Chinese Immigration and Chinese in the United States," is available at https://www.archives.gov/research /chinese-americans/guide.html. Several acts were passed to restrict or halt the immigration of Chinese to the United States.

LEGISLATION	YEAR	IMPACT
Chinese Exclusion Act	1882	Chinese laborers not allowed to immigrate for ten years. Chinese were not allowed to become citizens.
Act to Prohibit the Coming of Chinese Persons into the United States: "Geary Act"	May 1892	Chinese exclusion extended for ten years. Illegal removal of Chinese in the United States. Chinese Laborers were required to get a Certificate of Residence as proof of their right to be in the United States.
Scott Act	1902	An extension of the Chinese Exclusion Act. The Scott Act extended exclusion to the US territories of the Philippines and Hawaii.

The exclusion became permanent in 1904 and was in place for almost forty years until 1943 during World War II. During this time, China was an ally of the United States, and the exclusion was repealed with the 1943 Magnuson Act. Chinese immigrants were then allowed to become naturalized citizens. The act still restricted the immigration of Chinese to only one hundred per year.

TITLE	PUBLICATION NO. /INFORMATION	LOCATION
Chinese Case Files for District No. 9., Chicago, 1898–1940		NARA at Chicago
List of Chinese Exclusion Case Files for District No. 10, St. Paul, 1906–1942		NARA at Chicago
List of Chinese Passengers Arriving at San Francisco, 1888–1914	Publication No. M1414	National Archives and Records Administration
Registers of Chinese Laborers Arriving at San Francisco, CA, 1882–1888	Publication No. M1413	National Archives and Records Administration
List of Chinese Passengers Arriving at Seattle (Port Townsend), Washington, 1882–1916	Publication No. M1364	National Archives and Records Administration
Philadelphia, Pennsylvania, Case Files for Chinese Immigrants, 1900–1923	Publication No. M1144	Familysearch.org
Lists of Chinese Applying for Admission to the United States through the Port of San Francisco	Publication No. M1476	National Archives and Records Administration
Passenger List of Chinese Arrivals at Vancouver, British Columbia, Canada, January 1906–June 1912	Publication No. A3414	National Archives and Records Administration Ancestry.com
Lists of Chinese Passengers Arriving at Vancouver and Victoria British Columbia, Canada, January 1929–January 1941	Publication No. A3446	National Archives and Records Administration Ancestry.com
Chinese immigration Case Files 1883–1924	Publication No. M1610, M1144 & A3381	Ancestry.com
New York, Index to Chinese Exclusion Case Files, 1898–1943	Case Files from the Immigration and Naturalization New York District office	Ancestry.com

WOMEN AND CITIZENSHIP

For single women who immigrated to the United States in the early nineteenth and twentieth centuries, their status was dependent on the status of their husbands. An act passed in 1855 provided that an alien woman who married a United States citizen, or whose husband was a naturalized citizen, acquired automatic citizenship. According to the Expatriation Act (1907), a woman with United States citizenship could lose that citizenship if she married a noncitizen. Her legal identity was attached to her husband's. By 1922, the citizenship of a woman was no longer tied to the citizenship of her husband.

WORLD WAR I NATURALIZATIONS

World War I vets were given a special, shortened path to citizenship:

> *"any alien serving in the military or naval service of the United States during the time this country is engaged in the present war may file his petition for naturalization without making the preliminary declaration of intention and without proof of the required five years residence within the United States."*[17]

We have reviewed a lot of information on immigration and naturalization, and it is probably overwhelming. Do not worry! The good news is that you have time to repeat this process for all of your immigrant ancestors. And by the end, you will be an expert! Now that you have the tools you need to find immigration and naturalization records for your ancestors, you can continue on your journey to discovering your family history and building your biographical narrative.

---

17 "Washington, DC Military Naturalization Petitions, 1918-1924, http://search.ancestry.com/search/db.aspx?dbid=3034.

CHAPTER 5

US MILITARY RESEARCH

Finding the records of your ancestor's military service will help put their service in the context of historical events. The United States has participated in several military conflicts, some large and some small, that have left a paper trail. In this chapter, we will cover the Revolutionary War, the War of 1812, the Indian Wars, the Mexican War, the Civil War, World War I, World War II, the Korean War, and the Vietnam War. You will learn how to find draft registrations, military service records, prisoner of war records, pension files, and other records related to your ancestor's military service. A great place to start when looking for your military ancestors is *An Overview of Records at the National Archives Relating to Military Service* by Trevor K. Plante.[1] Most records can be found at the National Archives and Records Administration (NARA) in Washington, DC, or at regional NARA facilities in the United States. Records are available online at Ancestry.com, Fold3.com, Familysearch.org, MyHeritage.com, and other websites.

THE REVOLUTIONARY WAR (1775–1783)

The American Revolution was fought between the American colonists and the British colonial government represented by the Crown to gain independence. At

---

1 https://www.archives.gov/publications/prologue/2002/fall/military-records-overview.html.

the time of the War of Independence, there were thirteen North American colonies. The fighting started with the battles of Lexington and Concord in April 1775. On September 3, 1783, the Treaty of Paris was signed ending the Revolutionary War.[2] *Forgotten Patriots: African American and American Indian Patriots in the Revolutionary War: A Guide to Service, Sources and Studies* identifies over 6,600 names of African Americans and American Indians. Not only does it provide a list of names, but also the clues to finding forgotten patriots and historical context useful in family history research.[3]

On November 7, 1775, John Murray, 4th Earl of Dunmore, Royal Governor of the British Colony of Virginia, signed Lord Dunmore's Proclamation. The proclamation promised freedom for the enslaved of the revolutionaries who left their owners and fought for the British.[4] What happened to those African American soldiers who fought for the British? Once the Revolutionary War was over, some three thousand Black Loyalists were evacuated from New York and moved to Nova Scotia. The British gave them certificates of freedom and arranged for their transport. The *Book of Negroes* lists the Black Loyalists and is available online at http://www.blackloyalist.info/sources.

How do you find records for your Revolutionary War ancestor?

The National Archives and Records Administration (NARA) has a list of microfilm records related to the Revolutionary War (1775–1783) available for research in Washington, DC.[5]

---

2 "Treaty of Paris (1783)," https://www.ourdocuments.gov/doc.php?flash=false&doc=6.

3 "Forgotten Patriots Book," https://www.dar.org/library/forgotten-patriots/forgotten-patriots-book.

4 "Proclamation of Earl of Dunmore," http://www.pbs.org/wgbh/aia/part2/2h42.html.

5 "Revolutionary War Service, 1775-1783, https://www.archives.gov/files/research/military/american-revolution/service-records.pdf.

COLLECTION	LOCATION
General Index to Compiled Military Service Records of the Revolutionary War Soldiers	M860, National Archives and Records Administration
Index to Compiled Service Records of American Naval Personnel Who Served During the Revolutionary War	M879, National Archives and Records Administration
Index to Compiled Service Records of Revolutionary War Soldiers Who Served with the American Army in Connecticut Military Organizations	M920, National Archives and Records Administration
Index to Compiled Service Records of Revolutionary War Soldiers Who Served with the American Army in Georgia Military Organizations	M1051, National Archives and Records Administration
Index to Compiled Military Service Records of Volunteer Soldiers Who Served During the Revolutionary War in Organizations from the State of North Carolina	M257, National Archives and Records Administration
United States Revolutionary War Compiled Service Records, 1775–1783	Familysearch.org

REVOLUTIONARY WAR SERVICE RECORDS

Service records include muster rolls, payrolls, strength returns, and other miscellaneous information. Depending on how your ancestor served in the Revolutionary War, they might appear on more than one muster roll.

COLLECTION	LOCATION
US Compiled Revolutionary War Military Service Records, 1775–1783	Ancestry.com
US Compiled Service Records, Post-Revolutionary War Volunteer Soldiers, 1784–1811	Ancestry.com
US Revolutionary War Rolls, 1775–1783	Ancestry.com
Revolutionary War Service and Imprisonment Cards	Fold3.com
Compiled Service Records of Soldiers who Served in the American Army During the Revolutionary War	M881, National Archives and Records Administration Ancestry.com; Familysearch.org & Fold3.com
Revolutionary War Rolls, 1775–1783	M246, National Archives and Records Administration Ancestry.com; Familysearch.org & Fold3.com
Compiled Service Records of American Naval Personnel and Members of the Departments of the Quartermaster General and the Commissary General of Military Stores Who Served During the Revolutionary War	M880, National Archives and Records Administration Ancestry.com & Fold3.com

PENSION AND BOUNTY LAND WARRANT APPLICATIONS

There were three types of pensions provided by the United States to soldiers and their dependents:[6]

- Disability pensions awarded to those who were injured during service
- Service pensions awarded to veterans who served for a period of time
- Widow's pensions awarded to women whose husbands were killed during the war or were veterans who served for a period of time

---

6 https://www.fold3.com/title_467/revolutionary_war_pensions#description.

The United States Revolutionary War Pension and Bounty Land Warrant Application Files, 1800-1900 (NARA Microfilm 804), including eighty thousand pension and bounty land applications, are available online at Ancestry.com, Fold3.com, and Familysearch.org.

REVOLUTIONARY WAR FINAL PAYMENT VOUCHERS

Another resource to help you find information on your Revolutionary War ancestor is the Index to Selected Final Payment Vouchers Index for Military Pensions, 1818–1864 (RG 217, Inv. 14, Series 722A). The cards were created as an index for the final payments made to either the veteran or his widow. They provide family migrations, maiden names, and death dates of veterans, widows, or dependent children.[7] If a star is found on the index card, request the final payment voucher file from Selected Final Payments Vouchers, 1818–1864 (RG 217, Inventory 14, Series 722).

"Act of April 6, 1838"

This allowed heirs of pensioners to claim from the Treasury Department the pension amount that accrued between the date of last payment and the date of death. The Settled Accounts for Payment of Accrued Pensions (Final Payments), August 1838–September 1865, identify the pensioner's death date, death location, and names of heirs and include supporting documentation. An alphabetical name index was published by Craig R. Scott, *The "Lost" Pensions: Settled Accounts of the Act of 6 April 1838.*[8]

THE WAR OF 1812, "SECOND WAR OF INDEPENDENCE"

Americans fought the British, Canadian, and Native American soldiers for almost three years during the "Second War of Independence." During this time, the British burned down Washington, DC, forcing Dolly Madison to flee the White House. The next day, a thunderstorm helped stop the flames. Francis Scott Key wrote the "Star Spangled Banner" during the British bombardment of Fort McHenry in Baltimore. The verses were printed in Baltimore newspapers after the Battle.[9] The

---

7 https://www.fold3.com/title_654/final_payment_vouchers_index_for_military_pensions_18181864#overview.

8 Scott, Craig R. *The "Lost" Pensions: Settled Accounts of the Act of 6 April 1838.* Lovettsville, VA: Willow Bend Books, 1996; Prechtel-Kluskens, 2008.

9 Klein, Christopher, "9 Things You May Not Know About The Star-Spangled Banner, History Channel, http://www.history.com/news/9-things-you-may-not-know-about-the-star-spangled-banner.

Smithsonian has a great website on the Star-Spangled Banner, the burning of Washington, DC, and the Battle of Baltimore.[10] The war ended with the ratification of the Treaty of Ghent on February 16, 1815.[11]

FINDING WAR OF 1812 ANCESTORS

Search the index to Compiled Service Records of Volunteer Soldiers who served during the War of 1812. The database of nearly 600,000 men mustered into the armed forces between 1812 and 1815 includes the soldier's name, company, rank at time of induction, rank at time of discharge, and other helpful information.[12] NARA has a list of microfilm records related to the War of 1812 available for research in Washington, DC.[13]

Index and Service Records for the War of 1812

COLLECTION	LOCATION
US, War of 1812 Index to Service Records	Ancestry.com, Familysearch.org
Index to Compiled Service Records of Volunteer Soldiers Who Served During the War of 1812	M602, National Archives and Records Administration Ancestry.com, Familysearch.org & Fold3.com
Index to Compiled Service Records of Volunteer Soldiers Who Served During the War of 1812 in Organizations from the State of Louisiana	M229, National Archives and Records Administration
Index to Compiled Service Records of Volunteer Soldiers Who Served During the War of 1812 in Organizations from the State of North Carolina	M250, National Archives and Records Administration
Index to Compiled Service Records of Volunteer Soldiers Who Served During the War of 1812 in Organizations from the State of South Carolina	M652, National Archives and Records Administration

10 "Three Cheers for the Red, White, and Blue: Star-Spangled Banner and the War of 1812," Smithsonian, https://www.si.edu/spotlight/flag-day/banner-facts.

11 "Treaty of Ghent (1814)", https://www.ourdocuments.gov/doc.php?flash=false&doc=20.

12 Record Group 94 Records of the Adjutant General's Office, microfilm publication M602, a total of 234 rolls of film.

13 "Volunteer Military Service during the War of 1812 (1812-1815)." https://www.archives.gov/files/research/military/war-of-1812/volunteers.pdf.

COMPILED MILITARY SERVICE RECORDS FOR WAR OF 1812

The Compiled Military Service records identify the soldier's name, dates of service, terms of service, rank, and other information. Native Americans fought in the War of 1812, and the compiled service records available online at Fold3.com are for the Chickasaw Indians, Creek Indians, Lake Erie area, and Mississippi. The full compiled military service record still needs to be pulled at NARA in Washington, DC.

Compiled Military Service Records

COLLECTION	LOCATION
War of 1812 Service Records	Ancestry.com & Fold3.com
Navy and Marine Corps Officers, 1775–1900	Ancestry.com & Fold3.com
Index to Compiled Service Records of Volunteer Soldiers Who Served during the War of 1812 in Organizations from the State of Louisiana	M229, National Archives and Records Administration
Index to Compiled Service Records of Volunteer Soldiers Who Served during the War of 1812 in Organizations from the State of North Carolina	M250, National Archives and Records Administration
Index to Compiled Service Records of Volunteer Soldiers Who Served during the War of 1812 in Organizations from the State of South Carolina	M652, National Archives and Records Administration

PRISONER OF WAR RECORDS FOR 1812

- Ancestry.com: War of 1812 Prisoner of War Records, 1812–1815. http://search.ancestry.com/search/db.aspx?dbid=1131. This record set contains information relating to American soldiers, civilians, and British soldiers. Some of the information included in this collection:
  - Prisoner lists
  - Clothing provided by US agents to prisoners held in Canada
  - When and where soldiers were captured
  - Lists of men exchanged
  - Correspondence

DARTMOOR PRISON

Dartmoor was a notorious prison located on the moors of Devonshire about seventeen miles from Plymouth. More than 6,500 American sailors were admitted to the prison including black crews of privateers, which accounted for about 15 percent of the Americans.[14]

WAR OF 1812 PENSION FILES

Pensions were granted to soldiers who were disabled while in service and to heirs of soldiers who died during the war. The process of applying for a pension usually started with the soldier (the invalid) who would state his service and injury. Widows or dependent applicants had to prove their relationship to the soldier, and these records sometimes included original wedding certificates or records from the county clerk.

In 1871, an act was passed that "granted pensions to all surviving soldiers or sailors of the War of 1812, who served sixty days and were honorably discharged, or who received personal mention by Congress for specific services in the War. Applicants were required to have been loyal during the War of 1812 and to take an oath to support the Constitution."[15] Pensions were also provided to widows who were married prior to the peace treaty and had not remarried.[16] In 1878, a pension act was passed: "Pensions were granted to all those persons who [were] in any branch of service, who served fourteen days in the War of 1812, or who were in any engagement and were honorably discharged, and to the surviving widows of such persons."[17] Bounty land is land given to soldiers for military service. To find the pension records and bounty land warrants, search the indexes in the table below. Information includes the soldier's service, age, place of residence, widow's name including maiden name, marriage date, acres granted, and soldier's death date.

---

14 "The War of 1812: Prisoners of the War in 1812", PBS. http://www.pbs.org/wned/war-of-1812/essays/prisoners -war/.

15 Glasson, William Henry. *History of Military Pension Legislation in the United States,* New York: Columbia University, 1900. pp. 61–62.

16 Ibid.

17 Ibid, p. 63.

Pension and Bounty Land Warrants for War of 1812

COLLECTION	LOCATION
United States War of 1812 Index to Pension Application Files, 1812–1910	Familysearch.org
War of 1812 Pension Application Files Index, 1812–1815	Ancestry.com
War of 1812 Pension Application Files	Fold3.com
Bounty-Land Warrants Application Index	Fold3.com
Index to Pension Application Files of Remarried Widows Based on Service in the War of 1812, Indian Wars, Mexican War, and Regular Army before 1861	M1784, National Archives and Records Administration

THE INDIAN WARS (1784-1858)

Often an overlooked collection of records, the Indian Wars were wars between Americans and Native Americans primarily in the Eastern United States. The Northwest Indian War, also known as the "Ohio War," was fought for control of the Northwest Territory between 1785 and 1795. The Native Americans had the support of the British during the War.[18] The Creek War, also known as the "Civil Creek War," started in 1813 and ended in August 1814.[19] After the signing of the Treaty of Paris, Spain regained control of Florida. The first Seminole War (1817–1818) was fought in Florida and Southern Georgia with General Andrew Jackson attacking Spanish Florida. In the Second Seminole War (1835–1842), the Seminole were fighting to retain their land and avoid heading West. The Third Seminole War started in 1855 over land disputes between whites and Seminoles. This war ended about 1858 when the Seminole population was only two hundred in Florida.[20]

In 1830, the Indian Removal Act was signed into law by President Andrew Jackson and gave the federal government power to remove all Indians from their lands east of the Mississippi River to territory west of the Mississippi. The Trail of

18 https://en.wikipedia.org/wiki/Northwest_Indian_War.

19 https://www.britannica.com/event/Creek-War.

20 http://dos.myflorida.com/florida-facts/florida-history/seminole-history/the-seminole-wars/.

Tears during the fall and winter of 1838 and 1839 forcibly removed Cherokees from their land and forced them West. To find ancestors who might have served during the Indian Wars, start by searching indexes to the Service Records, Pensions, and Bounty Land Warrants.

Service Records available online and microfilm indexes:

Ancestry.com: US Army Indian Campaign Service Records, Index, 1815–1858. https://search.ancestry.com/search/db.aspx?dbid=61592

Fold3.com: Indian Wars Service Record Index. https://www.fold3.com/browse/249/hZx2yvBIU

There are state level indexes for compiled military service records at NARA for the Indian Wars: [21]

Alabama: Creek War 1837 (M244); Cherokee Removal 1838 (M243); Second Seminole War, 1836–38 (M245)

Georgia: Cherokee Disturbances and Removal 1836–1838 (M907)

Louisiana: Second Seminole War 1836 (M239) and War of 1837–1838 (M241)

North Carolina: Cherokee Disturbances and Removal 1837–1838 (M256)

Tennessee: Cherokee Disturbances and Removal 1836–1839 (M908)

PENSION AND BOUNTY WARRANT LAND APPLICATIONS

An act passed in 1892 provided pensions for veterans of the Indian Wars "who served for thirty days in Black Hawk War, the Creek War, the Cherokee disturbances, or the Florida War with the Seminole Indians between 1832 and 1842 and were honorably discharged."[22] Search Familysearch.org: *United States Index to Indian Wars Pension Files, 1892–1926,* at https://www.familysearch.org/search/collection/1979427.

---

21 Deeben, John Paul. *Genealogy Tool Kit: Getting Started on Your Family History at the National Archives.* Accessed June 15, 2017.

22 Glasson, William Henry. *History of Military Pension Legislation in the United States,* New York: Columbia University, 1900. p. 66.

MEXICAN WAR (1846–1848)

The Mexican War started because of continued dispute with Texas over annexation and boundaries. The Mexican war ended in 1848 with the signing of the Treaty of Guadalupe Hidalgo giving United States sovereignty over Texas, establishing the US–Mexican border, and giving the United States a large portion of its territory. The area included Arizona, California, Nevada, Utah, and parts of Wyoming, Colorado, and New Mexico. Gold was discovered in California just days before Mexico ceded the land to the United States in the Treaty of Guadalupe Hidalgo. Search the records below to find ancestors who might have served in the Mexican War.

INDEX, SERVICE, AND PENSION RECORDS

COLLECTION	LOCATION
Mexican War Service Records	Fold3.com[23]
Index to Compiled Service Records of Volunteer Soldiers Who Served During the Mexican War	M616, National Archives and Records Administration
Compiled Service Records of Volunteer Solders Who Served During the Mexican War in Organizations from the State of Texas	M278, National Archives and Records Administration
United States Mexican War Pension Index, 1887–1926	Familysearch.org
Selected Pension Application Files relating to the Mormon Battalion, Mexican War, 1846–1848	T1196, National Archives and Records Administration Fold3.com

CIVIL WAR (1861–1865)

The Civil War started when the Confederates attacked Union troops at Fort Sumter near Charleston, South Carolina, on April 12, 1861, and ended with General Robert E. Lee's surrender to Ulysses S. Grant at Appomattox Courthouse in Virginia on April 9, 1865.[24] During the Civil War, over three million men served in

---

23 These records are only complete for Arkansas, Mississippi, Mormon Battalion, Pennsylvania, Tennessee, and Texas.

24 http://www.history.com/this-day-in-history/robert-e-lee-surrenders.

the Union and Confederate armies. One of the bloodiest wars fought in the United States, the Civil War claimed an estimated six hundred thousand lives. Americans continue to celebrate, discuss, interpret, and analyze the Civil War. Understanding the historical context surrounding the Civil War is essential to knowing how your ancestor fits into this piece of American history. Whether they were enslaved, a Northerner, or a Southerner, their lives were impacted by this war. Available Civil War records include draft registrations, military service records, prisoner of war records, and pensions for the widows and veterans. These records are great for exploring your family history because they leave a paper trail of facts and historical context about your ancestors.

UNITED STATES ARMY AND NAVY (UNION)

Congress authorized a volunteer army of 500,000 men and $500 million dollars in the summer session of 1861.[25] The Civil War Military Draft Act was enacted on March 3, 1863, to provide soldiers to the Union Army. The act required men between the ages of twenty and forty-five to register for the draft, including immigrants who filed for citizenship. The exceptions to this rule were substitution and commutation (paying $300 to not serve). These exceptions led to unrest in New York among the working class and were fueled by racism due to the Emancipation Proclamation. In New York City, a riot resulted in about two thousand injuries and the burning of many structures, including an African American orphanage. The Union army would later grow to two million men.[26]

CONFEDERATE STATES OF AMERICA

In 1861, South Carolina was the first state to secede from the United States of America. Secession for South Carolina was about the preservation of slavery in the South. Many of the other Southern states soon followed and created the Confederate States of America (CSA). The border states of Delaware, Kentucky, Maryland, and Missouri did not officially join the Confederacy. The CSA was comprised of eleven slave-holding states that seceded from the United States: Alabama,

---

25 "1861-1865: A Devastating Civil War," United States Capitol Visitor's Center - https://www.visitthecapitol.gov/civilwar/html/section2.html.

26 "How many soldiers fought in the Civil War?" https://www.civilwar.org/learn/articles/civil-war-facts.

Arkansas, Florida, Georgia, Louisiana, Mississippi, North Carolina, South Carolina, Tennessee, Texas, and Virginia. West Virginia was formed because they refused to secede.[27] Richmond, Virginia, was the capitol of the Confederacy, and Jefferson Davis was the president.

UNITED STATES COLORED TROOPS (USCT)

General Order No. 329 was issued by the War Department on October 3, 1863. Section 6 of the order stated that if any citizen (enslaver) should offer his or her slave for enlistment into the military service, the enslaver, if said slave was accepted, would receive a certificate and would be entitled to compensation not to exceed the sum of $300. The enslaver would need to make proof of title and file a deed of manumission and release.[28] General Order no. 143 was signed on May 22, 1863, establishing the Bureau of Colored Troops to organize and coordinate colored regiments. The United States Colored Troops consisted of the following regiments and soldiers:[29]

- Seven Cavalry Regiments
- Fourteen Artillery Regiments
- 144 Infantry Regiments
- Brigade Bands Nos. 1 & 2
- Powell's Regiment Colored Infantry
- Southard's Company Colored Infantry
- Quartermaster Detachment
- Pioneer Corps—1st Division and 16th Army Corps
- Eighty-seven African American officers

More than 179,000 men served in the Union Army, and approximately 37,000 men died from disease and battle. The USCT fought in about forty major

27 Secession Acts of the Thirteen Confederate states. https://www.civilwar.org/learn/primary-sources/secession-acts-thirteen-confederate-states.

28 Weidman, Budge, "Black Soldiers in the Civil War: Preserving the Legacy of the United States." https://www.archives.gov/education/lessons/blacks-civil-war/article.html.

29 Compiled Military Service Records of Volunteer Union Soldiers Who Served with the United States Colored Troops: 1st through 5th United States Colored Cavalry, 5th Massachusetts Cavalry (Colored), 6th United States Colored Cavalry, Publication Number: M-1817, National Archives and Records Administration, 1997. https://www.fold3.com/pdf/M1817.pdf.

engagements and over four hundred lesser engagements. Sixteen African American soldiers received Medals of Honor.[30] The last United States Colored Troops were mustered out of federal service in December 1867.

Finding Your Civil War Ancestor

To find your Civil War ancestor, search the available indexes online or at the National Archives and Records Administration (NARA). Make sure you write down whether your ancestor was a Confederate or Union soldier, as well as their rank, state, unit, and company.

Civil War Soldiers and Sailors Indexes

COLLECTION TITLE	BRANCH	INFORMATION	LOCATION
Civil War Soldiers and Sailors Database	Army	Soldiers: Battle Unit Name, Side; Company: Soldier's Rank In, Soldier's Rank Out, Alternate Name, Film No., Plaque Number & Notes	National Park Service: Civil War Soldiers and Sailors Database Online *Familysearch.org*
Civil War Soldiers and Sailors Database	Navy	Place of Birth, Age, Complexion, Occupation, Height, Place of Enlistment, Date of Enlistment, Term of Enlistment, Rating and Detailed Muster Records	*Familysearch.org*
United States Civil War Soldiers Index, 1861–1865	Army	Name, Regiment, Union or Confederate, Company, Soldier's Rank, and Possible Alternate Names	*Familysearch.org* National Archives and Records Administration

---

30 "The Civil War's Black Soldiers: Contribution to Union Victory." National Park Service. https://www.nps.gov /parkhistory/online_books/civil_war_series/2/sec21.htm.

COMPILED MILITARY SERVICE RECORDS

These records include the soldier's hospital stays, injuries, attendance, and prisoner of war information. A soldier's birth date, birth location, and citizenship may be included in these records. After finding an ancestor's Compiled Military Service Record (CMSR), look for regimental histories to find out where the regiment fought. Based on the dates of your ancestor's enlistment period, try to determine when they mustered in or were paid as well as other information such as the battles they fought in.

Compiled Service Records for Union and Confederate Soldiers

For the Confederate, the compiled service records are available online at Fold3.com.

COLLECTION TITLE	BRANCH	INFORMATION	LOCATION
United States Civil War Service Records of Confederate Soldiers, 1861–1865	Confederate Army	Name, rank, and unit	*Familysearch.org*
United States Civil War Service Records of Union Soldiers, 1864–1866	Union	Union records of Confederate prisoners of war who served in the 1st–6th US Volunteer Infantry Regiments	*Familysearch.org*
United States Civil War Records of Confederate Non-regiment Soldiers, 1861–1865	Confederate	Name, rank, and unit	*Familysearch.org*
Alabama Civil War Service Cards Files	Confederate	Name, date of birth, date of death, marital status, occupation, enlistment date, discharge date, branch, regiment, company, unit, engagements, pension, remarks, and other information	Alabama Department of Archives and History
Index to Virginia Confederate Rosters	Confederate	Name, rank, company, regiment, biographical notes, and other information	Library of Virginia *Familysearch.org*

PRISONER OF WAR RECORDS

The Union and Confederate armies maintained prison camps during the Civil War. Andersonville, located in Georgia, was one of the most notorious Confederate military prison camps. It was originally built to house ten thousand prisoners, but that number eventually grew to more than forty thousand. Most of the prisoners were thin, starving, and died from injuries they incurred during battle that were not treated. A guest on *Genealogy Roadshow* believed her ancestor was imprisoned at Andersonville, and we were able to confirm that the family story was true.

To find an ancestor in Prisoner of War Records, you will need their full name, regiment, rank, unit, and the location of the prison. If you do not have that information, search the resources in the following table.

Prisoner of War Records from Andersonville and Fort McHenry

COLLECTION TITLE	INFORMATION	LOCATION
Georgia, Andersonville Prison Records, 1862–1865	Claims, reports, death, burials, departures, and hospital records	*Familysearch.org*
National Park Service: The Civil War	Andersonville and Fort McHenry information	National Park Service
Andersonville Prisoners of War	Name, rank, company, regiment, state, arm of service, page, code, grave, and remarks	*Ancestry.com*

CIVIL WAR PENSION RECORDS

The first Pension Act was passed in 1862 for veterans with war-related disabilities. Pensions were available to widows, children under sixteen, and other relatives. In 1872, an act was passed to allow veterans and widows to collect a lump-sum payment based on the date of death or discharge. A pension act was passed in 1890 for disabled veterans. Veterans had to have served ninety days or more during the Civil War and received an honorable discharge. A widow received a pension if she was married to the Civil War veteran prior to June 27, 1890, and was dependent upon him for support. If a widow remarried, she was no longer eligible for benefits.

Children were paid a pension up until the age of sixteen unless they were declared idiotic, insane, or permanently helpless. Then the pension payments continued throughout their life. In 1904, President Roosevelt issued Executive Order No. 78 declaring that old age was a disability covered by the 1890 act. In 1907, the Service and Age Pension Act passed, granting pensions to all veterans over sixty-two.[31]

Union Soldiers

When searching for the pension records of your Union Civil War ancestor, make note of all the information on the index card. Soldiers applied for pensions as invalids or for a disability.

Indexes to Pensions for Union Soldiers

COLLECTION TITLE	INFORMATION	LOCATION
US, Civil War Pension Index: General Index to Pension Files, 1861–1934	Name of soldier, name of dependent, service, date of filing, class, application number, certificate number, state from which filed, attorney and remarks	*Ancestry.com* *Findmypast.com*
United States Civil War and Later Pension Index, 1861–1917	Name, application number, certificate number, and regiment	*Familysearch.org*
Civil War Pensions Index	Name of soldier, name of dependent, service, date of filing, class, application number, certificate number, state from which filed, attorney and remarks	*Fold3.com*

CONFEDERATE PENSION AND SOLDIERS' HOME RECORDS

The former Confederate States passed laws approving pensions for former Confederate soldiers at the state level. Confederate veterans were eligible to apply for

---

31 Glasson, William Henry. *Federal Military Pensions in the United States*, New York: Oxford University Press, American Branch, 1918.

a pension in the state where they lived, even if they served the Confederate Army in a different state. Pension records can help you locate your ancestors during the twenty-year gap in the United States Federal Census. Pension applications for Confederate soldiers were typically governed by a Board of Commissioners. These records contain a vast amount of family history and provide insight into life after the war. Use the resources listed below by state to find the Confederate Pension for your ancestor. Start by searching the available indexes and then access the applications online or order a copy from the state library or archives. Be sure to research the laws associated with Confederate pensions for your ancestor's state, as these laws changed over time.

Alabama

In 1867, Alabama began granting pensions to Confederate veterans who had lost arms or legs. In 1886, the State began granting pensions to veterans' widows. In 1891, the law was amended to grant pensions to indigent veterans or their widows.[32] In 1899, the State Legislature authorized pensions for Confederate veterans who were not disabled and residents of Alabama or for their widows.[33]

To search Alabama Pension and Service Records online: Ancestry: Alabama, Confederate Pension and Service Records, 1862–1947 http://search.ancestry.com/search /db.aspx?dbid=1593.

This collection contains records of Confederate veterans' pensions in Alabama between 1865 and 1940. Until 1900, only disabled veterans were receiving a pension from the State of Alabama. Confederate pension applications from 1880 to 1940 are also available at the Microfilm Reading Room at the Alabama Department of Archives and History.

This resource can help you uncover some of the following information:

- Name
- Number
- Occupation

---

32 https://www.archives.gov/research/military/civil-war/confederate/pension.html.
33 http://search.ancestry.com/search/db.aspx?dbid=1593.

- Where wounded
- Date of wound
- Whether a widow or veteran
- Company
- Regiment
- Branch of service

Arkansas

Arkansas began providing pensions to Confederate veterans who were destitute in 1891. In 1915, widows and mothers of veterans became eligible for pension payments. This digital database from the Arkansas History Commission (AHC) extracts details on Confederate veterans and widows from Arkansas Confederate pension records from the years 1891 to 1939. *To search Arkansas Pension Applications online:* Ancestry: Arkansas, Confederate Pension Records, 1891–1935 http:// search.ancestry.com/search/db.aspx?dbid=2281.

Information from records collected by the Arkansas State Pensions Board includes the following details:

- Name of veteran
- Application number
- Name of widow
- Company
- Regiment
- State served from
- Division
- County where received pension
- Veteran's death date
- Widow's death date
- Application year (veteran)
- Comments (approved, widow application date, etc.)

Familysearch.org: Arkansas Ex-Confederate Pension Records, 1891–1939 Index and image of administrative records from the Arkansas State Auditor that authorized and dispersed pension payments. Records in Pension Board Minutes and Pension Lists. https://familysearch.org/search/collection/1921864.

Florida

In 1885, Florida began granting pensions to Confederate veterans in the sum of $5.00 per month. Widows were eligible for pensions four years later. Pensions were governed by a three-member board consisting of the governor, comptroller, and treasurer.[34]

To Search Pension Application Files: Florida Confederate Pension Application Files are available at https://www.floridamemory.com/collections/pensionfiles/.

Information is indexed by the following items:

- Application number
- Last name
- First name
- Unit
- Wife's maiden name
- Wife's first name
- Application county
- Year

Familysearch.org: Florida Confederate Veterans and Widows Pension Applications, 1885–1955 https://familysearch.org/search/collection/1913411.

The following information can be found on the veteran or his widow:

- Name
- Date and place of birth
- Unit dates and places of enlistment and discharge

---

34 https://www.floridamemory.com/collections/pensionfiles/.

- Brief description of service
- Wounds received
- Sworn statements on proof of service by comrades
- Place and length of residency in the state
- Widow's full name
- Date and place of marriage to the veteran
- Date and place of the veteran's death

Ordering copies of a Confederate Pension Application

Official copies are available from the State Archives of Florida for $7.50 per file. Checks should be payable to the Department of State and mailed to the address below. Make sure you review the State Archives website prior to your order for updates on fees and the processing of your request.

Florida Department of State

State Archives of Florida

500 S. Bronough St.

Tallahassee, FL 32399-0250

Georgia

Georgia began granting pensions to soldiers with artificial limbs in 1870, and by 1879, the pensions extended to other veterans and their widows residing in Georgia.

To search Georgia Pension Applications online: Ancestry: Georgia, Confederate Pension Applications, 1879–1960 are available at http://search.ancestry.com/search/db.aspx?dbid=1560.

Information contained in the database includes:

- Name of applicant (soldier or widow)
- Approximate application year
- Application type (Indigent Soldier, Indigent Widow, Indigent Colored, Widow, Soldier, or Colored)

Digital Library of Georgia: Confederate Pension Applications, 1879–1960 http://dlg.galileo.usg.edu/CollectionsA-Z/confpension_search.html?Welcome&Welcome.

Kentucky

On March 4, 1912, the Confederate Pension Act was passed by Kentucky General Assembly. The act provided aid to indigent and disabled Confederate veterans and their widows.[35]

To search Confederate Pension Applications online: Familysearch.org: Kentucky Confederate Pension Applications, 1912–1950 https://familysearch.org/search/collection/1916017.

Information contained in the Pension Applications:[36]

- Application number
- Full name of widow (applicant)
- Residence
- Length of residence in Kentucky
- Birth date and place
- Maiden name
- Full name of soldier
- Person who performed the marriage ceremony (copy of the marriage certificate might be included)
- Enlistment date
- Company and regiment
- Length of service
- When and where the company and regiment surrendered
- Was the soldier present at the time of surrender?

---

35 http://www.e-archives.ky.gov/Confederate_pension.htm.
36 https://familysearch.org/wiki/en/Kentucky_Confederate_Pension_Applications_(FamilySearch_Historical_Records)#What_Can_this_Collection_Tell_Me.3F.

- Reason if not present at the time of surrender
- Death date and place of soldier
- If the couple was living together at the time of death
- Second marriage information
- Property owned by the widow
- Family of the widow
- Witness for the widow
- Date and place of signing

Confederate Pensions (1912–1946) are located at the Kentucky Department for Libraries and Archives and are available online at http://www.e-archives.ky.gov /Confederate_pension.htm. Some applications contain supporting documentation such as letters, birth information, marriage licenses, affidavits, and other records. You can browse by date, name, application number, and unit.

The application includes the following information:

- Name
- Address
- Age at the time of application
- Military service history
- Superior officer's name
- Statements of witnesses
- County judge verification

Louisiana

In 1898, Louisiana began granting pensions to Confederate veterans and their widows. The index has over forty-nine thousand names included in applications submitted to the Board of Pension Commissioners.[37]

---

37 http://www.sos.la.gov/HistoricalResources/ResearchHistoricalRecords/LocateHistoricalRecords/Pages /ConfederatePensionDatabase.aspx.

To search the Confederate Pension Applications Index: The Confederate Pension Applications Index provides the following information on the applicant:

- Name
- State enlisted
- Service information: branch, unit, and company
- Parish
- Number of pages in the applicant's file

https://www.sos.la.gov/HistoricalResources/ResearchHistoricalRecords
/LocateHistoricalRecords/Pages/ConfederatePensionDatabase.aspx

To browse the Confederate Applications online or order a copy: Louisiana Confederate Pensions, 1898–1950, at Familysearch.org are arranged in alphabetical order. To order a copy of a pension application, complete the Request for Confederate Pension Application and send a $20.00 check for each individual and application. For credit cards, add a $5.00 service fee. Applications are available from the Louisiana Secretary of State, and make sure you check their website for updates. You will need the following information:

- Applicant's full name
- Target card name
- Military unit
- Residence (parish or town)

Submit form via email or snail mail to:
Research Library
Secretary of State
P.O. Box 94125
Baton Rouge, LA 70804-9125
Email: Library@sos.la.gov
https://www.sos.la.gov/HistoricalResources/PublishedDocuments
/LFP4RequestForConfederatePensionApplication.pdf

In 1888, Mississippi began granting pensions to indigent Confederate veterans or their widows. Mississippi was the only former Confederate state to include African American servants in its pension program from the beginning. Over 1,700 applications were submitted by African Americans.[38]

Browse the Confederate Pension Applications arranged in alphabetical order
Mississippi Office of the State Auditor Series 1201: Confederate Pension Applications, 1889–1932. http://www.mdah.ms.gov/arrec/digital_archives/pensions/. Applications include the following information:

- Name
- Age
- Place of residence
- Military service: unit, officers, dates of enlistment, and discharge
- Current circumstances for eligibility
- Signature of applicant
- Pension board members
- Witnesses
- Correspondence

Mississippi Confederate Veterans and Widows Pension Applications 1900–1974 at Familysearch.org are arranged in alphabetical order. The applications contain the following information:[39]

- Name of soldier, widow, or dependents
- Date and place of birth
- Dates and places of enlistment and discharge
- Company in which served and its captain

---

38 http://www.mdah.ms.gov/arrec/digital_archives/pensions/desc.

39 "Mississippi, Confederate Veterans and Widows Pension Applications," Familysearch Wiki https://familysearch org/wiki/en/Mississippi,_Confederate_Veterans_and_Widows_Pension_Applications_(FamilySearch_Historical _Records)#What_Can_these_Records_Tell_Me.3F.

- Length of service
- Name of regiment and its commander
- Details on wounds received
- Sworn statements on proof of service by comrades
- War Department service abstracts
- Place and length of residency in the state
- Date and place of marriage
- Date and place of the veteran's death

Missouri

Missouri offered pensions to destitute Confederate veterans and established a veterans' home for disabled Confederate soldiers, wives, widows, and orphans.

Browse the Pension and Soldiers Home Applications arranged alphabetically
Familysearch.org: Missouri, Confederate Pension Applications and Soldiers Home Applications.

This collection was acquired from the Missouri Department of Records and Archives in Jefferson City and covers 1911 to 1938. https://familysearch.org/search /collection/1865475.

North Carolina

Although some pensions were granted earlier, in 1885, the State of North Carolina began granting pensions for soldiers who were at least three-fourths incapacitated by wounds and widows whose husbands died in the war. Beginning in 1889, those applicants eligible for pensions were divided based on disability: pensioners who were totally disabled ($72 annually); pensioners who lost a leg or an arm ($60); pensioners who lost a hand or a foot ($48); pensioners who lost an eye or were partially incapacitated due to other wounds ($30); and widows. All persons entitled to pensions under the act, whether previously drawing pensions or not, were to appear before their county Board of Pensions on or before the first Monday in July 1901 for examination and classification. Applications for admission to the Soldiers' Home are included with pension applications and may date prior to

1901. Applicants who owned more than $500 worth of property or earned an annual salary of $300 or more were not eligible for a pension. Inmates of the Soldiers' Home, recipients of pensions from other states, and deserters were also excluded from benefits under the pension acts.[40]

Search the 1901 Confederate Pension Applications

Applications from the State Archives of North Carolina formally referred to as "Pension Bureau: Act of 1901 Pension Applications" are part of a digital collection with 35,717 applications.[41] Microfilm of the pension applications are available at State Archives of North Carolina located in Raleigh, North Carolina. http://digital.ncdcr.gov/cdm/home/collections/confederate-pension-applications.

Information found in the 1901 Pension Application:[42]

- Name
- Age at the time of application
- Place of residence
- Service information: regiment, length of service, wounds, or disability
- Name of witness
- Date of application
- Documents related to disabilities
- Correspondence relating to the application
- Application approved or disallowed by the state board

Browse the North Carolina, Confederate Soldiers & Widows Pension Applications 1885–1953, at Familysearch.org. The applications are arranged in alphabetical order.

Oklahoma

In 1915, the Fifth Legislature approved the Confederate Soldier's Pension Bill providing pensions for disabled and indigent Confederate soldiers, sailors, and

---

40 https://ncarchives.wordpress.com/2015/07/27/1901-confederate-pension-applications-digital-collection/.

41 http://digital.ncdcr.gov/cdm/home/collections/confederate-pension-applications.

42 https://ncarchives.wordpress.com/2014/06/23/1901-confederate-pension-applications-online/.

their widows. The Board of Pension Commissioners was created to hear and determine all applications for pensions. The board made their decision based on established criteria including the applicant's residence in Oklahoma for twelve months prior to the passage of the Pension Act.[43]

Index to Applications for Pensions from the State of Oklahoma, Submitted by Confederate Soldiers, Sailors, and Their Widows (Oklahoma City, OK: Oklahoma Genealogical Society Projects Committee, 1969).

Search the Oklahoma Confederate Pension Index

Index to Oklahoma Confederate Pension Records from the Oklahoma Digital Prairie. http://www.digitalprairie.ok.gov/cdm/landingpage/collection/pensioncard.

Information about the Oklahoma Confederate veterans includes:

- Name of soldier
- Spouse's name
- Address
- Date of marriage
- Date of death
- Military service

Search Confederate Pension Records

Application and Pension records have been combined and are housed in the State Archives of Oklahoma Department of Libraries. http://digitalprairie.ok.gov/cdm/landingpage/collection/pensions.

South Carolina

Confederate soldiers and widows in financial need were able to apply for a pension based on the 1887 law. In 1889, the South Carolina comptroller started publishing a county pension roll for veterans. These reports can help you determine if your ancestor received a pension. Most of the applications from 1888 to 1918 are not available. Starting in 1919, South Carolina granted Confederate pensions to

---

43 http://www.digitalprairie.ok.gov/cdm/landingpage/collection/pensioncard.

veterans and widows regardless of finances. The Confederate Home and Infirmary was opened in Columbia in 1909 and closed in 1958. Widows and wives were admitted beginning in 1925, with other female relatives such as sisters, daughters, and nieces admitted in later years. The applications provide name, age, residence, occupation, relationship (if female), unit, dates of service, and name of closest relative.

To search the Pension Records:
Confederate Pension Applications, 1919–1938, at South Carolina Department of Archives and History and online. This collection contains over ten thousand items and is available at http://www.archivesindex.sc.gov. Other record sets include:

- Artificial Limb Records: Comptroller General, Pension Department, Artificial Limbs Applications and Vouchers, 1879–1889
- Comptroller General, Pension Department, Pension Applications 1919–1925

To search Confederate Home and Infirmary Applications online: http://www .archivesindex.sc.gov/onlinearchives/search.aspx.
South Carolina, Confederate Home Records, 1909–1958 https://www .familysearch.org/search/collection/2126716.

Tennessee

The Board of Pension Examiners was established in 1891 to determine the eligibility of Confederate veterans applying for a petition. What were the requirements for eligibility? The requirements included not being able to support oneself, honorable discharge from service, and residence in the state for one year prior to their application.[44]

To search the Tennessee Confederate Pension Applications, Soldiers & Widows:
You can view these records by name or by county http://sos.tn.gov/products/tsla /tennessee-confederate-pension-applications-soldiers-widows.

---

44 http://sos.tn.gov/products/tsla/tennessee-confederate-pension-applications-soldiers-widows.

Information contained in the application:

- Name of soldier
- Place of birth
- Number of children
- Location of enlistment
- Regiment
- Periods of service
- Battles participated in
- Value of personal and real property

On April 9, 1921, Tennessee passed an act providing pensions of $10.00 a month for "those colored men who served as servants and cooks in the Confederate Army in the War Between the States."[45]

If your ancestor was formerly enslaved and served a Confederate soldier, search the African American "Colored" Confederate Pension Applications (CCPA) Index. http://sostngovbuckets.s3.amazonaws.com/tsla/history/military/civil_war/CCPA _Index.pdf.

The index contains the following information:

- Applicant's first name and surname
- County of residence at the time of application
- Unit in which he served
- Pension application number

To browse the images of pension applications:
Tennessee Confederate Pension Applications, Soldiers & Widows, 1891–1965, at Familysearch.org. These records are arranged by Colored Troops, filed by Soldiers, Widows, and Miscellaneous.

---

45 Tennessee 1921 Public Acts, Ch. 129 http://sostngovbuckets.s3.amazonaws.com/tsla/history/military/civil _war/ColoredConfederatePensionApplications.pdf.

To order a copy of Tennessee Confederate Pension Application:
Complete Form SS-2236 Military Records Search Request and send your request to Tennessee State Library and Archives, Public Services, 403 Seventh Avenue North, Nashville TN 37243-0312.

For additional information on ordering Confederate Pension records: https://sos.tn.gov /products/tsla/ordering-records-tennessee-state-library-and-archives.

To search index for Tennessee Confederate Soldiers' Home: Applications and Ledgers: https://sharetngov.tnsosfiles.com/tsla/history/military/csh1.htm.

The Tennessee Confederate Soldiers' Home opened on the ground of the Hermitage, the former plantation of President Andrew Jackson. Confederate veterans had to apply for admission to the Tennessee Confederate Soldiers' Home, which provided care and housing. Ledger One has the following information on the soldier:[46]

- Name
- Date application received
- Date of birth
- Place of birth
- Date of enlistment
- Rank
- Company and unit
- Wounded, captured, or released as a POW
- Date of discharge
- Occupation
- Date of death
- Remarks
- Ledger Two contains brief paragraphs on soldiers including name, age at time of admission, unit, dates of admission, discharge from the home, date of death, and burial place.[47]

---

46 http://sos.tn.gov/products/tsla/tennessee-confederate-soldiers-home-applications-and-ledgers.
47 Ibid.

Ordering Tennessee Confederate Soldiers' Home Applications and Ledgers
Use form SS-2236 Military Records Search Request to order photocopies of a *Tennessee Confederate Soldiers' Home Applications or Ledgers*. Make sure you review the Tennessee State Library and Archives website for any changes regarding fees and forms. http://sostngovbuckets.s3.amazonaws.com/tsla/general/forms/ss-2236.pdf.

The $10 fee covers copying up to twenty pages, and each additional copy after twenty pages is fifty cents. If there is an application file and an entry in a ledger for one soldier, the Library and Archives will copy both records for one fee. Payment is required in advance by check, money order, or credit card. Send form SS-2236 to Tennessee State Library and Archives, Research Department, 403 Seventh Avenue North, Nashville, TN 37243-0312.

Tennessee Civil War Veterans' Questionnaires
These were started in 1914 to record the experiences of veterans in the Civil War, by a Tennessee State Archivist who developed them and contacted living Civil War veterans asking them to return the questionnaires to Nashville. The project was completed in 1922 with 1,650 questionnaires.[48] The questionnaires are in alphabetical order with the Confederate soldiers' responses followed by Federal soldiers' responses. The index and sample questionnaires are available at http://share.tn.gov/tsla/history/military/quest.htm.[49]

Sistler, Samuel. *Index to Tennessee Confederate Pension Applications* (Nashville, TN: Sistler & Assoc., 1995)

Texas

Search Index of Confederate Pension Applications
The Index contains 54,634 approved and rejected home pensions issued by the Texas government between 1899 and 1975. The index provides name, county of residence, and pension number.[50]

---

48 http://sos.tn.gov/products/tsla/tennessee-civil-war-veterans-questionnaires.

49 Sistler, Samuel. *Index to Tennessee Confederate Pension Applications.* Nashville, TN: Sistler & Assoc., 1995.

50 https://www.tsl.texas.gov/arc/pensions/introcpi.html.

Search by Name or Keyword: https://www.tsl.texas.gov/apps/arc/pensions/index .php?formType=name.

Search the Confederate Pension Records
Ancestry.com: Alabama, Texas, and Virginia Confederate Pensions, 1884–1958 http://search.ancestry.com/search/db.aspx?dbid=1677.

Virginia

Search the Confederate Pension Records
Confederate Pension acts were passed in 1888, 1900, and 1902 by the Virginia General Assembly. The Act of 1888 provided pensions to Confederate soldiers, sailors, and marines disabled in action and widows of soldiers killed in action. Later pensions were broadened to include all veterans, their widows, and their unmarried or widowed daughters. The database has more than 46,000 entries linked to more than 220,000 application pages. Information contained in the pension files includes:[51]

- Name
- Medical evaluations
- Service records
- Information on income and property
- Date and place of marriages

Claims submitted by over five hundred African Americans who worked as cooks, herdsmen, laborers, servants, or teamsters in the Confederate Army are included in this collection.

Library of Virginia: Confederate Pension Records
http://lva1.hosted.exlibrisgroup.com/F/?func=file&file_name=find-b-clas10 &local_base=CLAS10.

Ancestry.com: Alabama, Texas, and Virginia Confederate Pensions, 1884–1958 http://search.ancestry.com/search/db.aspx?dbid=1677.

---

51 http://www.lva.virginia.gov/public/guides/opac/conpenabout.htm?_ga=1.256533451.1523300520.1491163263 #Names.

OTHER CIVIL WAR RECORDS

There are several other Civil War records sets that provide historical data about the Civil War and its impact on the United States. The three record sets Amnesty Records, Confederate Citizens, and Southern Claims Commission are available online.

Amnesty Records

In May 1865, President Andrew Johnson issued an Amnesty Proclamation for those who participated in the rebellion after taking an oath or affirmation. There were fourteen classes of people who were "excepted from the benefits of this proclamation":[52]

- Civil/diplomatic officers, domestic or foreign agents of the Confederate government
- All who left the judiciary in the United States to aid in the rebellion
- Military or naval officers above the rank of colonel in the army or lieutenant in the navy of the Confederacy
- All who left seats in Congress in the United States to aid the Confederacy
- All who resigned commissions in the United States Army or Navy to evade their duties to resist the rebellion
- Those who treated prisoners of war unlawfully
- All persons who have been or were absent from the United States for the purpose of aiding the rebellion
- Military and Naval officers of Confederacy who were educated at West Point or the United States Naval Academy
- All persons who were governors of the Confederate States during the Civil War
- All persons who left their homes in the United States to aid the Confederate States
- All parties engaged in the destruction of the United States commerce on the high seas, and persons who made raids on the United States through

---

52 http://www.nytimes.com/1865/05/30/news/president-johnson-s-amnesty-proclamation-restoration-rights-property -except.html.

Canada or engaged in destroying the United States commerce on lakes and rivers that separate the British provinces from the United States

- All persons who are seeking to take the oath and are in the custody of civil, military, or naval authorities or agents of the United States as prisoners of wars or detained for offenses
- All persons who have voluntarily participated in the rebellion and have taxable property over $20,000
- All persons who have taken the oath of amnesty in the president's proclamation on December 8, 1863, or an oath of allegiance to the United States since the dates of said proclamation. Special applications can be made to the president for pardon by any person belonging to such classes, and such may be liberally extended as consistent with the facts of the case.[53]

Records available online

- United States, Civil War Confederate Applications for Pardons, 1865–1867, at Familysearch.org
- Confederate Amnesty Papers at Fold3.com
- Confederate Applications for Presidential Pardons, 1865–1867, at Ancestry .com

Confederate Citizen's Files

These files contain documents related to the goods and services provided to the Confederacy by private individuals and businesses. These records are searchable and available online.

- Confederate Citizen's File at Fold3.com
- United States, Civil War Confederate Papers of Citizens or Businesses 1861–1865 at Familysearch.org

---

53 http://www.nytimes.com/1865/05/30/news/president-johnson-s-amnesty-proclamation-restoration-rights
-property-except.html.

Southern Claims Commission

The Southern Claims Commission was organized to compensate Southerners loyal to the Union Army during the Civil War. Individuals from Arkansas, Alabama, Georgia, Florida, Louisiana, Mississippi, North Carolina, South Carolina, Tennessee, Texas, Virginia, and West Virginia filed claims stating they were loyal and had taken or furnished supplies to the Union Army or had them taken. Claimants had to provide witnesses, and some of those witnesses were formerly enslaved. Below is a table of the Southern Claims Commission Index, Approved and Disallowed:

COLLECTION	LOCATION
US Southern Claims Commission Master Index, 1871–1880	Ancestry.com
US Southern Claims Commission Allowed Claims, 1871–1880	Ancestry.com Fold3.com
Southern Claims Barred and Disallowed	Ancestry.com Fold3.com
Southern Claims—Approved—Alabama	Fold3.com
Southern Claims—Approved—Georgia	Fold3.com
Southern Claims—Approved—Virginia	Fold3.com
Southern Claims—Approved—West Virginia	Fold3.com

SPANISH-AMERICAN WAR

On April 26, 1898, the United States declared war on Spain over the sinking of the battleship USS *Maine* in Havana harbor. The fighting ended on December 10, 1898, and Spain ceded all former Spanish colonies (Guam, Puerto Rico, and the Philippines). To find Spanish-American War ancestors, start by searching the indexes and service records listed in the table below:

Indexes and Service Records for the Spanish-American War

COLLECTION	LOCATION
General Index to Compiled Service Records of Volunteer Soldiers Who Served During the War with Spain	Microfilm Publication M871—National Archives and Records Administration
United States Index to Service Records, War with Spain, 1898	*Familysearch.org*
Index to Compiled Military Service Records of Volunteer Soldiers Who Served During the War with Spain in Organizations from the State of Louisiana	Microfilm Publication M240—National Archives and Records Administration
Index to Compiled Military Service Records of Volunteer Soldiers Who Served During the War with Spain in Organizations from the State of North Carolina	Microfilm Publication M413—National Archives and Records Administration *Ancestry.com*
Compiled Service Records of Volunteer Soldiers Who Served in the Florida Infantry During the War With Spain	Microfilm Publication M1087—National Archives and Records Administration *Ancestry.com*
Spanish-American War Service Record Index	*Fold3.com*

WORLD WAR I

World War I, also known as "The Great War," started in July 1914 and ended in November 1918. According to the US Department of Veterans Affairs "America's Wars" fact sheet: Over 4.5 million service members served in the Great War, over 53,000 died in battle, about 63,000 died in service, and about 204,000 suffered nonmortal wounds.[54] Records are available at the National Personnel Records Center, although a fire in 1973 and the resulting action to contain the fire damaged or destroyed a significant portion of Army Service records for personnel between November 1912 and January 1960. Seventy-five percent of the records for

---

54 United States Department of Veteran's Affairs America's Wars https://www.va.gov/opa/publications/factsheets/fs_americas_wars.pdf.

Air Force personnel discharged between September 1947 and January 1964 were also destroyed.[55]

AFRICAN AMERICAN TROOPS IN WORLD WAR I

More than three hundred thousand African Americans who were part of segregated troops served in World War I and were primarily in support roles. The "Harlem Hellfighters" (369th Infantry) were on the front line for six months with the French Army.[56] African American soldiers fought for freedom during World War I but faced discrimination when they returned home after the war. On *Genealogy Roadshow*, we discussed the "Red Summer" of 1919, the year my grandfather Lavell Nathaniel Jones was born in Junction City, Arkansas. There were race riots across the country based on social tensions after World War I. The competition for jobs and housing among blacks and whites returning from the war was part of the catalyst for Red Summer.

NATIVE AMERICANS IN WORLD WAR I

Many Native Americans volunteered even though they were not considered citizens. On November 6, 1919, Congress enacted legislation offering citizenship to Native Americans who were veterans of World War I. Choctaw Indians from 142nd Infantry Regiment, 36th Division, were the first code talkers. The Army enlisted soldiers from Cheyenne, Comanche, Cherokee, Osage, and Yankton Sioux tribes.[57]

RECORDS RELATED TO WORLD WAR I

A great resource is "Finding Your World War I Veteran at the National Archives at St. Louis," by Theresa Fitzgerald. You can find the article online at https://www.archives.gov/files/st-louis/pdf/finding-your-wwl-veteran.pdf. A list of WWI records is available at the National Personnel Records Center at the National Archives in St. Louis at https://www.archives.gov/research/military/ww1/st-louis-wwl-series.

55 "The 1973 Fire, National Personnel Records Center," National Archives and Records Administration https://www.archives.gov/st-louis/military-personnel/fire-1973.html.

56 "100 Amazing Facts About the Negro: Who Were the Harlem Hellfighters?" by Henry Louis Gates, Jr. http://www.pbs.org/wnet/african-americans-many-rivers-to-cross/history/who-were-the-harlem-hellfighters/.

57 "Code Talkers," National Archives and Records Administration https://www.archives.gov/research/native-americans/military/code-talkers.html.

Draft registrations are very useful in doing your family history research. The World War I Selective Service system was in place from May 1917 to May 1919. Registrations for June 5, 1917, included all men ages twenty-one through thirty-one; June 5, 1918, all men over the age of twenty-one after the first draft; and September 1918, all men between eighteen and forty-five. A supplemental registration was held on August 24, 1918, for those becoming twenty-one years old after June 5, 1918. From a draft registration, you can uncover vital information such as birth name, birth location, citizenship, residence, occupation, employer, dependents, marital status, race, build, height, eye color, hair color, etc. Below is the World War I draft registration for my great-grandfather Nathaniel Lockhart Hawthorne Jones. He was born in Spearsville, Louisiana, on November 15, 1895, but lived in Junction City, Arkansas, where my grandfather Lavell Nathaniel Jones was born. At the time of the registration, he was married and had two children. Fun fact: the ends of my great-grandfather's draft registration were clipped because he was African American.

"United States World War I Draft Registration Cards, 1917–1918," database with images, FamilySearch (https://familysearch.org/ark:/61903/1:1:K354-MMC : 12 December 2014), Nathaniel Lockhart Hawthorne Jones, 1917-1918; citing Union County, Arkansas, United States, NARA microfilm publication M1509 (Washington DC: National Archives and Records Administration, n.d.); FHL microfilm 1,530,647.

World War I Records: Casualties, Draft Registrations, Enemy Alien Affidavits, Naturalizations, and Service Records

COLLECTION TITLE	INFORMATION	LOCATION
United States World War I Draft Registrations	Biographical information	Ancestry.com, Fold3.com & Familysearch.org
United States Index to Naturalizations of World War I Soldiers	Naturalization information for 18,000 soldiers	Familysearch.org
United States, YMCA World War I Service Cards	Name, age, and occupation of 27,000 individuals who served with the YMCA	Familysearch.org
California, San Francisco World War I Enemy Alien Registration Affidavits, 1918	Name, gender, birth date, residence, year, father's name, and mother's name	Familysearch.org
Louisiana World War I Service Records, 1917–1920	Name, age, birthplace, birth year, residence, military service, and other information	Familysearch.org
Maine World War I Draft Registration Index, 1917–1919	Name, age, residence, birth date, birthplace, occupation, race, relative, relationship, and other information	Familysearch.org
World War I New York Army Cards	Name, birth date, age, birthplace, military service, and other information	Fold3.com
North Carolina, World War I Service Cards, 1917–1919, located at the North Carolina Archives	Name, birth year, birthplace, age, date, place, and residence	Familysearch.org
Texas World War I Records acquired from the Texas Military Forces Museum in Austin	Name, date, place, birth date, race, and birthplace	Familysearch.org
WWI, WWII, and Korean War Casualty Listings	Names, birth date, birthplace, death, death location, death description, military service, and notes	Ancestry.com

VETERANS HOMES

In Los Angeles, the Sawtelle Disabled Veterans Home was established in 1888 on the corner of Wilshire and Sawtelle. The home sheltered veterans from the Civil War, Spanish-American War, Indian Conflicts, and World War I. The surviving case files from 1888 to 1933 are at the National Archives and Records Administration in Riverside, California, and the names are listed online at https://www.archives.gov/riverside/finding-aids/disabled-veterans-files.html. The files from the Leavenworth Kansas Soldiers Home from 1885 to 1933 are available at the National Archives and Records Administration (NARA) regional facility in Kansas City. Order records from the National Personnel Records Center in St. Louis by completing Military Record Requests using Standard Form 180.

WORLD WAR II

Known as the Second World War, World War II was a global war that lasted from 1939 to 1945. More than sixteen million Americans fought in World War II. On September 16, 1940, President Roosevelt signed into law Proclamation 2425—Selective Service Registration.[58] Men who had reached their twenty-first birthday but not their thirty-sixth birthday registered with their local draft board. When the United States entered the war after the attack on Pearl Harbor, all men from the age of eighteen until the day before their forty-fifth birthday were subject to military service. On April 27, 1942, the fourth draft, also known as the "Old Man's Draft," was conducted for men ages forty-five to sixty-four.[59] All men from their eighteenth birthday to their sixty-fifth birthday were required to register. Multiple draft registrations were held between November 1940 and October 1946. The government selected men through a lottery system, and if drafted you would serve for twelve months. The Selective Training and Service Act provided that not more than nine hundred thousand men were to be in training at any one time, and it limited service to twelve months.[60] Six drafts were conducted by the federal government during World War II.

---

58 http://www.presidency.ucsb.edu/ws/?pid=15858.

59 "Selective Service Records," National Archives and Records Administration https://www.archives.gov/st-louis/archival-programs/other-records/selective-service.html.

60 https://en.wikipedia.org/wiki/Selective_Training_and_Service_Act_of_1940.

Upon discharge from the military, veterans received a brief one-page summary of their service. This document included their rank, service number, inclusive dates of service, overseas service, military occupation, battles, campaigns, decorations, and awards. The National Personnel Records Center (NPRC) has custody of the personnel files of individuals serving in the Army, Army Air Forces, Navy, Marine Corps, and Coast Guard. Review the NPRC website for a list of available records from World War II.

FINDING YOUR WORLD WAR II ANCESTOR

Start by reviewing the article "Finding Information on Personal Participation in World War II"—National Archives and Records Administration Publication at https://www.archives.gov/files/research/military/ww2/ww2-participation.pdf.

World War II Records: Causalities, Draft Registrations, Enlistment Records, Missing in Action, Muster Rolls, and Prisoner of War Records

COLLECTION	INFORMATION	LOCATION
World War II Draft Registrations	Name, serial number, address, telephone, age, place of birth, country of citizenship, employer's name, place of employment, name and address of person who will always know registrant's address, relationship to registrant, description (race, eye color, weight, complexion, hair color, and year of registration)	Ancestry.com, Familysearch.org, and Fold3.com
US WWII Draft Cards, Young Men, 1940–1947	Name, serial number, address, telephone, age, place of birth, country of citizenship, employer's name, place of employment, name and address of person who will always know registrant's address, relationship to registrant, year of registration, description (race, eye color, weight, complexion, and hair color)	Ancestry.com

COLLECTION	INFORMATION	LOCATION
US World War II Navy Muster Rolls, 1938–1949	Name, occupation/specialty, service number, date of enlistment, date reported for duty, ship or station, ship number, and date of muster roll	Ancestry.com
WWII Prisoners of the Japanese, 1941–1945	Name, rank, service number, arm of service, unit information, POW camp notes, and other information	Ancestry.com
US, World War II Army Enlistment Records, 1938–1946	Name, serial number, army branch, enlistment information, birth year and location, race, height, weight, education, marital status, and other information	Ancestry.com
US WWII Military Personnel Missing in Action or Lost at Sea, 1941–1946	Name of military personnel, date of loss, branch, rank, service number, and status	Ancestry.com

Search WWII Electronic Records on archives.gov

The electronic database of World War II Army Enrollment records contains approximately nine million records of men and women who enlisted in the Army between 1938 and 1946. Click the link below and click the "search" button next to the database name. https://aad.archives.gov/aad/series-list.jsp?cat=WR26.

What information is contained in this record? Below is the information for my paternal grandfather Lavell Nathaniel Jones. The database also provides information on each data element associated with the WWII enlistee.

- Army Serial Number: 38179208
- Name: Jones, Lavell N.
- Residence state: Arkansas
- Residence county: Union
- Place of enlistment: CP Joseph T. Robinson, Little Rock, Arkansas
- Date of enlistment day: 28
- Date of enlistment month: 6

- Date of enlistment year: 42
- Grade: Alpha Designation: Undefined Code
- Grade: Code: Private
- Branch: Alpha Designation: Branch Immaterial—Warrant Officers, USA
- Branch: Code: Branch Immaterial—Warrant Officers, USA
- Term of enlistment: Enlistment for the duration of the war or other emergency, plus six months, subject to the discretion of the President or otherwise according to law.
- Source of army personnel: Civil Life
- Nativity: Arkansas
- Year of birth: 19
- Race and citizenship: Negro, citizen
- Education: Grammar school
- Civilian occupation: Semiskilled routeman
- Marital status: Single, no dependents
- Component of the army: Selected (Enlisted Men)
- Box number: 1299
- Film reel number: 6.65

Ordering Military Records from National Archives and Records Administration (NARA)

To order military service records, use NATF Form 86, which can be downloaded or ordered online at https://www.archives.gov/forms. Look for (Pre-WWI) Military Service Records and click the appropriate link.

JAPANESE AMERICAN INTERNMENT

In February 1942, President Roosevelt signed Executive Order 9066 forcing about 117,000 Japanese Americans to leave their homes, businesses, and livelihood.[61] Japanese Americans were evacuated from California, Oregon, and Washington and interned in camps in Arizona, Arkansas, California, Colorado, Idaho, Utah, and Wyoming. The War Relocation Authority (WRA) was established to handle Japanese Internment during World War II. This action generated documentation

---

61 Transcript of Executive Order 9066: Resulting in the Relocation of Japanese (1942) https://www.ourdocuments.gov /doc.php?flash=true&doc=74&page=transcript.

essential to researching Japanese American ancestors in the United States during World War II. The National Archives has an excellent resource on researching WWII Japanese Internment and Relocation Records at https://www.archives.gov /research/japanese-americans/internment-intro.

Searching for Japanese American Evacuees

You will need to know both the Japanese and English names of the individual interned. Search the Access Archival Database (AAD) for World War II records, then search the "Records about Japanese Americans created During World War II."[62] Information collection on each individual includes:

- Name
- Assembly center
- Relocation project
- Previous address
- Birthplace of parents
- Father's occupation
- Education
- Foreign residence
- Military service
- Physical defects
- Public assistance or pension
- Age, sex, and marital status
- Birth date and location
- Alien registration number or social security number
- Did they attend Japanese language school? Where?
- Highest grade completed in school
- Occupation
- Religion
- Language proficiency

---

62 National Archives and Records Administration, "Search the Database of Japanese American Evacuees (Record Group 210)." https://www.archives.gov/research/japanese-americans/wra.

If you do not find your ancestor in the index, it's suggested that you search the Alien Enemy Detention and Internment Case Files Index from the Department of Justice online at https://www.archives.gov/research/japanese-americans/internment -files.

Order Copies of Japanese Internment Records

Once you locate your ancestor, order their case file from the National Archives and Records Administration. Instructions on ordering records can be found at https://www.archives.gov/research/japanese-americans/order.

In 1948, the Congress passed and signed into law the Japanese-American Claims Act to compensate Japanese Americans for the property they lost when they were removed to internment camps. Search the Compensation and Reparations for the Evacuation, Relocation, and Internment Index (Redress Case Files) online at https://www.archives.gov/research/japanese-americans/redress.

OTHER CONFLICTS

If your ancestor participated in more recent conflicts such as the Korean War or the Vietnam War, below are a few resources to help you locate information about their participation.

KOREAN WAR (1950–1953)

Start by searching the Korean War records at the Access to Archival Databases (AAD) at archives.gov. Click on the link for the Korean War to access records about deceased, injured, wounded, prisoners of war, and other information. Review state level lists of fatal casualties of the Korean War at https://www.archives .gov/research/military/korean-war/casualty-lists/state-level-alpha.html. A list of Korean War casualties and veterans affairs, BIRLS Death files, is available online at Fold3.com.

VIETNAM WAR (1954–1975)

A conflict that was very controversial at the time and still is today. During the Vietnam War, over fifty-eight thousand American soldiers died or were missing in action. Start by searching the Vietnam Records at the Access to Archival Databases (AAD) at archives.gov. Click on the link for the Vietnam War to access records about deceased, injured, wounded, incidents, contracts, and other records. Fold3.com has Vietnam Service Records and Vietnam War Milestone documents.

To find ancestors who were casualties, missing in action, or prisoners of war during the Vietnam War, review the Electronic Records Reference Report from the National Archives. https://www.archives.gov/research/military/vietnam-war /electronic-records.html. There are state level lists of fatal casualties of the Vietnam War at https://www.archives.gov/research/military/vietnam-war/casualty -lists/state-level-alpha.html.

CHAPTER 6
ETHNIC ANCESTRY

AFRICAN AMERICAN FAMILY HISTORY

African American research can be challenging and overwhelming and seem impossible because of slavery. Not every person of African ancestry in the United States was bound in chains. There were free people of color in the North and the South. Not every white person was an enslaver; African American men, women, and children were enslaved by African Americans and Native Americans, too. One of the major myths of African American family history is that records do not exist because our ancestors were enslaved. That is simply not true. I would argue it is the opposite. Enslaved individuals were property, and as property, their movements or the movements of their enslavers generated records. These records are useful in finding enslaved and free ancestors.

When you research people of African ancestry in the United States, it's important to understand key events in African American history that helped to shape laws that governed free people of color and the enslaved. While it can be emotional, understanding the Transatlantic and Domestic slave trade is critical. The Reconstruction Era is a fascinating period in history and one that all family history researchers need to study. Records generated during this period can be a great source of information and can provide insight into the conditions of the formerly enslaved and southern whites.

Key Events in African American History

1619: August—First African slaves arrive in Jamestowne, Virginia: thirty-two Africans in 1620 and twenty-three Africans according to a 1625 census.[1]

1654: John Casor becomes the first legally recognized slave in the United States.[2]

1705: In October, Virginia declares all negro, mulatto, and Indian slaves should be held as real estate.[3]

1800: Gabriel's conspiracy as it is known was a slave rebellion lead by an enslaved man named Gabriel.[4] African American men who were enslaved planned to attack Richmond to destroy slavery in Virginia. The rebellion originated in a Henrico County neighborhood and extended primarily to Hanover and Caroline Colonies.

1807: The Abolition of the Slave Trade Act of 1807 went into effect on January 1, 1808.

1822: Denmark Vesey is hanged for planning a slave rebellion in Charleston, South Carolina.

1831: Nat Turner leads a slave rebellion in Virginia, and William Lloyd Garrison founds the abolitionist newspaper *The Liberator.*

1850: Fugitive slave laws require runaway slaves in free states to be returned to their enslavers. This law part of the Compromise of 1850 allowed California to enter the union as a "free" state and not a slave state.

1852: *Uncle Tom's Cabin* by Harriett Beecher Stowe is published.

1857: The Dred Scott decision: The United States Supreme Court rules people of African descent are not citizens of the United States and could not sue in Federal Court.[5]

1863 TO 1877: Reconstruction Era—Transformation of the South as directed by Congress

1863: Emancipation Proclamation takes effect.

1865: 13th Amendment prohibits slavery.

1865: The Bureau of Refugees, Freedmen, and Abandoned Lands (a.k.a. Freedmen's Bureau) is established.

---

1 http://historicjamestowne.org/history/the-first-africans/.

2 Eschner, Kat. "The Horrible Fate of John Casor, The First Black Man to be Declared a Slave for Life in America," Smithsonian.com, March 8, 2017 - https://www.smithsonianmag.com/smart-news/horrible-fate-john-casor-180962352/.

3 "The Slave Experience: Legal Rights & Government," PBS - http://www.pbs.org/wnet/slavery/experience/legal/docs1.html.

4 https://www.encyclopediavirginia.org/Gabriel_s_Conspiracy_1800.

5 "Dred Scott's fight for freedom," Africans in America, https://www.pbs.org/wgbh/aia/part4/4p2932.html.

TRANSATLANTIC SLAVE TRADE

The Transatlantic Slave Trade was the forced migration of over twelve million Africans to the Caribbean, North America, and South America. The records generated from the Atlantic and domestic slave trade include ship records, diaries, inventories, wills, account books, bills of sale, runaway newspaper ads, manumission papers, deeds, family papers, and other documents. These records are valuable and provide historical context regarding the lives of the enslaved and the enslavers. Most of these records are in the enslaver's name and not the name of the enslaved.

DOMESTIC SLAVE TRADE

In 1790, 45 percent of all those enslaved in the South lived in Virginia, 28 percent in 1820, and 12 percent in 1860. During the 1830s, one out of every five enslaved people was forcibly removed to the Lower South. I always say all roads lead to Virginia when it comes to researching enslaved ancestors. The number of enslaved removed from Virginia in the 1830s equated to the entire black population in 1790. It's estimated about nine hundred thousand individuals who were enslaved were removed from the Upper South to the Lower South.[6]

Select list of records related to Slave Trade at Ancestry.com.

COLLECTION TITLE	INFORMATION
Adams County, Mississippi, Slave Certificates, 1858–1861	Slave trader, slave name, gender, color, age, and other information
Edgefield, South Carolina Slave Records, 1774–1866	Slave's name, description, owner, new owner, date bought, value/price, and source
Louisiana Slave Records, 1719–1820	Name, master's name, gender, race, birthplace, age, family, name of seller, name of buyer, value, and selling currency
New Orleans Louisiana Slave Manifests, 1807–1860	Slave's age, height, slave owners name, shipper's name, slave owner's residence, captain's name, port of destination, and dates of certification

---

6 Deyle, Steven. *Carry Me Back: The Domestic Slave Trade in American Life*, New York: Oxford University Press, 2006.

COLLECTION TITLE	INFORMATION
US Southeast Coastwise Inward and Outward Slave Manifests, 1790–1860	Name of ship, master, port of departure, port of destination, slave name, age, description, shipper or owner, and their place of residence
Washington, DC, Slave Emancipation Records, 1851–1863	Name, age, family members, residence, date of manumission, description, and owner information.
Washington, DC, Slave Owner Petitions, 1862-1863	Slave owner, petition date, slave names, and case number

TIP

Did the ancestors of the enslavers migrate from the Upper South to the Lower South during the height of the Domestic Slave Trade? Make sure you track their real estate purchases during their migration along with their census profile data.

PLANTATION SYSTEM

When you research African American ancestry, it's important to understand the plantation economy and community. A child's status as a slave was based on the status of its mother. In 1662, Virginia enacted a law "that all children borne in this country shall be held bond or free only according to the condition of the mother."[7] If the mother was free, the child was free, even if the father was a slave. If the mother was enslaved, then all of her children would be enslaved, thus increasing the wealth of the enslaver. The plantations in the South grew based on enslaved labor and the sale of products to the North. In South Carolina, there were rice and indigo plantations. In Maryland and Virginia, it was tobacco. In Louisiana, it was sugar cane, while King Cotton was prominent in Alabama, Georgia, and

---

7 Slave Law in Colonial Virginia: A Timeline," Sam Houston State University http://www.shsu.edu/~jll004/vabeach course_spring09/bacons_rebellion/slavelawincolonialvirginiatimeline.pdf.

Mississippi. Those enslaved in urban areas worked in factories or were domestic or skilled tradesmen hired out to families.

According to the United States Census Bureau, the plantation system in the South consisted of twenty to two hundred enslaved individuals with several hundred acres of land. There were overseers who directed the work through several enslaved known as drivers. Those enslaved on plantations were skilled tradesmen, mechanics, field hands, house servants, and anyone over the age of twelve years old.[8] With emancipation, "a billion and a half of capital invested in slaves disappeared."[9]

The Fugitive Slave Act of 1850 required citizens to assist in the recovery of fugitive slaves. It denied a fugitive's right to a jury trial. (Cases would instead be handled by special commissioners—commissioners were paid $5 if an alleged fugitive was released and $10 if he or she was sent away with the claimant.) The act called for changes in filing for a claim, making the process easier for slave owners. Also, according to the act, there would be more federal officials responsible for enforcing the law. This put free people of color in a dangerous position with no right to plead their cases if captured and sold into slavery.

RECONSTRUCTION (1863–1877)

The period after the Civil War and Emancipation of the formerly enslaved when the United States sought to restore the South with a government presence is known as the Reconstruction. Tensions flared between those who were formerly enslaved and whites who were competing for jobs. June 19th (Juneteenth) commemorates the abolition of slavery in the US State of Texas in 1865. General Granger and his soldiers were there to take possession of the state and enforce emancipation of the enslaved. After his arrival, former slaves rejoiced in the street, and annual Juneteenth celebrations began in 1866. This holiday was mostly recognized in the state of Texas and became a state holiday in 1980. Today, thirty-one states and the District of Columbia recognized Juneteenth as a state holiday.

8 Census 1904, *Bulletin 8 Negroes in the United States.*, p. 79.
9 Census 1904, *Bulletin 8 Negroes in the United States.*, p. 80.

FREEDMEN'S BUREAU

On March 3, 1865, Congress established the Bureau of Refugees, Freedmen and Abandoned Lands, also known as the Freedmen's Bureau, as part of the War Department. The Freedmen's Bureau was charged with helping formerly enslaved men, women, and children integrate into society as free people. Charged with supervising the aid and relief efforts for those formerly enslaved, the Freedmen's Bureau established over 4,300 schools and one hundred hospitals; issued food and clothing; operated refugee camps; issued marriage certificates for slave marriages previously not recognized by law; supervised labor contracts; and worked with African American soldiers, sailors, and their heirs to secure back pay, bounty payments, and pensions for their service in the Civil War.[10]

The Freedmen's Savings and Trust Company, also known as the Freedmen's Savings Bank, was established by Congress on March 3, 1865. By 1871, the Freedmen's Bank had thirty-seven branches in seventeen states and the District of Columbia. During its nine-year history, the bank received more than $57 million in deposits and served nearly seventy thousand depositors.[11] In the Financial Panic of 1873, mismanagement, fraud, and other factors caused the bank to nearly collapse in 1874. The bank officially closed on June 29, 1874.[12]

> ## SLAVE MARRIAGES
>
> In May 1865, General Otis Howard, Commissioner of the Freedmen's Bureau issued orders legitimizing slave marriages.[13]
>
> ___
>
> 13 Washington, Reginald. "Sealing the Sacred Bonds of Holy Matrimony Freedmen's Bureau Marriage Records," *Prologue*, Vol. 37, No. 1, Spring 2005. https://www.archives.gov /publications/prologue/2005/spring/freedman-marriage -recs.html.

Freedmen's Bureau Records are available at the National Archives and Records Administration (NARA) in Washington, DC, and online at free and subscription-based sites such as Familysearch.org and Ancestry.com.

---

10 "African American Freedmen's Bureau Records", Familysearch.org.

11 Freedmen's Savings Bank, http://freedmansbank.org/.

12 Washington, Reginald. "The Freedmen's Savings and Trust Company and African American Genealogical Research," *Prologue*, Vol. 29, No. 2, Summer 1997. https://www.archives.gov/publications/prologue/1997/summer/freedmans -savings-and-trust.html.

Freedmen's Bureau Records: Microfilm and Online

RECORD COLLECTION	DESCRIPTION	LOCATION
Records of Superintendents of Education	Alabama, Arkansas, District of Columbia, Georgia, Louisiana, North Carolina, Tennessee, Texas, Virginia	Microfilm at National Archives and Records Administration (NARA), Washington, DC
Records of Assistant Commissioners	Alabama, Arkansas, District of Columbia, Florida, Georgia, Louisiana, Mississippi, North Carolina, South Carolina, Tennessee, Texas, Virginia	Microfilm at National Archives and Records Administration (NARA), Washington, DC
Freedmen's Bureau, Records of the Commission, 1865–1872	Selected Series of Records Issued by the Commissioner of the Freedmen's Bureau and Registers and Letters Received by the Commissioner of the Freedmen's Bureau. Microfilm Publications M742 and M752 from NARA.	Browse records online at Familysearch.org
Field Office Records: Provide a window into the life of the formerly enslaved in the South.	Alabama, Arkansas, District of Columbia, Florida, Georgia, Kentucky, Louisiana, Maryland/Delaware, Mississippi, Missouri, North Carolina, South Carolina, Tennessee, Texas, and Virginia	Microfilm at National Archives and Records Administration (NARA), Washington, DC
Marriage Records of the Office of the Commissioner, Washington Headquarters of the Bureau of Refugees, Freedmen, and Abandoned Lands, 1861–1869	Record types include unbound marriage certificates, marriage licenses, monthly reports of marriages, and other proofs of marriages. Record type and quantity vary with each state. NARA Publication: M1875	Familysearch.org Microfilm at National Archives and Records Administration (NARA), Washington, DC

Freedmen's Bureau Records: Microfilm and Online

RECORD COLLECTION	DESCRIPTION	LOCATION
Selected Series of Records Issued by the Commissioner of the Bureau of Refugees, Freedmen, and Abandoned Lands, 1865–1872	Files that document the overall administration and operation of the Bureau. NARA Publication: M742 Collection Title: United States, Freedmen's Bureau, Records of the Commissioner, 1865–1872, at Familysearch.org	Microfilm at National Archives and Records Administration (NARA), Washington, DC Familysearch.org
Registers and Letters Received by the Commissioner of the Bureau of Refugees, Freedmen, and Abandoned Lands, 1865–1872	Files that document the overall administration and operation of the Bureau. NARA Publication: M752 Collection Title: United States, Freedmen's Bureau, Records of the Commissioner, 1865–1872, at Familysearch.org	Microfilm at National Archives and Records Administration (NARA), Washington, DC Familysearch.org
Records of the Education Division of the Bureau of Refugees, Freedmen, and Abandoned Lands, 1865–1871	Letters sent, Letters Received, Reports of Schools by the State Superintendents of education on a monthly, quarterly, and annual basis. NARA Publication: M803 Collection Title: United States, Freedmen's Bureau, Records of the Superintendent of Education and Division of Education, 1865–1872, at Familysearch.org	Microfilm at National Archives and Records Administration (NARA), Washington, DC Familysearch.org
Records of the Field Offices of the Freedmen's Branch, Office of the Adjutant General, 1872–1878	Some of the records include documents and letters submitted by African American soldiers and sailors for bounty, pension, arrears of pay, and other items related to military service. Microfilm publication M2029.	Microfilm at National Archives and Records Administration (NARA), Washington, DC. Browse the collection at Familysearch.org

RECORD COLLECTION	INFORMATION
Freedmen's Bureau Field Office Records	Alabama, Arkansas, District of Columbia, Georgia, Kentucky, Louisiana, Mississippi, Missouri, North Carolina, South Carolina, Tennessee, Texas, Virginia
Labor Contracts Indenture and Apprentice Records (1865–1872)	Given name, surname, age, birth dates, death dates, race, residence, and occupation
Records of Freedmen's Complaints (1865–1872)	Civil Rights Complaints including date, complainant, action, when taken, result of action, and final action
Freedmen's Bureau Marriages	Marriage licenses, marriage certificates, monthly reports of marriages, and other proof of marriage
Freedmen's Bureau Hospital and Medical Records	Patient information, sick and wounded, prescription books, and other medical records from Freedmen's hospitals
Freedmen's Bureau Ration Records (1865–1872)	Rations and other supplies provided to freedmen and refugees
Freedmen's Bureau Records of Persons and Articles Hired (1865–1872)	Persons and articles hired by the Field Office
Virginia and DC Freedmen's Bureau Field Office Records (1863/1865–1872)	Field office records from Washington, DC, and Virginia
Freedmen's Bank Records (1865–1874)	Registers for over sixty-seven thousand formerly enslaved people who opened accounts with the bank. Information includes name, date account opened, birthplace, residence, age, complexion, occupation, name of employer, spouse's name, children's name, father, mother, and siblings.

THE 1870 BRICK WALL

I am sure that during your research, you have heard about the "1870 Brick Wall." The 1870 Federal Census was the first census that enumerated the four million formerly enslaved African Americans. When beginning their family history, most African Americans can only trace their family back to 1870, if they were enslaved. Most researchers assume former enslaved individuals took the surname of their last enslaver. Surnames were derived from a variety of sources: the surnames of an enslaved parent who was deceased or sold off or a completely new name to remove themselves from their enslaved past and embrace freedom. Or the name of a previous enslaver who might have been their father. Lawyers always say there is an exception to every rule. That is also the case for researching enslaved individuals. If your ancestor had an unusual name such as Ailes, Dwelle, or Simkins, then the name might have come from a former enslaver. How do you determine if your ancestor was formerly enslaved? Were you able to find them in the 1860 Census, or do you have emancipation papers? Are there any family stories about your ancestors being free people of color?

Finding the Last Enslaver

If your ancestor has an unusual surname, start by looking for whites with the same surname in the same county as your ancestors in 1870. Document the census information for all white families with same surname. Make a note of how close the white and black families lived to one another. You may also want to keep a running list of African Americans who are not directly related with the same surname in the county. It's important to get to know the county where your ancestors lived in 1870 by reviewing county histories. These histories might cover prominent families in the town or county with the same surname as your ancestor. I have found these very useful in my family history research.

TIP

Go back to the United States Vital Records Research in Chapter 2 and also review the Census Records Research section to create a census profile for whites in the county with the same surname.

Unusual Surnames

Now that you have candidates for the last enslaver, make a special note of the family members who might have been adults in 1860. Note this on the census profile you created for each enslaver. While children could inherit property such as enslaved individuals, they were generally appointed a guardian until they came of age. Search for the "white families" with the same surname in the 1860 census, both free population and slave schedules. For each possible enslaver, document the number of enslaved individuals and the value of their property both real and personal.

TIP

Create an Excel spreadsheet with a list of the enslavers with the same unusual surname and the number of enslaved individuals in 1850 and 1860.

Look for the enslaved listed in the 1860 Slave Schedule who are within the same age range of your enslaved ancestor. The ages of enslaved could be off by five to ten years. Research the enslavers in the 1850 US Census Free Population and Slave Schedules. Make note if the number of enslaved individuals increased or decreased each year for each enslaver. An increase in enslaved people could mean an inheritance from a family member, purchase of enslaved individuals, or natural increase. A decrease in enslaved individuals could mean a sale of enslaved people, natural decrease due to death, or other reasons. As you continue your research, you might need to repeat this process with US Federal Census records from 1790 to 1840.

Common Surnames

If your ancestors have a common surname like Berry, Jones, or Smith, look for Labor contracts from the Freedmen's Bureau Records in the location where your ancestor was formerly enslaved. Labor contracts name the sharecropper, date of agreement, terms of the agreement, and owner of the farm. Typically, these formerly enslaved individuals entered sharecropping agreements with their former enslavers. These contracts are available online, and this is one way to find a former enslaver. For example, Louis (Lewis) Carter, my fourth great-grandfather, entered a sharecropping agreement on January 8, 1866, with Dr. John W. Taylor of Madison County, Virginia, for one year. With this information, I can start to research John W. Taylor and his family to find documents related to my Carter family. This additional information will help prove or disprove my theory that Dr. John W. Taylor was the last enslaver.

Cohabitation Records

Another resource for uncovering the last enslaver is Cohabitation Records. Alabama, Georgia, Kentucky, Mississippi, North Carolina, and Virginia required newly freed slaves to register their marriages and their children at the county courthouse. It was illegal for the enslaved to get married and to inherit or own property. They often had to get permission from their enslaver to "marry" or "take up" with another enslaved person. Cohabitation records were an attempt after emancipation by the state to recognize formerly enslaved men and women who were living together during slavery as "husband and wife." These records are available at county courthouses, state archives, libraries, and online within the Freedmen's Bureau records collection at Familysearch.org. The Cohabitation Act of 1866, passed by the Virginia Assembly, legalized the marriages of formerly enslaved people in Virginia and declared their children to be legitimate.[14]

Once you find the last enslaver or possible candidates for the last enslaver, search probate and estate records for any first names and ages of the enslaved that match your ancestor's. It's important to start a tree for the possible enslavers. You will need to research this family just like you are researching your own by documenting their lives. For the enslavers, keep track of any property, deeds, or conveyance of land over their lifetime; census profiles; church affiliation; military service; tax entries; newspaper articles; accounts books; personal papers; and estate records. If your ancestor was an enslaver, use the documents you have in your collection to identify the enslaved by name, including wills, inventories,

---

14 "Cohabitation Act of 1866," Encyclopedia of Virginia, Accessed April 15, 2017, https://www.encyclopediavirginia .org/Cohabitation_Act_of_1866; Berry, Kenyatta D. "Reconstructing the Family Unit: Repairing Bonds Broken by Slavery," Mercy Street Revealed Blog (PBS), March 7, 2017. http://www.pbs.org/mercy-street/blogs/mercy-street -revealed/reconstructing-the-family-unit-repairing-bonds-broken-by-slavery/.

personal papers, and other documents. You might be able to trace the descendants and provide them with valuable information about their family tree.

RESEARCHING FREE PEOPLE OF COLOR

What does it mean to be a free person of color?

The term "free people of color (French: *gens de couleur libres*)," in the context of the history of slavery in the Americas, at first specifically referred to persons of partial African and European descent who were not enslaved. The term was especially used in the French colonies, including La Louisiane and settlements on Caribbean islands such as Saint-Domingue, Guadeloupe, Martinique, and Jamaica.[15] In the United States, a free negro or free black was the legal status of an African American person who was not enslaved. The term was used in the Thirteen Colonies and in the United States until the abolition of slavery in 1865.

EMANCIPATION AND FREEDOM

How did your ancestor become a free person of color?

Typically, the formerly enslaved were freed by manumission, purchasing their freedom, running away, serving in the Revolutionary War, or through the will of their enslaver. Manumission is the act of the enslaver freeing an enslaved person, but the process could be complex. Historically, manumissions have been seen as sentimental or benevolent gestures. Fathers manumitted their children, and some of the enslaved were manumitted after years of service. However, once the enslaver died, it was up to the administrator of his estate and/or relatives to follow through with the request. If the estate was in debt, the most valuable property was enslaved people, so there was no guarantee of freedom.

In 1782, the Virginia Assembly passed an act that allowed enslavers to free enslaved people through their wills and other documents that were proved in a county courthouse with two witnesses. Before this law, a special act of the

---

15 Gehman, Mary. *The Free People of Color of New Orleans: An Introduction,* New Orleans: Margaret Media, 1994.

assembly was required to set an enslaved person free.[16] In Southern states, free people of color were required to register at the county courthouse and carry their freedom papers. In 1793, the Virginia legislature passed a law that "required every free negro or mulatto to register with the city or county clerk and obtain at a cost of twenty-five cents a certificate confirming their status."[17] Get to know the manumission laws for the state where your ancestor was freed. Manumission laws were part of a series of Black Codes passed by northern and southern states. Manumission papers can provide details on the enslaver, the enslaved person, color, stature, marks, and scars. These papers are often housed in county courthouses, family papers, universities, and public and genealogical libraries.

I caught the genealogy bug while in law school researching George Dwelle of Augusta and Atlanta, Georgia. George was born a slave in Georgia and sold twice, including to Alabama. After his white father, C. J. Cook, died, he was hired out and eventually purchased his freedom and his mother's freedom.

Remember the status of the child is tied to the status of the mother. So, if a mixed child is born to a white mother, that child is considered free. Records related to mulatto children with white mothers are in the county courthouse and state records.

The Bundy Family

As mentioned previously, my second great-grandaunt Delilah Virginia Sellers married into the Bundy Family of Middlesex County, Virginia. Samuel Bundy and Mary Jane Ariberson were the parents of eighteen (known) children, all born free. In 1840, Samuel was living in Russell County, Virginia, presumably with his wife and two young daughters. Remember the 1840 US census only listed the name for the head of household and age/sex for other members of the household. My next step is to learn as much as possible about the Free People of Color in Russell and Middlesex counties to determine how Samuel and Mary Bundy obtained their freedom.

---

16 Education at Library of Virginia, "Deed of Manumission for Francis Drake, May 23, 1791."http://edu.lva .virginia.gov/online_classroom/shaping_the_constitution/doc/drake.

17 Library of Virginia, "A Guide to Sussex County (Va.), Free Negro and Slave Records, 1787–1850." http://ead.lib .virginia.edu/vivaxtf/view?docId=lva/vi04015.xml.

CARIBBEAN

During Season 3 of *Genealogy Roadshow,* I revealed the first immigrant ancestor of a father and daughter with Caribbean ancestry. They had no idea their ancestor immigrated through Ellis Island from the Bahamas! That was a learning experience for me because when you think of Ellis Island, you think of European immigrants and not Afro-Caribbean immigrants. It clearly broadens our perspectives! As a result of your research in Immigration and Naturalization records, you should have the following information on your Caribbean ancestor.

- Full name of your immigrant ancestor, birth date, and country of origin
- Year of immigration and arrival
- Where they settled in the United States
- Names of any relatives identified on passenger lists

Using these data, you can find additional information about them in their ancestral home and the records set available. As with most research, it's important to know the history of the island, including whether or not it changed hands between the Dutch, English, French, or Spanish. Like African American research in the United States, key events in Caribbean history shaped laws for free and enslaved people of color.

It is estimated that 1.6 million enslaved individuals were transported between Africa and the Caribbean between 1640 and 1807. However, the Transatlantic slave trade continued illegally for several years.

Slavery officially ended in the British Caribbean on August 1, 1834, and most former slaves were apprenticed to their former masters for a period of four years. Only children under the age of six and the enslaved in Antigua and the Bahamas (who had passed local laws abolishing apprenticeship) were freed immediately. For most people in the British Caribbean, slavery did not officially end until August 1, 1838. France and Demark abolished slavery in their colonies in 1848.

Key Events in Caribbean History:

- **1789:** The enslaved on various islands colonized by the French rebel during the French Revolution.
- **1791:** The enslaved revolt in Dominica, Jamaica, and Hispaniola—later known as Saint-Domingue.
- **1791–1804:** Haitian Revolution an important revolution in shaping and framing the history of enslaved people in the Caribbean. Enslaved and Free People of Color defeat British, French, and Spanish forces to gain independence.
- **1804:** Slavery is abolished in Haiti.
- **1816:** Bussa's rebellion was the largest slave revolt in the history of Barbados, involving thousands of enslaved people.
- **1831:** Baptist War in Jamaica, when more than sixty thousand enslaved individuals refused to work until they were given their freedom and a basic living wage. The enslaved were led by Samuel Sharpe, a Baptist Preacher.
- **1832–1834:** Pompey's Slave Rebellion took place on Exuma Island in Bahamas.

Select List of Caribbean Resources Online

How to find your enslaved Caribbean ancestors?

There were a number of absentee enslavers in the Caribbean who went back to their respective countries and hired overseers and managers for the day-to-day operations. When you are looking for information on your enslaved ancestor, the records might be in the archives of the colonizing country. Learn about the slave trade in that region, including ports of entry. If your ancestors were freed prior to 1834, review church records, colonial records, and slave registers. The British Online Archives has slave trade records from Liverpool 1754 to 1792. The records are from the slave ships' logs and other slave trade records from Liverpool.[18]

---

18 "Slave trade records from Liverpool, 1754-1792," British Online Archives, https://microform.digital/boa/collections/5/slave-trade-records-from-liverpool-1754-1792.

The following databases can be helpful in finding your Caribbean ancestors:

COLLECTION	LOCATION
Caribbean Births and Baptisms, 1590–1928	Ancestry.com & Familysearch.org
Jamaica Civil Registrations, 1880–1999	Familysearch.org
US Virgin Islands, Danish West Indies Slave Records, 1672–1917	Ancestry.com
Caribbean, Select Deaths & Burials, 1709–1906	Ancestry.com
Caribbean, Select Marriages, 1591–1905	Ancestry.com
St. Croix, US Virgin Islands, Slave and Free People Records, 1799–1921	Ancestry.com
Barbados, Select Marriages, 1854–1879	Ancestry.com
Barbados, Select Burials, 1854–1885	Ancestry.com

For information on the enslaved, the Slave Registers of former British Colonial Dependencies, 1813–1834, at Ancestry.com provides for each of the countries and years listed in the table. Information includes: name of owner; place of residence; and name (usually given name unless baptized), gender, age and nationality of slave.[19]

COUNTRY/ISLAND	YEARS
Antigua	1817–1818, 1821, 1824, 1828, 1832
Bahamas	1822, 1825, 1828, 1831, 1834
Barbados	1817, 1820, 1823, 1826, 1829, 1832, 1834
Berbice (Guyana)	1818–1819, 1822
Dominica	1817, 1820, 1823
Grenada	1817–1834
Honduras	1834
Jamaica	1817, 1820, 1823, 1826, 1829, 1832, 1834
Mauritius	1817, 1819, 1822, 1826, 1830, 1832, 1835
Nevis	1817, 1822, 1825, 1828, 1831

---

19 "Slave Registers of former British Colonial Dependencies, 1813-1834," Ancestry.com. http://search.ancestry.com /search/db.aspx?dbid=1129.

COUNTRY/ISLAND	YEARS
Sri Lanka (Ceylon)	1818–1832
St. Christopher	1817, 1822, 1825, 1827–1828, 1831, 1834
St. Lucia	1815, 1819
St. Vincent	1817, 1822, 1825, 1828, 1831, 1834
Tobago	1819–1834
Trindad	1813, 1815–1816, 1819, 1822, 1825, 1828, 1831, 1834
Virgin Islands	1818, 1822, 1825, 1828, 1831, 1834

NATIVE AMERICAN ANCESTRY

Native Americans, also known as American Indians, are the indigenous people of North America. This research will cross several of the records we have already covered in this book, including census, land, and vital records. I receive emails all the time asking about Native American ancestry. The Bureau of Indian Affairs (BIA) was established on March 11, 1824, by Secretary of War John C. Calhoun, to "oversee and carry out the Federal government's trade and treaty relations with the tribes."[20] According to the BIA, there are 567 federally recognized tribes, and the Bureau provides services to 1.9 million American Indian and Alaska Natives.[21] "Federally recognized" Native American tribes are tribes that have a relationship with the United States Government and the Bureau of Indian Affairs. The Bureau works with tribes to get federal recognition. The National Archives has an extensive collection of records on the Bureau of Indian Affairs.[22] Critical to understanding Native American history and family history are the treaties signed between Native tribes and the United States government.

"From 1774 until about 1832, treaties between individual sovereign American Indian nations and the US were negotiated to establish borders and prescribe conditions of behavior between the parties. The negotiations ended in a mutually

---

20 Mission Statement and History, Bureau of Indian Affairs - https://www.bia.gov/bia.

21 United States Department of Interior, Indian Affairs Homepage - https://www.bia.gov/.

22 Records of the Bureau of Indian Affairs (BIA) - https://www.archives.gov/research/guide-fed-records/groups/075.html.

signed pact which had to be approved by the US Congress. Non-tribal citizens were required to have a passport to cross sovereign Indian lands. In 1871, the House of Representatives ceased recognition of individual tribes within the US as independent nations with whom the United States could contract by treaty, ending the nearly one-hundred-year-old practice of treaty-making between the US and American Indian tribes."[23]

IDENTIFYING THE TRIBE

Oral history is important in family history research, especially Native American research. Interview family members to verify the family story of Native American ancestry. Identify as much information as possible about the ancestor you believe to be Native American. Where did your ancestor live? What tribes also lived in the area? Were they a member of Cherokee, Creek, Chickasaw, Choctaw, Seminole, or another tribe? Were your ancestors enslaved by an Indian nation? Become very familiar with the tribes that lived in the state where your ancestor resided. Not all American Indian tribes have been recognized by the federal government.

FIVE CIVILIZED TRIBES, DAWES COMMISSION, AND ROLLS

On March 3, 1893, Congress established a commission to negotiate agreements with the Cherokee, Chickasaw, Choctaw, Creek, and Seminole tribes. This commission would later become known as the Dawes Commission after Henry Dawes of Massachusetts:[24] "Officially known as The Final Rolls of the Citizens and Freedmen of the Five Civilized Tribes in Indian Territory, the Dawes Rolls list individuals who applied and were approved for membership in the Five Civilized Tribes (Cherokee, Chickasaw, Choctaw, Creek, and Seminole). Enrollment for the Dawes Rolls began in 1898 and ended in 1906."[25]

On June 10, 1896, Congress authorized the Dawes Commission to receive written applications and add names to preexisting rolls. Individuals could appeal

---

23 "*American Indian Treaties*," National Archives and Records Administration. Accessed April 21, 2017 https://www .archives.gov/research/native-americans/treaties.

24 "Dawes Records: Five Civilized Tribes—Cherokee, Chickasaw, Choctaw, Creek and Seminole Tribes in Oklahoma," National Archives and Records Administration, accessed April 21, 2017, https://www.archives.gov/research/native -americans/dawes.

25 Oklahoma Historical Society, 2016.

decisions to the United States District Courts of Indian Territory: "The Seminole Tribe made arrangements with the Commission and bypassed the 1896 application process; there are no 1896 Applications for Seminole Indians."[26]

In 1898, the Curtis Act, required all individuals to apply to the Dawes Commission even if they had applied in 1896.

The Dawes Rolls contain information on the 101,000 individuals who were accepted between 1898 and 1914 for tribal membership. Over 250,000 individuals applied for land allotments.[27] The Dawes Rolls cover the enrollee's name, sex, blood degree, and census card number. The census card may provide family history information and contain references to earlier rolls, such as the 1880 Cherokee census. The land allotment information for approved enrollees is available at the National Archives and Records Administration (NARA) in Fort Worth, Texas. These records contain an enrollment jacket, census card, and land Allotment Jacket. They are arranged by the enrollment category and enrollment number, but the Seminoles are arranged by census card number.[28]

Information submitted by individuals and family groups was recorded on enrollment cards or "census cards." Documented information on individuals: name, roll number, age, sex, degree of Indian blood, relationship to the head of the family, and their parents' names.[29] References to other family members cover changes in marital status, birth, and death information. The enrollment cards are arranged by tribe, enrollment category, and then by whether the application was approved, doubtful, or rejected. The tribes are Cherokee, Choctaw, Mississippi Choctaw, Chickasaw, Creek, and Seminole. The categories are citizens by blood, citizens by marriage, newborn citizens by blood, minor citizens by blood, freedmen, newborn freedman, and minor freedman. Applications were marked either "Straight," "D," or "R." Straight applications were accepted, "D" applications were

26 "Dawes Records; 1896 Applications and Choctaw-Citizenship Court Pertaining to Cherokee, Chickasaw, Choctaw, & Creek Tribes in Oklahoma," National Archives and Records Administration, accessed April 21, 2017. https://www .archives.gov/research/native-americans/dawes/dawes-1896.html.

27 Familysearch, 2017.

28 "Applications for Allotment, 1889-1907," National Archives Catalog, accessed on April 21, 2017. https://catalog .archives.gov/id/559520.

29 "Dawes Records: Five Civilized Tribes—Cherokee, Chickasaw, Choctaw, Creek and Seminole Tribes in Oklahoma," National Archives and Records Administration, accessed April 21, 2017. https://www.archives.gov/research/native -americans/dawes.

doubtful, and "R" applications were rejected. "D" cards later became Straight or "R" depending on the commission's decision.

Finding your ancestor in the Dawes Commission Records
Search the index for their name and write down the tribe and enrollment number. Once you have this information, try to locate them on the Enrollment and Census Cards.

Index to the Final Rolls of Citizens and Freedmen of the Five Civilized Tribes in Indian Territory

https://www.archives.gov/research/native-americans/rolls/final-rolls.html.

Enrollment and Census Cards
- US, Native American Enrollment Cards for the Five Civilized Tribes, 1898–1914. This includes their age, sex, blood, and census card number. http://search.ancestry.com/search/db.aspx?dbid=1241
- US, Native American Citizens, and Freedmen of the Five Civilized Tribes, 1895–1914. Information on Native Americans who can claim tribal membership by blood or marriage. This roll includes the names of individuals approved and disapproved. http://search.ancestry.com/search/db.aspx?dbid=2976
- US, Native American Applications for Enrollment in Five Civilized Tribes (overturned), 1896. Applications for enrollment from the Muskogee Area Office of the Bureau of Indian Affairs that was responsible for working with the Five Civilized Tribes. The applications are organized numerically, and applications from Cherokee and Choctaw freedmen are filed separately. These records include affidavits, depositions, correspondence, evidence, lists, and notice of appeal. http://search.ancestry.com/search/db.aspx?dbid=1238
- Ancestry.com: Oklahoma and Indian Territory, Dawes Census Cards for Five Civilized Tribes, 1898–1914 http://search.ancestry.com/search/db.aspx?dbid=60543

Search Census Records

Below are a few online census resources to help you find Native American ancestors. Make sure you read the database description and source information before searching:

- US, Indian Census Rolls, 1885–1940: information includes their name, gender, age, birth date, marital status, head of household relationship, tribe name, agency, and reservation name. http://search.ancestry.com/search/db.aspx?dbid=1059

- California, Index to Census Roll of Indian, 1928–1933: contains information similar to Indian Census Rolls. http://search.ancestry.com/search/db.aspx?dbid=61006

- North Carolina, Native American Census Selected Tribes, 1894–1913. Every year, superintendents in charge of Native American reservations submitted Indian Census rolls. http://search.ancestry.com/search/db.aspx?dbid=1692

- Oklahoma and Indian Territory, Indian Censuses and Rolls, 1851–1959: information from the Bureau of Indian Affairs held at NARA in Fort Worth, Texas. Covers the Arapaho, Cherokee, Eastern Cherokee, Cheyenne, Chickasaw, Choctaw, Creek, Delaware, Kickapoo, Miami, Muskogee, Osage, Potawatomi, Sac and Fox, Seminole, and Shawnee tribes. http://search.ancestry.com/search/db.aspx?dbid=8810

- Census of the Blackfeet, Montana, 1897–1898: George B. McLaughlin and Thomas P. Fuller, US Indian Agents, took a census of about 2,000 Piegan Indians in Montana in 1897 and 1898. Arranged by household, the census provides their English name, sex, age, and relationship to the head of household. http://search.ancestry.com/search/db.aspx?dbid=49103

- Minnesota, Indian Allotment Records, 1888–1919: Allotment records for Native Americans in the Crookston, Saint Cloud, and Duluth Land Districts. Records might include name, date of application, age, tribe, location, sex, name of child if applying for a minor, and description of land. http://search.ancestry.com/search/db.aspx?dbid=2339

Ancestry.com has partnered with the Oklahoma Historical Society to make the following resource available:

> *Oklahoma and Indian Territory, Marriage, Citizenship and Census Records, 1841–1927. The collection contains records held by the Oklahoma Historical Society. Most of the marriage records include name, spouse, marriage date, and location. Tribes and Nations included are the Arapaho, Cherokee, Cheyenne, Choctaw, Creek, Fox, Kiowa, Quapaw, Sac, and Shawnee. http://search.ancestry.com/search/db.aspx?dbid=9026*

Take a DNA Test

An autosomal DNA test provides your ethnic mix and marker test for Native American. Ancestry.com, 23andMe, FamilyTreeDNA, and MyHeritage.com all provide autosomal DNA tests that can be used to determine your Native American ancestry. Depending on which ancestor was Native American, it may or may not show up in your test results. The DNA chapter discusses testing and the percentage of DNA you inherit from your relatives. Taking a DNA test will not provide information on your ancestor's tribe. That information is uncovered during traditional family history research. Use the results from the DNA test along with your research to prove or disprove a family story of Native American ancestry.

SLAVERY AMONG THE FIVE CIVILIZED TRIBES

Most people do not realize that Native Americans were also enslavers. They resided in the slave states of Georgia, Mississippi, Alabama, and Tennessee. It is estimated that 15,000 enslaved individuals were on the "Trail of Tears." Only 8 percent of Cherokee households were enslavers, according to the 1835 Cherokee census, and only three Cherokee households enslaved more than fifty individuals. Of the slaveholding Cherokee, 83 percent held fewer than ten slaves.[30] The Choctaw brought many of their slaves from Georgia. They did not recognize anyone of

---

30 Seybert, Tony. "Slavery and Native Americans in British North America and the United States:1600 to 1865," Slavery in America. Accessed on April 22, 2017, https://web.archive.org/web/20040804001522/http://www.slaveryinamerica.org/history/hs_es_indians_slavery.htm.

partial African heritage as being a Choctaw citizen. The Chickasaw obtained slaves born in Georgia, Virginia, and Tennessee.[31]

Resources for the Five Civilized Tribes
Cherokee

The Cherokee inhabited Alabama, Georgia, North Carolina, South Carolina, and Tennessee. The Cherokee Nation, Eastern Band of Cherokee, and the United Keetowah Band of Cherokee are recognized by the federal government. The Indian Removal Act signed in 1830 by President Andrew Jackson forced Native Americans to move west. Indian Removal to Oklahoma, known as the "Trail of Tears," occurred during the winter of 1838–39. To find your Cherokee ancestors online, search the following resources:

- Access Genealogy: 1817 Reservation Roll https://www.accessgenealogy.com/native/1817-cherokee-reservation-roll.htm
- Access Genealogy: 1835 Henderson Roll—this collection contains almost 22,000 names http://www.accessgenealogy.com/native/1835-henderson-roll.htm
- Access Genealogy: 1851 Old Settler Roll—a list of Cherokees residing in Oklahoma when most of the Cherokee arrived in the winter of 1839 http://www.accessgenealogy.com/native/old-settlers-roll.htm.
- Ancestry.com: US Census Records and Cherokee Muster Rolls, 1835–1838 http://search.ancestry.com/search/db.aspx?dbid=26356
- Ancestry.com: US Census Records and Cherokee Muster Rolls, 1835–1838 http://search.ancestry.com/search/db.aspx?dbid=26356
- Ancestry.com: US Cherokee Baker Roll and Records, 1924–1929—the final roll for obtaining membership in the Eastern Band of North Carolina Cherokee. http://search.ancestry.com/search/db.aspx?dbid=2398

---

31 Krauthamer, Barbara. *Black Slaves, Indian Masters: Slavery, Emancipation, and Citizenship in the Native American South.* Chapel Hill: The University of North Carolina Press, 2013.

- Cherokee Emigration Rolls, 1817–1838—lists of Cherokee Indians involved in the removal from Georgia and Southeastern United States to west of the Mississippi
  https://catalog.archives.gov/id/595427
- 1848 Mullay Roll is a list of Cherokees who remained in North Carolina, Eastern Cherokee Census Rolls, 1835–1884
  https://www.archives.gov/files/research/microfilm/m1773.pdf
- Guion Miller Roll, 1906–1911, "Eastern Cherokee Court of Claims": on May 18, 1905, the US Court of Claims ruled in favor of the Eastern Cherokee Tribe, awarding them $1 million. More than 125,000 people applied, and the court approved about thirty-five thousand individuals.[32]
  A free online index is available for searching from the National Archives and Records Administration at https://www.archives.gov/research /native-americans/rolls/guion-miller.html#list.
- The 1928 Baker Roll and Records of the Eastern Cherokee Enrolling Commission, 1924–1929, Descriptive Pamphlet
  https://www.archives.gov/files/research/microfilm/m2104.pdf

Chickasaw

Chickasaw were located in northern Alabama, eastern Arkansas, western Kentucky, northern Mississippi, and western Tennessee and now reside in Oklahoma.[33] Below are online resources that are helpful for learning more about the Chickasaw:

- Chickasaw Nation Records are available on microfilm from the Family History Library published by the Oklahoma Historical Society, Indian Archives Division (1971). http://familysearch.org/search/catalog/544208 ?availability=Family%20History%20Library
- Chickasaw Schools, Oklahoma Historical Society—http://www.okhistory .org/publications/enc/entry.php?entry=CH034

32 "Guion Miller Roll, 1906-1911, Eastern Cherokee Court of Clams," National Archives and Records Administration, Accessed on April 22, 2017 https://www.archives.gov/research/native-americans/rolls/guion-miller-rolls.html.

33 Pritzker, Barry. *Native Americans: An Encyclopedia of History, Culture and People, Volume 1*, ABC-CLIO, 1998.

Choctaw

The Choctaw were located in southeastern United States including Mississippi, Alabama, Florida, and Louisiana. The Choctaw code talkers used their native language in World War I to transmit messages while on the front lines. Here are a few resources that can help you discover Choctaw ancestors and learn more about Choctaw schools:

- 1830 Armstrong Roll, also known as the Census Concerning Choctaw Removal.
  https://www.accessgenealogy.com/native/armstrong-rolls.htm
- Choctaw Nation Schools (1904)
  https://www.accessgenealogy.com/native/choctaw-nation-schools-in -1904.htm

Creek

Creek Indians are also known as Muscogee and trace their ancestry through their maternal line. Six districts function as counties: Coweta, Deep Fork, Eufaula, Muscogee, Okmulgee, and Wewoka.[34]

- Oklahoma, Creek Equalization Records, 1912–1921. Applications to provide heirship by descendants of members of the Creek Nation. The records include family members and relationships. The records were generated for payments authorized by Congress in 1914 and 1918 to equalize allotments provided to the Creeks. Proof Heirship forms include deceased allottee, date of death, death location, and spouse and children of the deceased.
  http://search.ancestry.com/search/db.aspx?dbid=60542

---

34 "Creek Indians," Familysearch.org Wiki, Accessed May 2, 2017, https://familysearch.org/wiki/en/Creek_Indians.

Seminole

The Seminole were part of the Creek tribes located in southern Georgia, northern Florida, and Alabama.[35] Seminole Emigration Records: Transcription of records from NARA microfilm series M234, rolls 290, 291, 806, and 807. http://www.seminolenation-indianterritory.org/seminole_emigration_records.htm

Enumeration of Seminole Indians in Florida, 1880–1940, National Archives and Records Administration reference report #1009—https://www.archives.gov/files/research/native-americans/reference-reports/florida-seminole-enumeration.pdf.

---

35 "Seminole," The Encyclopedia of Oklahoma History and Culture, Oklahoma Historical Society - http://www.okhistory.org/publications/enc/entry.php?entry=SE011

CHAPTER 7

EUROPEAN RESEARCH

Using the information you've gathered so far, you will have a starting point to "jump across the pond" to find your European ancestry. I believe there are three key things you need to know before "jumping the pond" to find your European roots: your ancestor's birth name, birth location, and year of immigration to the United States. Before you dive into records, research in your ancestor's homeland. It's important to take a step back and learn more about their country and its origin, language, naming patterns, and people. Due to conflicts, major wars, and other events, the geographic boundaries of European countries shifted over time. Each region and family within Europe may be unique regarding the catalyst for immigration to the United States. In this chapter, I will touch on records related to English, Irish, German, and Italian ancestry. These represent four of the top five single ancestries reported on the 2015 American Community Survey (ACS) by the United States Census Bureau. I will also briefly touch on the Jewish genealogy and the resources available.

Like research within the United States, you will need to familiarize yourself with civil registrations (vital records), census records, church records, land records, parish records, and other records in your ancestor's home country.

ENGLISH, WELSH, AND SCOTTISH

According to *The Family Tree Guidebook to Europe: Your Essential Guide to Trace Your Genealogy in Europe* by Allison Dolan and the *Family Tree* magazine editors, it is estimated that twenty-five million Americans have English ancestry and about 9.2 million claim Scott or Scotts-Irish ancestry. Personally, I was surprised when my AncestryDNA results came back 7 percent British, although I should not have been surprised, since my ancestors were enslaved. According to 23andMe, my 100 percent British and Irish ancestor was likely born between 1760 and 1850. This ancestor could be as far back as my fourth or fifth great-grandparent.

A great resource for researching your British and Northern Ireland ancestors is the National Archives and can be found here: http://www.nationalarchives.gov.uk/. They have research guides online. Click "Menu" and then click "Help with your research." Under the "Find a research guide" tab, select "Family History." There are more than two hundred guides available. According to the Birth, Marriage, Death (BMD) guide in England and Wales, all records since July 1, 1837, are kept at the General Register Office (GRO). If you are researching for BMD records prior to July 1, 1837, look for parish registers in local archives. The guide also lets you know what records are online and where to find them in other archives and organizations. The General Register Office for Scotland (GROS) has birth, marriage, death, and other records. Below is a list of select resources to get you started with discovering your English, Welsh, and Scottish ancestors:

BIRTH, MARRIAGE, AND DEATH RECORDS

COUNTRY	COLLECTION	LOCATION
England & Wales	Civil Registration Birth Index, 1837–1915	Ancestry.com
England & Wales	Births, Marriages, and Deaths, 1837–1983	Findmypast.com
England & Wales	Births, 1837–2006	Findmypast.com
England & Wales	Marriages, 1837–2005	Findmypast.com
Scotland	Select Births & Baptisms, 1564–1950	Ancestry.com, Familysearch.org & Myheritage.com

COUNTRY	COLLECTION	LOCATION
England & Wales	Christening Index, 1530–1980	Ancestry.com
England & Wales	Marriages, 1538–1988	Ancestry.com
England & Wales	Civil Registration Marriage Index, 1837–1915	Ancestry.com
England & Wales	Birth Registration Index, 1837–2008	Familysearch.org
England & Wales	Civil Registration Marriage Index, 1916–2005	Ancestry.com
Scotland	Select Marriages, 1561–1910	Ancestry.com, Familysearch.org & Myheritage.com
England & Wales	England Marriages, 1538–1975	Familysearch.org
England & Wales	Civil Registration Death Index, 1837–1915	Ancestry.com
England & Wales	FreeREG Parish Registers	https://www.freereg.org.uk
England & Wales	Free BMD	https://www.freebmd.org.uk/
England & Wales	Civil Registration Death Index, 1916–2007	Ancestry.com
England & Wales	Death Index, 2007–2015	Ancestry.com
Scotland	Scottish Deaths, 1747–1868	Myheritage.com

CENSUS RESOURCES

Census records for England, Scotland, and Wales can be found at Ancestry.com, Findmypast.com, Familysearch.org, and Myheritage.com. Access the data for free or for a fee depends on the website. The 1841 census identified the address; house (inhabited or uninhabited); names of each person who spent the preceding night in the household; age (if over fifteen years, then rounded down to the nearest five years); sex; occupation; and whether born in the same county or Ireland, Scotland, or Foreign parts. From the 1851 census forward, enumeration forms included address, name of each person who spent the night in that household, relationship to the head of household, marital status, age at last birthday, sex, occupation, place of birth, and whether blind, deaf, or idiot.

COLLECTION TITLE	LOCATION
1911 England & Wales Census	Findmypast.com & Familysearch.org
1901 England & Wales Census	Findmypast.com & Familysearch.org
1891 England, Scotland & Wales Census	Ancestry.com & Findmypast.com
1881 England, Scotland & Wales Census	Ancestry.com & Findmypast.com
1871 England, Scotland & Wales Census	Ancestry.com & Findmypast.com
1861 England, Scotland & Wales Census	Ancestry.com & Findmypast.com
1851 England, Scotland & Wales Census	Ancestry.com & Findmypast.com
1841 England, Scotland & Wales Census	Ancestry.com & Findmypast.com

IRISH

According to the United States Census Bureau, an estimated thirty-four million Americans claim Irish ancestry. While growing up in Detroit, I was always told that I had Irish ancestry, and my DNA results came back 3 percent Irish. The rumors of Irish ancestry came from my paternal side and my grandmother's Murphy ancestors. However, to confirm my Irish heritage, I need more than a DNA test. Ireland is divided between the Republic of Ireland and Northern Ireland, which is part of the United Kingdom. Civil registrations of births, marriages, and deaths started in 1864 for all religions. Ancestry.com, Familysearch.org, Findmypast.com, and Myheritage.com have parish, civil registration, and other records to help you uncover your Irish roots. RootsIreland at http://www.rootsireland.ie/ has a number of Irish Catholic and other church records. The Irish census was taken every ten years from 1821 through 1911. The National Archives of Ireland has a number of resources available online at http://www.nationalarchives.ie /digital-resources/introduction/ including the 1901 and 1911 censuses. The census was not taken in 1921 because of the Irish Civil War and was resumed in 1926. Below is a list of select Civil Registrations and Census resources for your Irish ancestors:

IRISH CIVIL REGISTRATIONS

COLLECTION TITLE	LOCATION
Ireland, Catholic Parish Registers, 1655–1915	Ancestry.com
Ireland, Select Births and Baptisms, 1620–1911	Ancestry.com
Ireland, Select Catholic Birth and Baptism Registers, 1763–1912	Ancestry.com
Ireland, Civil Registration Births Index, 1864–1958	Ancestry.com
Ireland, Civil Registration Deaths Index, 1864–1958	Ancestry.com & Familysearch.org
Ireland Marriages, 1619–1898	Familysearch.org, Myheritage.com, Findmypast.com & Ancestry.com
Ireland, Civil Registration Marriages Index, 1845–1958	Ancestry.com

IRISH CENSUS RESOURCES

The National Archives of Ireland at http://www.census.nationalarchives.ie/ has fragments/substitutes from 1821 to 1851 and the 1901 and 1911 Ireland Censuses. Some of the census data includes address, names within the household, sex, age, and relation to head of household.

COLLECTION TITLE	LOCATION
Ireland, Census, 1911	Findmypast.com
Ireland, Census, 1901	Findmypast.com
Ireland Census 1821–1851	Findmypast.com & Familysearch.org

ITALIAN

October is Italian American heritage month in the United States. More than sixteen million Americans reported Italian ancestry, according to the 2016 American Community Survey by the United States Census Bureau. A great place to start when researching your Italian ancestors is the "Italy Genealogy" page on the Familysearch.org Wiki https://www.familysearch.org/wiki/en/Italy_Genealogy#Getting_Started_with_Italy_Research. The wiki provides information on how to get started, research tools, strategies, and a clickable map of the twenty Italian regions. Civil registrations for birth, marriage, and death began in 1809 for most of Italy, about 1820 for Sicily, and in 1866 for the remaining areas.[1] Below is a list of Civil Registration and Passenger records to help find your Italian ancestors:

ITALIAN CIVIL REGISTRATIONS

COLLECTION TITLE	LOCATION
Italy, Select Births and Baptisms, 1806–1900 (in Italian)	Ancestry.com
Italy, Select Marriages, 1809–1900 (in Italian)	Ancestry.com
Italy, Select Deaths and Burials, 1809–1900 (in Italian)	Ancestry.com
Italy Births and Baptisms, 1806–1900	Familysearch.org & Myheritage.com
Italy Marriages, 1809–1900	Familysearch.org & Myheritage.com
Italy Deaths and Burials, 1809–1900	Familysearch.org & Myheritage.com

The Italians to America Passenger Data File, 1855–1900, National Archives & Records Administration (NARA) (https://aad.archives.gov/aad/fielded-search .jsp?dt=2123&tf=F&cat=GP44&bc=sl) is a series of records of over 845,000 passengers who arrived in the United States between 1855 and 1900. About 99 percent identified their country of origin or nationality as Italy or one of the following Italian regions: Lombardy, Piedmont, Sardinia, Sicily, or Tuscany. Some passengers identified their country of origin as England, France, Germany, Spain, or the United States.

There are some records of passengers who were US citizens or non-US citizens planning to continue their travels, returning to the United States, or staying in the United States. Most arrivals were at the Port of New York, and others arrived in Baltimore, Boston, New Orleans, and Philadelphia. The passenger record may include name, age, town of last residence, destination, and codes for passenger's sex, occupation, literacy, country of origin, and other information. The ship manifest identification number (indicates the port of arrival), the name of the ship,

---

1 Carmack, Sharon DeBartolo. "Italy," *In The Family Tree Guidebook to Europe: Your Essential Guide to Trace Your Genealogy in Europe*. Edited by Allison Dolan and the editors of Family Tree Magazine, Cincinnati: Family Tree Books, 2013.

the code for its port of departure, and date of arrival are included in the ship manifest header file.

GERMAN

According to the US Census Bureau, more than forty million Americans claimed German roots in the American Community Survey. In 1871, Germany was unified when the various principalities, states, and kingdoms merged, with the exception of Austria. Each of these various principalities, states, and kingdoms had their own laws and record-keeping system. To find records related to your German ancestor, you will need to know their home village. Make sure you study maps of Germany for the period prior to your ancestor's immigration to the United States.

This will help you establish which records are available, including those kept by the Lutheran or Catholic churches. The "German Genealogy" article on the Familysearch Wiki has research strategies, tutorials, a clickable map, a records finder, and more. You can access the article at https://www.familysearch.org /wiki/en/Germany_Genealogy. Below is a list of select birth, marriage, and death resources to help find your German ancestors:

GERMAN RECORDS

COLLECTION	LOCATION
German, Lutheran Baptisms, Marriages, and Burials, 1500–1971 (German)	Ancestry.com
German Births and Baptisms, 1558–1898	Familysearch.org & Myheritage.com
Germany, Prussia, Westphalia, Minden, Miscellaneous Collections from Municipal Archives	Familysearch.org
Germany Select Marriages, 1558–1929	Familysearch.org & Myheritage.com
Germany Deaths and Burials, 1582–1958	Familysearch.org & Myheritage.com
Eastern Prussian Provinces, Germany (Poland), Selected Civil Vitals, 1874–1945 (in German)	Ancestry.com

"The largest Jewish cultural group in the United States and Canada today are the Ashkenazim, who can trace their Jewish ancestry to Northern and Eastern Europe (German, Austria-Hungary, Poland, and the Russian 'Pale of Settlement).' [2]

Ancestry.com has partnered with JewishGen, the American Jewish Joint Distribution Committee (JDC), the American Jewish Historical Society, and The Miriam Weiner Routes to Roots Foundation to create the Jewish Family History Collection http://www.ancestry.com/cs/jewishgen-all. Before you start researching your Jewish ancestors, I would highly recommend reading "Where to Start" written by Gary Mokotoff for Ancestry. To access the article, click "Where do I begin?" on the Jewish Family History Collection homepage at Ancestry.com. Gary provides tips for interviewing family members, information on Jewish naming patterns, Jewish tombstones, and other resources to help you tackle the challenges unique to researching your Jewish ancestors. Due to the border changes in Eastern Europe, it's important to verify the location of the town or village where your ancestor lived. As mentioned previously, maps and gazetteers for the time period in question will be helpful in narrowing down the location and whether or not it still exists.

HOLOCAUST RESEARCH (SHOAH)

To assist with this difficult research, review Mr. Mokotoff's work on *How to Document Victims and Locate Survivors of the Holocaust* published by Avotaynu and available at http://www.avotaynu.com/holocaust/. His article on "Holocaust Research" is accessible by clicking "Learn More" in the Holocaust (Shoah) section within the Jewish Family History Collection on Ancestry.com. As part of this collection, Ancestry and JewishGen have more than 120 databases available in relation to the Holocaust.

---

2 New York Genealogical and Biographical Society, New York Family History Research Guide and Gazetter (New York, NYG&B, 2015), 189.

CHAPTER 8
ADOPTION RESEARCH

Adults who were adopted as infants or young children are the most common group of people searching for adoption information and birth relatives.[1] I often receive emails asking for help from individuals who were adopted or have a parent who was adopted. In each email, there is a need to connect with their birth family and their genetic ancestry. They are also searching for an answer to a burning question: why? *Why was I placed up for adoption? Why did my grandparents place my parent up for adoption? Did they do it willingly? What were the circumstances surrounding the adoption? Did they think about their child? Do my birth parents think about me? Are they alive, and will I be able to find them?* The circumstances involving adoption vary, and some, or all, of these questions may or may not be answered on your journey to discover your birth family. There is no guarantee that the search will be successful or that the birth parent(s) will want to meet. Embarking on this journey can be emotional, overwhelming, and stressful. It's important to garner support from family, friends, and other loved ones.

Start by gathering as much information as possible from your parents about your birth family and the circumstances of your adoption. If you are researching the adoption of a parent or grandparent, ask your parent about their childhood, where they were born, their adoptive parents, and whether there were other

---

1 Child Welfare Information Gateway. "Searching for Birth Relatives", US Department of Health and Human Services, Children's Bureau (2011), p. 2.

children in the family adopted. For grandparents who were adopted, ask your parents if they recall any information related to the adoption or any family members coming to visit from the birth family.

Adoptees, along with other family historians, have benefited from the growth and popularity of DNA. The accessibility of DNA has made it a popular tool used by adoptees to find their birth parents, siblings, grandparents, cousins, and other relatives. The Autosomal DNA test (atDNA) is one of the most common and provides DNA results inherited from the birth mother and birth father. Your DNA is matched against other DNA tests within the database to find possible relatives. There are third-party tools that allow you to compare your DNA with someone who has tested at a different company. Of course, they need to have their DNA uploaded to the same third-party tool. This is covered in more detail in the DNA chapter. This blog post can further explain which tests are helpful for adoptees: http://adoptiondna.blogspot.com/p/recommended-tests.html. While DNA can be very useful when looking for relatives, it's important to employ traditional genealogy research techniques to find the birth family.

Some adoptees start their search for medical reasons because this typically is an unknown factor. Laws vary from state to state on the release of medical history to the adoptee and their adoptive parents. When researching the adoption of a deceased parent or grandparent, medical history information may not be as easily accessible. Once you are able to discover the names of your grandparents or other relatives, death certificates are a useful tool for building a medical family history using the cause of death and contributory factors. Create a medical history profile for each ancestor tracking the cause of death, age, genetic diseases, and ongoing illness prior to death.

There are pieces of information useful when searching for the birth family: (a) birth name and/or adopted name; (b) birth date and location; (c) location of adoption; (d) name of birth mother; and (e) hospital where the adopted child was born. Most adoptees or someone researching an adopted person will have one or two pieces of information related to their adoption or the adoptee. How do you find the missing pieces of information? You need to understand the laws of the state where you or the other person was adopted. The American Adoption Congress has a list of adoption laws for each state, which can be found here:

http://www.americanadoptioncongress.org/state.php. This varies by state, but the following information is available about the adoption and the adoptee's birth date and birth location. For the birth parents, their age, physical description, religion, race and ethnicity, medical history, education, occupation, reason for adoption, and other children of each birth parent.[2]

USEFUL DOCUMENTS WHEN RESEARCHING ADOPTEES

- **Adoption Agency records:** Adoptions can take place via a state or private agency responsible for placement of the adopted child. Depending on when and where the adoption took place, this information might be available from state agencies. Once you have the name of the adoption agency, search the local archives, historical societies, and libraries to see if they have records related to this agency. If you do not know the name of the agency, determine if there were any child welfare agencies in the neighborhood, town, or city where the adopted child was born. This is particularly useful when researching a parent or a grandparent who was adopted.
- **Birth Records:** The original birth certificate and the amended birth certificate with the adoptive parents' names. Access to the original birth certificate is restricted, and some states require a court order.

TIP

Note: If the adoptive family had the birth certificate amended, the original birth certificate may not exist. Some agencies may require permission from both biological parents.

- **Records for Religious Institutions:** If your ancestor was Catholic, their birth mother might have spent time in a Catholic home for unwed mothers, and the adoption would have been handled by the Church. These

---

2 Access to Adoption Records. Child Welfare Information Gateway. https://www.childwelfare.gov/topics /systemwide/laws-policies/statutes/infoaccessap/.

records may not be as accessible, so contacting the state where the adoption took place for the amended birth certificate might prove fruitful.

- **Guardianships papers:** A guardian is someone appointed by the court to take care of a minor child. Information on guardianship is typically found in the county courthouse where the child was adopted.
- **Hospital records:** Access to these records may vary from state to state and according to time period. Hospital records require knowledge of the birth name, birth date, and hospital.
- **Consents:** Some states require the birth parents and/or the adoptee to consent to disclose their contact information at a future date.
- **Court Decrees:** Required for access to information about the birth parents in some states.

TIP

If you were born in one state and adopted in another, know the adoption laws and access to birth records for both states. Some agencies have multiple offices, so there can be more information in one state office versus another office.

ORGANIZATIONS TO HELP YOU WITH YOUR RESEARCH

- Join groups like DNA Detectives that help adoptees find their birth parents
- Association of Professional Genealogists—http://www.apgen.org
- American Adoption Congress—http://www.americanadoptioncongress.org
- Child Welfare Information Gateway—http://www.childwelfare.gov

Now that you have information on the birth parents, how do you locate them? First, you need to determine if the birth parents are still living. Below is a list of the various resources for locating living relatives. The US Vital Records at a Glance chart in the US Records Research chapter is useful for locating marriage, divorce, and death records.

- Marriage and divorce records: Check marriage and divorce records for the birth parent based on the information you gathered from the state or adoption agency. Depending on the state law, these records are available to determine if a birth parent married or remarried after the adoption.

- Death certificates: As mentioned previously, these records are useful for creating a family medical history. Depending on state law, these records are available fifty to one hundred years after the death date. There are exceptions for immediate family members in some states.

- Obituaries: In lieu of a death certificate, obituaries can provide useful information such as married name, age, death date and location, occupation, surviving family members, and funeral and burial information. For more information on obituaries, see the chapter on Other Records, Newspapers section.

- Funeral home records: Contact the funeral home mentioned in the obituary or on the death certificate to obtain records. If the funeral home is no longer in business, check local historical societies and universities to see if the records have been donated.

- Cemetery records: Findagrave.com and Billiongraves.com are excellent online resources for finding burial locations and cemetery information. Not all tombstones have been photographed and recorded online. Contact the cemetery for more information on deceased family members. If the cemetery is historic, a copy of the older records could be at the local library or historical society. For more information, see Other Records chapter, Cemetery Research section.

- Probate records: Once you have located information about a deceased birth parent, check probate records for the county where they died. These records contain information about surviving relatives and personal and real property. Review the county courthouse's guidelines for access to probate records before contacting the court clerk. These are often available online; for more information on probate records, see the United States Records Research chapter, section on the United States Court System and Court Records.

- City directories, as well as high school and university yearbooks, are a great way to locate birth parents or their relatives. Most of these are available online at subscription-based sites and some regional sites.

As you connect with your birth relatives via DNA, gather family information from your connections to assist in the search. You may want to consider a third-party mediator to make it less stressful for all parties. Discovering the ancestry of your birth family can bring you closure and add to your sense of identity. Revealing, connecting, and understanding one's family history can fuse a void that has existed and started with the question *Why?*

CHAPTER 9

DNA

DNA is the fastest-growing segment in family history! It reminds me of the explosion in popularity of family history over a decade ago, when records became easily accessible online. Today, more people are starting with DNA tests as a first step to discovering their family history. However, this leads to more questions and not the definitive answers they were seeking. What that means for the average American is that you have a plethora of options and opportunities to learn more about your ancestors. The growth of DNA has given rise to the field of Genetic Genealogy, which is "the use of DNA testing in combination with traditional genealogical and historical records."[1]

On February 22, 2016, I appeared on the talk show *The Real,* where I revealed the DNA of the hosts. The segment was titled "Who Am I?" and can be viewed on *The Real*'s YouTube channel. This is the question that most Americans have about their ancestry. During and after the episode airing, I received thousands of emails asking for help on DNA. It was impossible to answer all the emails, but there were some universal themes: Can you help me find my ancestry? What DNA test should I take? I have taken a DNA test; what should I do next? While I cannot recommend one test over another, they each offer a unique value proposition that we will discuss later in the chapter.

---

1 "Genetic Genealogy," International Society of Genetic Genealogy Wiki. Accessed June 1, 2017. https://isogg.org /wiki/Genetic_genealogy.

DNA will continue to evolve over the years as more people get tested and DNA companies build stronger databases to compare customer samples. Technology companies are developing tools to make it easier for consumers to analyze their DNA results. This is an area to watch, since it's not always easy to identify the common ancestor you share with a DNA cousin. What does DNA do for us today? DNA allows you to connect with your ancestral home as well as identify cousins you might've missed on your family tree. Using DNA alone cannot solve your family history mystery, but it is a tool you can use in conjunction with traditional research.

DNA BASICS

DNA or deoxyribonucleic acid is a long molecule that contains our unique genetic code.[2] Three types of DNA tests are used in combination with your family history research: mitochondrial DNA, Y-chromosomal DNA, and autosomal DNA.

- Mitochondrial DNA (mtDNA)—reveals information about the direct maternal line from mother to daughter without recombination.
- Y-chromosomal DNA (Y-DNA)—found only in men who inherit almost unchanged from their fathers.
- Autosomal DNA (atDNA)—inherited from both parents, 50 percent from your mother and 50 percent from your father.

DNA COMPANIES

The most popular test for consumers is Autosomal DNA, which is offered by Ancestry.com, 23andMe, FamilyTree DNA, and Myheritage.com. The Autosomal DNA test provides percentages of Sub-Saharan African, Middle Eastern, European, Native American, Asian, and Jewish ancestry. Ancestry.com only offers the Autosomal DNA test (AncestryDNA), and it is one of the most popular sites with almost ten million tests sold. Ancestry has recently launched Genetic Communities, which is a group of AncestryDNA members who are connected through DNA. Using data from these genetic communities, they look for patterns in

2 "What is DNA?", Your Genome. Accessed June 1, 2017. http://www.yourgenome.org/facts/what-is-dna.

ethnicity as well as compile and compare birth dates and locations from trees linked to DNA results to identify common migration routes.[3]

23andMe offers two types of tests: "Ancestry," based on autosomal DNA, and "Health + Ancestry." The Ancestry test includes five reports: ancestry composition, your DNA family (DNA matches), maternal Haplogroup, neanderthal ancestry, and paternal Haplogroup. The Health + Ancestry includes four reports: carrier status, genetic health risks, traits, and wellness. If you are looking for information on your health and genetic health risks, then 23andMe is the test for you.

Founded in 2000, FamilyTreeDNA offers three types of DNA tests: (1) Family Finder, which tests your autosomal DNA; (2) Y-DNA; and (3) mt-DNA. FamilyTree DNA boasts the largest MtDNA and Y-DNA databases in the world. At FamilyTreeDNA, you can join free surname, geographical, and lineage research projects. These projects are run by volunteer administrators responsible for organizing and managing their project. MyHeritage's DNA test analyzes your sample against forty-two supported ethnicities to reveal your ethnic origins. Each company is constantly updating the way they analyze DNA, so your results may change slightly.

Each company uses their database to compare your DNA sample with others. By doing this comparison, they are able to provide you with a list of genetic cousins and an estimate of the most recent common ancestor (MRCA). CentiMorgans (cMs) are used to measure genetic distance and imply distance on a shared chromosome. They will not provide you with the name of the MRCA, only the possible relationship between you and your DNA match. You will need to connect with your genetic cousins to find the most recent common ancestor.

There are third-party tools that you can use to analyze your DNA such as GedMatch. You can upload your raw DNA data from multiple companies to GedMatch, and it will be compared with others who have uploaded their DNA data no matter where they have tested. This broadens the scope of possible DNA cousins that can help you discover your MRCA.

MY DNA RESULTS

I have tested with 23&Me, AncestryDNA, and FamilyTreeDNA. My mtDNA results from FamilyTreeDNA revealed my Haplogroup: L0a1b1a1. The mtDNA Haplogroup

---

3 "What are migrations?". Ancestry.com, https://www.ancestry.com/cs/dna-help/communities/write-history.

is a group of maternally related individuals who have a common ancestor. All members of the Haplogroup can trace their line back to a single maternal ancestor who lived in Eastern or Central Africa thousands of years ago. Others in my Haplogroup L0a1b1a1 live in Cuba, Kenya, Mozambique, South Africa, and Venezuela.

ANCESTRYDNA RESULTS

Ancestry.com is one of the most popular websites, and they have invested heavily in DNA over the past few years. I have had most of my relatives tested at AncestryDNA because it's where most of my known second cousins and other relatives have been tested. How does Ancestry estimate ethnicity? Below is a statement from Ancestry on their database and genetic profiles:

> *AncestryDNA has built a database of genetic profiles for 26 regions around the world, which is called a "reference panel." This panel is made up of people known to have deep-rooted ancestry in a particular area. We use this panel to create a genetic profile for a region and then compare your profile against each regional profile to see what percentage of your DNA came from a particular region.*[4]

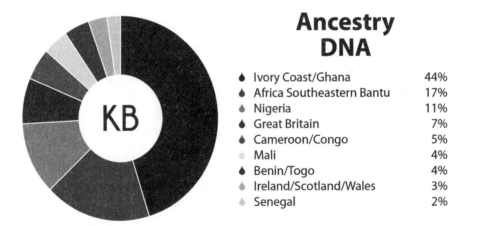

Ancestry DNA	
Ivory Coast/Ghana	44%
Africa Southeastern Bantu	17%
Nigeria	11%
Great Britain	7%
Cameroon/Congo	5%
Mali	4%
Benin/Togo	4%
Ireland/Scotland/Wales	3%
Senegal	2%

Kenyatta's AncestryDNA Results, Chart by Lori Susi

For my chart above, I am 88 percent Sub-Saharan African and 10 percent European. Ancestry recently changed the wording to "Low Confidence Region."

---

4 AncestryDNA 101: The Insider's Guide to DNA, https://www.ancestrycdn.com/support/us/2016/11/ancestrydna101.pdf.

According to Ancestry.com, *"Low confidence regions are areas for which there's a small amount of DNA evidence found in your sample. All ethnicities with predicted percentages of less than 4.5% appear as low confidence regions."*[5]

Digging into the African Ancestry, the low-confidence regions are Cameroon/Congo, Mali, Benin/Togo, and Senegal. I was not surprised by the percentage of Southeastern African ancestry because my mtDNA results at FamilyTreeDNA had East African ancestry. Based on my results, Ancestry has placed me in two migration groups, Northern and Central Virginia African Americans and Southern State African Americans. Both of these groups fit into my research on my maternal and paternal ancestors.

23ANDME RESULTS

23andMe tested my DNA against thirty-one populations, and below is a summary of my results and information on the specific populations. The test results are about the same with some variations, especially on how 23andMe defines West African. Looking at the scientific detail at 23andMe, I have selected the regions in my DNA profile.

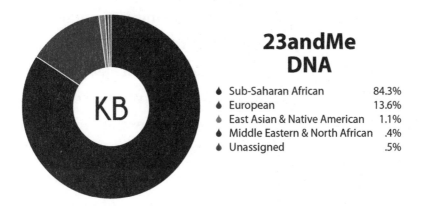

Kenyatta's 23andMe DNA Results, Chart by Lori Susi

East Asian and Native American
Native American (Colombian, Karitiana, Maya, Pima, Surui);
Southeast Asian (Burmese, Cambodian, Indonesian, Lao, Malaysian, Filipino, Thai, Vietnamese)

---

5 Getting the Most from AncestryDNA: Ethnicity, Ancestry Support. Ancestry.com. Accessed on June 1, 2017. https://support.ancestry.com/s/article/ka215000000U0IiAAK/Getting-the-Most-from-your-AncestryDNA-Test-Results-Part-2-of-3-1460089700555.

Northwestern European, British, and Irish
Northwestern European, British, and Irish (Irish, United Kingdom);
Southern European, Italian (Italian, Northern Italian, Tuscan)

Middle Eastern and North African
North African (Algerian, Bahrani, Bedouin, Egyptian, Jordanian, Kuwaiti, Moroccan, Mozabite, Palestinian, Saudi Arabian, Tunisian, Emirati, Yemeni)

Sub-Saharan African
West African (Bantu, Cameroonian, Ghanian, Ivorian, Liberian, Luhya, Mandenka, Nigerian, Sierra Leonean, Yoruba); East African (Eritrean, Ethiopian, Maasai, Somali); Central and South African (Biaka Pygmies, Mbuti Pygmies, San)

The International Society of Genetic Genealogy (ISOGG) was founded to promote and educate on Genetic Genealogy. The ISOGG Wiki (https://isogg.org/wiki/Wiki_Welcome_Page) is a great resource to learn more about DNA, the types of tools available, genetic genealogy resources, and much more. The cousin tree on the ISOGG wiki provides the percentages of DNA shared with immediate relatives to your third cousins. Access information on autosomal DNA Statistics at https://isogg.org/wiki/Autosomal_DNA_statistics. Now that you have an idea of the types of DNA tests, the DNA companies, ethnic percentages, and the percentages of DNA you share with family members, you can use this information as a guide to take a DNA test. If you have already taken a DNA test, use family history research and this additional information to help you make those connections to family members. I would start connecting with any close matches including first, second, and third cousins before moving to fourth cousins and beyond. I hope you have learned a lot and enjoyed this journey to discover your family history. Remember to share your discoveries and the stories of your ancestors with your family!

ACKNOWLEDGMENTS

I would like to thank my parents, family, and friends for supporting me over the past twenty years during my obsession and fascination with family history. I am truly blessed to have found my passion, and I continue to enjoy it each and every day. A big thanks to Renee Carl, Ariana Florio, Barry Kline, D. Joshua Taylor, and Stuart Wasilowski for reviewing portions of my manuscript and providing feedback and encouragement along the way. A special thanks goes to my mother, Denise M. Berry, for telling me that I could be and do anything. With every move, challenge, and success, you have been my biggest cheerleader. I cannot thank you enough for believing in me!

APPENDIX

—⊂※※⊃—

United States Quick Reference Guide to Census and Vital Records by State

STATE	TERRITORY & STATEHOOD	CAPITAL	CENSUS RECORDS (FEDERAL & STATE)	VITAL RECORDS (BIRTH, MARRIAGE & DEATH)
Alabama	Territory: 1817 Statehood: 1819 22nd State	Montgomery	Federal: 1820–1940 State: 1820, 1821, 1823, 1850, 1855, 1866, 1907 & 1921 Confederate Veterans	Birth: 1908 Marriage: 1908 Death: 1908
Alaska	Territory: 1912 Statehood: 1959 49th State	Juneau	Federal: 1900–1940 State: 1870, 1878, 1879, 1881, 1885, 1887, 1890–1895, 1904–1907, 1914, 1917	Birth: 1913 Marriage: 1913 Death: 1913
Arizona	Territory: 1863 Statehood: 1912 48th State	Phoenix	Federal: 1860 (included in New Mexico), 1870–1940 State: 1866, 1867, 1869, 1872, 1874, 1876, 1880, 1882	Birth: 1909 Marriage: 1909 Death: 1909
Arkansas	Territory: 1819 Statehood: 1836 25th State	Little Rock	Federal: 1830–1840 State: 1823, 1829, 1865, 1911	Birth: 1914 Marriage: 1914 Death: 1914

STATE	TERRITORY & STATEHOOD	CAPITAL	CENSUS RECORDS (FEDERAL & STATE)	VITAL RECORDS (BIRTH, MARRIAGE & DEATH)
California	Statehood: 1850 31st State	Sacramento	Federal: 1850–1940 State: 1816, 1836, 1844, 1852	Birth: 1905 Marriage: 1905 Death: 1905
Colorado	Territory: 1861 Statehood: 1876 38th State	Denver	Federal: 1870–1940 State: 1861, 1866, 1885	Birth: 1907 Marriage: 1907 Death: 1907
Connecticut	Statehood: 1788 5th State	Hartford	Federal: 1790–1940 State: 1907 Military Census	Birth: 1897 Marriage: 1897 Death: 1897
Delaware	First State: 1787	Dover	Federal: 1790–1940 State: 1782	Birth: 1881 Marriage: 1847 Death: 1881
District of Columbia	Organized in 1790, Seat of Government 1800		Federal: 1790–1940 State: 1803, 1867, 1878	Birth: 1874 Marriage: 1811 Death: 1874
Florida	Territory: 1822 Statehood: 1845 27th State	Tallahassee	Federal: 1850–1940 State: 1825, 1855, 1866, 1867, 1868, 1875, 1885, 1895, 1935, 1945	Birth: 1899 Marriage: 1927 Death: 1899
Georgia	Statehood: 1788 4th State	Atlanta	Federal: 1800–1940 State: 1798, 1800, 1810, 1827, 1834, 1838, 1845, 1852, 1853, 1859, 1865, 1879	Birth: 1919 Marriage: 1952 Death: 1919
Hawaii	Territory: 1900 Statehood: 1959 50th State	Honolulu	Federal: 1900–1940 Colonial Census: 1866, 1878, 1890, and 1896	Birth: 1842 Marriage: 1842 Death: 1842
Idaho	Territory: 1863 Statehood: 1890 43rd State	Boise	Federal: 1890–1940 Territory: Oregon Territory 1850, Washington Territory 1860, Idaho Territory 1870, 1880	Birth: 1911 Marriage: 1947 Death: 1911

STATE	TERRITORY & STATEHOOD	CAPITAL	CENSUS RECORDS (FEDERAL & STATE)	VITAL RECORDS (BIRTH, MARRIAGE & DEATH)
Illinois	Territory: 1809 Statehood: 1818 21st State	Springfield	Federal: 1810–1940 State: 1810, 1818, 1820, 1825, 1830, 1835, 1840, 1845, 1855, 1865	Birth: 1916 Marriage: 1962 Death: 1916
Indiana	Territory: 1800 Statehood: 1816 19th State	Indianapolis	Federal: 1820–1940 State: 1807, 1853, 1857, 1871, 1877, 1883, 1889, 1901, 1913, 1919, 1931	Birth: 1907 Marriage: 1800 Death: 1900
Iowa	Territory: 1838 Statehood: 1846 29th State	Des Moines	Federal: 1840–1940 State: 1836, 1838, 1844, 1846, 1847, 1849, 1851, 1852, 1854, 1856, 1885, 1895, 1905, 1915, 1925	Birth: 1880 Marriage: 1880 Death: 1880
Kansas	Territory: 1854 Statehood: 1861 34th State	Topeka	Federal: 1860–1940 State: 1855, 1865, 1875, 1885, 1895, 1905, 1915, 1925	Birth: 1911 Marriage: 1913 Death: 1911
Kentucky	Statehood: 1792 15th State	Frankfort	Federal: 1800–1940	Birth: 1911 Marriage: 1958 Death: 1911
Louisiana	Territory: 1805 Statehood: 1812 18th State	Baton Rouge	Federal: 1810–1940 State: 1853, 1858	Birth: 1918 Marriage: Located at parishes[1] Death: 1911
Maine	Statehood: 1820 23rd State	Augusta	Federal: 1820–1940 State: 1837	Birth: 1892 Marriage: 1892 Death:1892
Maryland	Statehood: 1788 7th State	Annapolis	Federal: 1790—1940 State: 1776, 1778	Birth: 1898 Marriage: 1777 Death: 1898
Massachusetts	Statehood: 1788 6th State	Boston	Federal: 1790–1940 State: 1855 & 1865	Birth: 1841 Marriage: 1841 Death: 1841

---

1 A statewide marriage index does not exist.

STATE	TERRITORY & STATEHOOD	CAPITAL	CENSUS RECORDS (FEDERAL & STATE)	VITAL RECORDS (BIRTH, MARRIAGE & DEATH)
Michigan	Territory: 1805 Statehood: 1837 26th State	Lansing	Federal: 1820—1940 State: 1837, 1845, 1854, 1864, 1874, 1884, 1888, 1894, 1904	Birth: 1867 Marriage: 1805 (county level) Death: 1867
Minnesota	Territory: 1849 Statehood: 1858 32nd State	St. Paul	Federal: 1850—1940 State: 1849, 1853, 1855, 1857, 1865, 1875, 1885, 1895, 1905	Birth: 1900 Marriage: 1958 Death: 1908
Mississippi	Territory: 1798 Statehood: 1817 20th State	Jackson	Federal: 1820—1940 State: 1801, 1805, 1808, 1810, 1816, 1818, 1820, 1822, 1823, 1824, 1825, 1830, 1833, 1837, 1840, 1841, 1845, 1850, 1853, 1860, 1866	Birth: 1912 Marriage: 1926 Death: 1912
Missouri	Territory: 1812 Statehood: 1821 24th State	Jefferson City	Federal: 1810—1940 State: 1797, 1803, 1817, 1819, 1840, 1844, 1852, 1856, 1860, 1864, 1876, 1880	Birth: 1910 Marriage: 1881 Death: 1910
Montana	Territory: 1864 Statehood: 1889 41st State	Helena	Federal: 1870—1940 State: 1862–63 Census of Miners	Birth: 1907 Marriage: Kept at county level Death: 1907
Nebraska	Territory: 1854 Statehood: 1867 37th State	Lincoln	Federal: 1860—1940 State: 1854, 1855, 1856, 1865, 1869, 1885	Birth: 1904 Marriage: Kept at county level Death: 1904
Nevada	Territory: 1861 Statehood: 1864 36th State	Carson City	Federal: 1860 Enumerated as part of Utah; 1870–1940 State: 1862, 1863, 1875	Birth: 1911 Marriage: Kept at county level Death: 1911

STATE	TERRITORY & STATEHOOD	CAPITAL	CENSUS RECORDS (FEDERAL & STATE)	VITAL RECORDS (BIRTH, MARRIAGE & DEATH)
New Hampshire	Statehood: 1788 9th State	Concord	Federal: 1790–1940	Birth: 1901 Marriage: 1901 Death: 1901
New Jersey	Statehood: 1787 3rd State	Trenton	Federal: 1790–1940 State: 1855, 1865, 1875, 1885, 1895, 1905, 1915	Birth: 1848 Marriage: 1848 Death: 1848
New Mexico	Territory: 1850 Statehood: 1912 47th State	Santa Fe	Federal: 1850–1940 State: 1790, 1823, 1845, 1885	Birth: 1920 Marriage: County formation Death: 1920
New York	Statehood: 1788 11th State	Albany	Federal: 1790–1940 State: 1790, 1825, 1835, 1845, 1855, 1865, 1875, 1892, 1905, 1915, 1925	Birth: 1880 Marriage: 1880 Death: 1880
North Carolina	Statehood: 1789 12th State	Raleigh	Federal: 1790–1940 State: 1786	Birth: 1913 Marriage: 1868 Death: 1913
North Dakota	Territory: 1861 Statehood: 1889 39th State	Bismarck	Federal: 1860 –1940 State: 1885, 1915, 1925	Birth: 1923 Marriage: 1925 Death: 1923
Ohio	Territory: 1799 Statehood: 1803 17th State	Columbus	Federal: 1800–1940	Birth: 1908 Marriage: 1949 Death: 1908
Oklahoma	Territory: 1890 Statehood: 1907 46th State	Oklahoma City	Federal: 1860–1940 State: 1890, 1907	Birth: 1908 Marriage: 1890 or county formation Death: 1908
Oregon	Territory: 1848 Statehood: 1859 33rd State	Salem	Federal: 1850–1940 State: 1842, 1843, 1845, 1849, 1850, 1853, 1854, 1855, 1856, 1857, 1858, 1859, 1865, 1870, 1875, 1885, 1895 1905	Birth: 1903 Marriage: 1906 Death: 1903

STATE	TERRITORY & STATEHOOD	CAPITAL	CENSUS RECORDS (FEDERAL & STATE)	VITAL RECORDS (BIRTH, MARRIAGE & DEATH)
Pennsylvania	Statehood: 1787 2nd State	Harrisburg	Federal: 1790–1940	Birth: 1906 Marriage: Kept at county level Death: 1906
Rhode Island	Statehood: 1790 13th State	Providence	Federal: 1790–1940 State: 1774, 1777, 1782, 1865, 1875, 1885, 1905, 1915, 1925, 1935	Birth: 1853 Marriage: 1853 Death: 1853
South Carolina	Statehood: 1788 8th State	Columbia	Federal: 1790–1840 State: 1825, 1839, 1869, 1875	Birth: 1915 Marriage: 1911 Death: 1915
South Dakota	Territory: 1861 Statehood: 1889 40th State	Pierre	Federal: 1860–1940 State: 1885, 1895, 1905, 1915, 1925, 1935, 1945	Birth: 1905 Marriage: 1905 Death: 1905
Tennessee	Statehood: 1796 16th State	Nashville	Federal: 1820–1940 State: 1891	Birth: 1914 Marriage: early records at county level and statewide in 1945 Death: 1914
Texas	Statehood: 1845 28th State	Austin	Federal: 1850–1940 State: 1829–1836	Birth: 1903 Marriage: 1836 Death: 1903
Utah	Territory: 1850 Statehood: 1896 45th State	Salt Lake City	Federal: 1850–1940 State: 1858	Birth: 1905 Marriage: 1887 at County level Death: 1905
Vermont	Statehood: 1791 14th State	Montpelier	Federal: 1790–1940	Birth: 1857 Marriage: 1857 Death: 1857
Virginia	Statehood: 1788 10th State	Richmond	Federal: 1790–1940 State: 1782, 1783, 1784, 1785, 1786	Birth: 1912 Marriage: 1853 Death: 1912

STATE	TERRITORY & STATEHOOD	CAPITAL	CENSUS RECORDS (FEDERAL & STATE)	VITAL RECORDS (BIRTH, MARRIAGE & DEATH)
Washington	Territory: 1853 Statehood: 1889 42nd State	Olympia	Federal: 1850 (enumerated as part of the Oregon Territory), 1860–1940 State: 1856, 1857, 1858, 1860, 1871, 1874, 1877, 1878, 1879, 1880, 1881, 1883, 1885, 1887, 1889, 1891, 1892, 1898	Birth: 1907 Marriage: County formation prior to 1968 Death: 1907
West Virginia	Statehood: 1863 35th State	Charleston	Federal: 1870–1940	Birth: 1917 Marriage: County level in 1853 Death: 1917
Wisconsin	Territory: 1836 Statehood: 1848 30th State	Madison	Federal: 1840–1940 State: 1836, 1838, 1842, 1846, 1847, 1855, 1865, 1875, 1885, 1895, 1905	Birth: 1907 Marriage: 1907 Death: 1907
Wyoming	Territory: 1868 Statehood: 1890 44th State	Cheyenne	Federal: 1850 (part of Utah Territory), 1860 (part of Nebraska or Utah Territory), 1870–1940 State: 1875, 1878	Birth: 1909 Marriage: May 1941 Death: 1909

NATIONAL ARCHIVES AND RECORDS ADMINISTRATION FACILITIES

NARA Washington, DC–area locations:

National Archives and Records Administration

700 Pennsylvania Avenue NW

Washington, DC 20408-0001

http://www.archives.gov

The National Archives at College Park

8601 Adelphi Rd.

College Park, MD 20740-6001

https://www.archives.gov/dc-metro/college-park

The Washington National Records Centre (WNRC)

4205 Suitland Rd.

Suitland, MD 20746-8001

https://www.archives.gov/dc-metro/suitland

NARA Regional Locations

The National Archives at Atlanta
5780 Jonesboro Rd.
Morrow, GA 30260-3806
Phone: (770) 968-2100
https://www.archives.gov/atlanta
States: Alabama, Florida, Georgia, Kentucky, Mississippi, North Carolina, South
Carolina, and Tennessee

The National Archives at Boston
380 Trapelo Rd.
Waltham, MA 02452-6399
Phone: (781) 663-0144
https://www.archives.gov/boston
States: Connecticut, Maine, Massachusetts, New Hampshire, Rhode Island, and
Vermont

The National Archives at Chicago
7358 S. Pulaski Rd.
Chicago, IL 60629-5898
Phone: (773) 948-9001
https://www.archives.gov/chicago
States: Illinois, Indiana, Michigan, Minnesota, Ohio, and Wisconsin

The National Archives at Denver
17101 Huron Street
Broomfield, CO 80023
Phone: (303) 604-4740
https://www.archives.gov/denver
States: Colorado, Montana, New Mexico, North Dakota, South Dakota, Utah,
and Wyoming

The National Archives at Fort Worth
1400 John Burgess Dr.
Fort Worth, TX 76140
Phone: (817) 551-2051
https://www.archives.gov/fort-worth
States: Arkansas, Louisiana, Oklahoma, and Texas

The National Archives at Kansas City
400 West Pershing Road
Kansas City, MO 64108
Phone: (816) 268-8000
https://www.archives.gov/kansas-city
States: Iowa, Kansas, Missouri, and Nebraska

The National Archives at New York City
One Bowling Green
New York, NY 10004
Phone: 1 (866) 840-1752
https://www.archives.gov/nyc
States: New York and New Jersey
Territories: Puerto Rico and US Virgin Islands

The National Archives at Philadelphia
14700 Townsend Road
Philadelphia, PA 19154-1096
Phone: (215) 305-2044
https://www.archives.gov/philadelphia
States: Delaware, Maryland, Pennsylvania, Virginia, and West Virginia

The National Archives at Riverside
National Archives at Riverside
23123 Cajalco Road
Perris, CA 92570-7298

Phone: (951) 956-2000

https://www.archives.gov/riverside

States: Southern California, Arizona, and Clark County, Nevada

The National Archives at San Francisco

Leo J. Ryan Memorial Federal Building

1000 Commodore Dr.

San Bruno, CA 94066-2350

Phone: (650) 238-3501

https://www.archives.gov/san-francisco

States: California (except southern California), Hawaii, Nevada (except Clark
   County)

Territories: American Samoa and Guam

The National Archives at Seattle

6125 Sand Point Way NE

Seattle, WA 98115-7999

Phone: (206) 336-5115

https://www.archives.gov/seattle

States: Alaska, Idaho, Oregon, and Washington

National Archives at St. Louis

National Personnel Records Center

1 Archives Drive

St. Louis, MO 63138

Phone: (314) 801-0800

https://www.archives.gov/st-louis

STATE ARCHIVES AND HISTORICAL SOCIETIES

STATE	ARCHIVES AND HISTORICAL SOCIETIES
Alabama	Alabama Department of Archives and History
Alaska	Alaska State Archives
Arizona	Arizona State Library, Archives and Public Records
Arkansas	Arkansas History Commission
California	California State Archives
Colorado	Colorado State Archives
Connecticut	Connecticut State Archives
Delaware	Delaware Public Archives
Florida	State Library and Archives of Florida
Georgia	Georgia Archives
Hawaii	Hawaii State Archives
Idaho	Idaho State Historical Society Library and Archives
Illinois	Illinois State Archives
Indiana	Indiana Archives and Records Administration
Iowa	State Historical Society of Iowa
Kansas	Kansas Historical Society
Kentucky	Kentucky Department of Libraries and Archives
Louisiana	Louisiana State Archive and Research Library
Maine	Maine State Archives

STATE	ARCHIVES AND HISTORICAL SOCIETIES
Maryland	Maryland State Archives
Massachusetts	Massachusetts Archives
Michigan	Archives of Michigan
Minnesota	Minnesota Historical Society
Mississippi	Mississippi Department of Archives and History
Missouri	Missouri State Archives
Montana	Montana Historical Society
Nebraska	Nebraska State Historical Society
Nevada	Nevada State Library and Archives
New Hampshire	New Hampshire Division of Archives and Records Management
New Jersey	New Jersey State Archives
New Mexico	New Mexico State Record Center and Archives
New York	New York State Archives
North Carolina	State Archives of North Carolina
North Dakota	State Historical Society of North Dakota
Ohio	Ohio History Connection Archives and Library
Oklahoma	Oklahoma State Archives and Records Management
Oregon	Oregon State Archives
Pennsylvania	Pennsylvania State Archives
Rhode Island	Rhode Island State Archives
South Carolina	South Carolina Department of Archives and History
South Dakota	South Dakota State Historical Society & State Archives
Tennessee	Tennessee State Library and Archives
Texas	Texas State Library and Archives Commission
Utah	Utah Division of Archives and Records Service
Vermont	Vermont State Archives and Records Administration
Virginia	Library of Virginia
Washington	Washington State Archives
West Virginia	West Virginia Archives and History
Wisconsin	Wisconsin State Historical Society
Wyoming	Wyoming State Archives

VITAL RECORDS OFFICES

STATE	VITAL RECORDS OFFICES
Alabama	Alabama Center for Health Statistics Alabama Department of Public Health The RSA Tower, 201 Monroe Street, Suite 1150 Montgomery, AL 36104
Alaska	Department of Health and Social Services Alaska Health Analytics & Vital Records Section 5441 Commercial Blvd. P.O. Box 110675 Juneau, AK 99811
Arizona	The Bureau of Vital Records Arizona Department of Health Services 1818 West Adams Street Phoenix, AZ 85007
Arkansas	Arkansas Department of Health Vital Records Section, Slot 44 4815 West Markham Street Little Rock, AR 72205
California	CA Department of Public Health—Vital Records MS: 5103 P.O. Box 997410 Sacramento, CA 95899

STATE	VITAL RECORDS OFFICES
Colorado	Vital Records Section Colorado Department of Public Health and Environment 4300 Cherry Creek Drive South Denver, CO 80246
Connecticut	Connecticut Department of Public Health 410 Capitol Avenue Hartford, CT 06134
Delaware	Delaware Public Archives Office of Vital Statistics Division of Public Health 417 Federal Street Dover, DE 19901
District of Columbia	Vital Records Division 899 North Capitol Street NE, First Floor Washington, DC 20002
Florida	Department of Health Bureau of Vital Statistics 1217 North Pearl Street Jacksonville, FL 32202
Georgia	Georgia Department of Public Health Vital Records 1680 Phoenix Blvd, Suite 100 Atlanta, GA 30349
Hawaii	State Department of Health Office of Health Status Monitoring Vital Records Section P.O. Box 3378 Honolulu, HI 96801
Idaho	Vital Records Unit Bureau of Vital Records and Health Statistics 450 W. State St. Boise, ID 83702

STATE	VITAL RECORDS OFFICES
Illinois	Division of Vital Records Illinois Department of Public Health 925 E Ridgely Avenue Springfield, IL 62702
Indiana	Vital Records Indiana State Department of Health 2 N. Meridian St. Indianapolis, IN 46231
Iowa	Iowa Department of Public Health Bureau of Health Statistics Lucas Office Building 321 East 12th Street Des Moines, IA 50319
Kansas	Office of Vital Statistics Curtis State Office Building 1000 SW Jackson Street, Suite 120 Topeka, Kansas 66612
Kentucky	Office of Vital Statistics Department for Public Health Cabinet for Health and Family Services 275 East Main Street 1E-A Frankfort, KY 40621
Louisiana	Bureau of Vital Records and Statistics 628 N. 4th St., Baton Rouge, LA 70802
Maine	Maine Center for Disease Control and Prevention Division of Data, Research and Vital Statistics 220 Capitol Street 11 State House Station Augusta, ME 04333-0011
Maryland	Division of Vital Records Department of Health 6764-B Reisterstown Road Baltimore, MD 21215

STATE	VITAL RECORDS OFFICES
Massachusetts	Registry of Vital Records and Statistics 150 Mount Vernon Street 1st Floor Dorchester, MA 02125
Michigan	Michigan Department of Health & Human Services Vital Records Office 333 S. Grand Ave., 1st floor Lansing, MI 48933
Minnesota	Minnesota Department of Health Central Cashiering - Vital Records P.O. Box 64499 St Paul, MN 55164-0499
Mississippi	Vital Records State Department of Health 222 Marketridge Drive Ridgeland, MS 39157
Missouri	Missouri Department of Health and Senior Services Bureau of Vital Records 930 Wildwood P.O. Box 570 Jefferson City, MO 65102-0570
Montana	Office of Vital Statistics MT Dept. of Public Health and Human Services 111 N Sanders, Rm. 6 P.O. Box 4210 Helena, MT 59604
Nebraska	Nebraska Vital Records 1033 O Street, Suite 130 Lincoln, NE 68509-5065
Nevada	Office of Vital Records 4150 Technology Way, Suite 104 Carson City, NV 89706
New Hampshire	Division of Vital Records Administration Archives Building 71 South Fruit Street Concord, NH 03301-2410

STATE	VITAL RECORDS OFFICES
New Jersey	New Jersey Department of Health Office of Vital Statistics & Registry 140 East Front Street Trenton, NJ 08625
New Mexico	New Mexico Vital Records 1105 S. St. Francis Dr. Santa Fe, NM 87505
New York	Certification Unit Vital Records Section/2nd floor 800 North Pearl Street Menands, NY 12204 NYC Health Department Office of Vital Records 125 Worth Street, CN4, Rm. 133 New York, NY 10013-4090
North Carolina	NC Vital Records Cooper Memorial Health Building 225 N. McDowell St. Raleigh, NC 27603-1382
North Dakota	North Dakota Department of Health Division of Vital Records 600 East Boulevard Avenue, Dept. 301 Bismarck, ND 58505
Ohio	Vital Statistics Ohio Department of Health 225 Neilston St. Columbus, OH 43215
Oklahoma	Vital Records Service State Department of Health 1000 NE 10th St. Oklahoma City, OK 73104
Oregon	Oregon Vital Records 800 NE Oregon St, Ste. 205 Portland, OR 97232

STATE	VITAL RECORDS OFFICES
Pennsylvania	Division of Vital Records 101 S. Mercer St. New Castle, PA. 16101
Rhode Island	RI Department of Health Office of Vital Records, Room 101 3 Capitol Hill Providence, RI 02908
South Carolina	Office of Vital Records SC DHEC 2600 Bull Street Columbia, SC 29201
South Dakota	Vital Records State Department of Health 207 East Missouri Avenue, Suite 1A Pierre, SD 57501
Tennessee	Tennessee Vital Records 1st Floor, Andrew Johnson Tower 710 James Robertson Parkway Nashville, TN 37243
Texas	Texas Vital Records Department of State Health Services 1000 W. 49th St. Austin, TX 78756
Utah	Office of Vital Records and Statistics Utah Department of Health 288 North 1460 West Salt Lake City, UT 84114
Vermont	Vermont Department of Health Vital Records Section 108 Cherry Street Burlington, VT 05402
Virginia	Virginia Department of Health Office of Vital Records 2001 Maywill St. Richmond, VA 23230

STATE	VITAL RECORDS OFFICES
Washington	Washington State Department of Health Center for Health Statistics Town Center 1 101 Israel Road SE Tumwater, WA 98501
West Virginia	Vital Registration Office Room 165 350 Capitol Street Charleston, WV 25301
Wisconsin	WI Vital Records Office 1 West Wilson Street Room 160 Madison, WI 53703
Wyoming	Vital Statistics Services 2300 Capital Avenue Cheyenne, WY 82002

ADDITIONAL RESEARCH
RESOURCES

CHAPTER 2: UNITED STATES RECORDS RESEARCH

Croom, Emily Anne. *The Genealogist's Companion and Sourcebook 2nd Edition.* Cincinnati: Betterway Books, 2003.

Szucs, Loretto Dennis, and Sandra Hargreaves Luebking. *The Source: A guidebook of American Genealogy.* Provo, UT: Ancestry, 2006.

Census Records

Blake, Kellee. "First in the Path of the Fireman: The Fate of the 1890 Population Census, Part 1." *Prologue,* vol. 28, no. 1 (Spring 1996) www.archives.gov/publications/prologue/1996/spring/1890-census-1.html.

Blake, Kellee. "First in the Path of the Fireman: The Fate of the 1890 Population Census, Part 2." *Prologue,* vol. 28, no. 1 (Spring 1996) www.archives.gov/publications/prologue/1996/spring/1890-census-2.html.

Blake, Kellee. "First in the Path of the Fireman: The Fate of the 1890 Population Census, Part 3." *Prologue,* vol. 28, no. 1 (Spring 1996) www.archives.gov/publications/prologue/1996/spring/1890-census-3.html.

Cadle, Farris W. *Georgia Land Surveying History and Law.* Athens, GA: University of Georgia Press, 1991.

Hemperley, Marion R. *The Georgia Surveyor General Department: A History and Inventory of Georgia's Land Office.* State Print. Office, 1982

Kluskens, Claire Prechtel. "Plans of Division: Describing the Enumeration Districts of 1930 Census." *Prologue,* vol. 35, no. 3 (Fall 2003). www.archives.gov/publications/prologue/2003/fall/1930-eds.html.

Kluskens, Claire Prechtel. "The WPA Census Soundexing Projects." *Prologue,* vol. 34, no. 1 (Spring 2002).

Chapter 4: Immigration and Naturalization Records

Barnes, Elizabeth, and Marie Louie. "The A-Files Finding Your Immigrant Ancestors." *Prologue*, Spring 2013.

Coldham, Peter W. *Emigrants from England to the American Colonies, 1773–1776*. Baltimore: Genealogical Publishing Co., 1998.

Colletta, John P. *They Came in Ships: A Guide to Finding Your Immigrant Ancestor's Arrival Record*. Salt Lake City: Ancestry, 2001.

Filby, P. William, and Mary K. Meyer, eds. *Passenger and Immigration Lists Index: A Guide to Published Arrival Records of about 500,000 Passengers Who Came into the United States and Canada in the Seventeenth, Eighteenth and Nineteenth Centuries*. Detroit: Gale Research Co., 1981. This book is available at the Family History Library in Salt Lake City, Utah.

Galenson, David W. *White Servitude in Colonial America: An Economic Analysis*. New York: Cambridge University Press, 1981.

Hacker, Meg. "When Saying 'I Do' Meant Giving Up Your US Citizenship." *Prologue*, Vol. 30, No. 2, NARA, Summer 1998. https://www.archives.gov/files/publications/prologue/2014/spring/citizenship.pdf.

Hickey, Walter V. "Genealogy Notes: A Gold Mine of Naturalization Records in New England." *Prologue*, Vol. 36, No 3, Fall 2004. https://www.archives.gov/publications/prologue/2004/fall/genealogy-2004-fall.html.

"Immigration, Migration, and Naturalization." *New York Family History Research Guide and Gazetteer*. 1st ed. New York: New York Genealogical and Biographical Society, 2015. 43–53. Print.

Salinger, Sharon. *"To serve well and faithfully": Labor and Indentured Servants in Pennsylvania 1662–1800*. Cambridge: Cambridge University Press, 1987.

Smith, Marian L. "Any woman who is now or may hereafter be married…" Women and Naturalization, ca. 1802–1940. *Prologue*, Vol. 30, No. 2, Summer 1998. https://www.archives.gov/publications/prologue/1998/summer/women-and-naturalization-1.html. https://www.archives.gov/publications/prologue/1998/summer/women-and-naturalization-2.html.

Szucs, Loretto Dennis, FUGA, Kory L. Meyerink, MLS, AG, FUGA, and Marian Smith. "Immigration Records." *The Source: American Guidebook to Genealogy*. 3rd ed. Provo: Ancestry, 2006. 355–430. Print.

Szucs, Loretta D. *They Became American: Finding Naturalization Records and Ethnic Origins*. Salt Lake City: Ancestry, Inc. 1998.

Wormser, Paul. "Documenting Immigrants: An Examination of Immigration and Naturalization Service Case Files." National Archives–Pacific Southwest Region (Laguna Nigel, CA), 2013. https://www.archives.gov/files/research/immigration/case-files.pdf.

Chapter 5: Military Research

Revolutionary War

"Revolutionary War Pension and Bounty-Land-Warrant Application Files." M804, National Archives and Records Administration. Washington, DC, 1974. https://www.fold3.com/pdf/M804.pdf.

War of 1812

Butler, Stuart L. "Genealogical Records of the War of 1812." *Prologue*, Vol. 23. No. 4, Winter 1991. https://www.archives.gov/publications/prologue/1991/winter/war-of-1812.html.

Collins, James P. "Native Americans in the Antebellum US Military." *Prologue*, Vol. 39, No 4, Winter 2007. https://www.archives.gov/publications/prologue/2007/winter/indians-military.html.

Dixon, Ruth Priest. "Genealogical Fallout from the War of 1812." *Prologue*, Vol. 24. No. 1, Spring 1992. https://www.archives.gov/publications/prologue/1992/spring/seamans-protection.html.

The War of 1812, PBS. http://www.pbs.org/wned/war-of-1812/home/.

Mexican War

"A Guide to the Mexican War," compiled by Kenneth Drexler, Digital Reference Specialist, Library of Congress - http://www.loc.gov/rr/program/bib/mexicanwar/.

Dear, Michael. "Monuments, Manifest Destiny, and Mexico." *Prologue*, Vol. 37, No. 2, Summer 2005. https://www.archives.gov/publications/prologue/2005/summer/mexico-1.html.

Descendants of Mexican War Veterans—http://dmwv.org/index.htm contains a Roll of Honor, information on how to obtain grave markers, a grave registry, and information on veterans buried in Mexico.

Military Resources: Mexican War, 1846–1848, National Archives and Records Administration (NARA) https://www.archives.gov/research/alic/reference/military/mexican-war.html.

Civil War

"Black Soldiers in the Civil War: Preserving the Legacy of the United States Colored Troops" by Budge Weiman, National Archives and Records Administration (NARA). https://www.archives.gov/education/lessons/blacks-civil-war/article.html.

Blanton, DeAnne. "Women Soldiers of the Civil War." *Prologue*, Vol. 25, No. 1, Spring 1993. https://www.archives.gov/publications/prologue/1993/spring/women-in-the-civil-war-1.html.

Glasson, William Henry. *Federal Military Pensions in the United States*. New York: Oxford University Press, American Branch, 1918.

Johns, John Edwards. *Florida in the Civil War*. Gainesville: University Press of Florida, 1963.

Meier, Michael T. "Civil War Draft Records: Exemptions and Enrollments." *Prologue*, Vol. 26, No. 4, Winter 1994. https://www.archives.gov/publications/prologue/1994/winter/civil-war-draft-records.html.

Plante, Trevor K. "Enhancing Your Family Tree with Civil War Maps." *Prologue*, Vol. 35, No. 2, Summer 2003. https://www.archives.gov/publications/prologue/2003/summer/civil-war-maps.html.

Plante, Trevor K. "Researching African Americans in the US Army, 1866–1890: Buffalo Soldiers and Black Infantryman." *Prologue*, Vol. 33, No. 1, Spring 2001. https://www .archives.gov/publications/prologue/2001/spring/buffalo-soldiers.html.

Plante, Trevor K. "*The Shady Side of the Family Tree:* Civil War Union Court-Martial Case Files." *Prologue*, Vol. 30, No. 4, Winter 1998. https://www.archives.gov/publications /prologue/1998/winter/union-court-martials.html.

Reidy, Joseph P. "Black Men in Navy Blue During the Civil War." *Prologue*, Vol. 33, No. 3, Fall 2001. https://www.archives.gov/publications/prologue/2001/fall/black-sailors-1 .html.

Rick, Alan. *Florida in the Civil War: 1860 Through Reconstruction.* Pensacola: University Press of Florida, 1961.

Shepherd, D. William, ed. *Florida Soldiers in the Civil War: A Reprint of Part II: Florida in the War Between the States, 1861–1865, Extracted from Soldiers of Florida Published by the State of Florida in 1903.* Panama City, FL: Norfield Publishing, 1998.

Wynne, Lewis, and Robert A. Taylor. *Florida in the Civil War.* Charleston: Arcadia Press, 2001.

Missouri and the Civil War

Fellman, Michael. *Inside War, The Guerrilla Conflict in Missouri During the American Civil War.* New York: Oxford University Press, 1989.

Records of the Missouri Provost Marshal Database documents the lives of the Missouri citizens who encountered the Union Army. https://s1.sos.mo.gov/records/archives /archivesdb/provost/.

Guide to Civil War Resources at the Missouri State Archives. https://www.sos.mo.gov /archives/resources/civilwar/.

Oklahoma and Civil War.

Abel, Annie Heloise. *The American Indian as Participant in the Civil War.* Cleveland: Arthur H. Clark, 1919.

Abel, Annie Heloise, *The American Indian as Slaveholder and Secessionist,* Reprint. Originally published: Cleveland: Arthur H. Clarke Co., 1915. Lincoln and London: University of Nebraska Press, c. 1992.

Fisher, LeRoy H., ed. *The Civil War Era in Indian Territory.* Los Angeles: Lorrin L. Morrison, 1974.

Index to Applications for Pensions from the State of Oklahoma, Submitted by Confederate Soldiers, Sailors, and Their Widows. Oklahoma City, OK: Oklahoma Genealogical Society Projects Committee, 1969.

South Carolina and the Civil War

Cauthen, Charles Edward. *South Carolina Goes to War, 1860–1865.* Columbia: University of South Carolina Press, 1950.

Helsley, Alexia Jones. *South Carolina's African American Confederate Pensioners, 1923–1925.* Columbia: South Carolina Department of Archives and History, 1998.

Kirkland, Randolph W. *Dark Hours: South Carolina Soldiers, Sailors and Citizens Who Were Held in Federal Prisons During the War for Southern Independence, 1861–1865*. Charleston: South Carolina Historical Society, c2002.

McCawley, Patrick. Guide *to Civil War Records: A Guide to the Records in the South Carolina Department of Archives and History*. Columbia: South Carolina Department of Archives and History, c. 1994.

Civil War Pensions

Prechtel-Kluskens, Claire. "Anatomy of Union Civil War Pension File." NGS Newsmagazine (2010). https://www.archives.gov/files/calendar/genealogy-fair/2010/handouts/anatomy-pension-file.pdf.

Florida Confederate Pension Records

A Guide to Civil War Records at the State Archives of Florida. https://www.floridamemory.com/collections/civilwarguide/published.php.

White, Virgil. *Register of Florida CSA Pension Applications*. Waynesboro, TN: National Historical Publishing Co., 1989.

Georgia Confederate Pension Records

White, Virgil D., and Georgia Dept. of Archives and History. *Index to Georgia Civil War Confederate Pension Files*. Waynesboro, TN: National Historical Pub. Co., 1996.

Mississippi Confederate Pensions

Hollandsworth, James G. Jr. 2008. "Black Confederate Pensioners After the Civil War." *Mississippi History Now*, http://www.mshistorynow.mdah.ms.gov/articles/289/black-confederate-pensioners-after-the-civil-war.

Wiltshire, Betty C. *Mississippi Confederate Pension Applications*. Carrollton, MS: Pioneer Publishing Co., 1994.

Spanish-American War

Bradford, James C., ed. *Crucible of Empire: The Spanish-American War and Its Aftermath*. Annapolis: Naval Institute Press, 1993.

Livingston, Rebecca. "Sailors, Soldiers, and Marines of the Spanish-American War: The Legacy of USS Maine" *Prologue*, Vol. 30. No. 1, NARA, Spring 1998.

Peuser, Richard W. "Documenting United States Naval Activities During Spanish-American War." *Prologue*, Vol. 30. No. 1, NARA, Spring 1998.

Plante, Trevor K. "New Glory to Its Already Gallant Record: The First Marine Battalion in the Spanish-American War." *Prologue*, Vol. 30. No. 1, NARA, Spring 1998.

World War I

Farwell, Byron. *Over There: The United States in the Great War, 1917–1918*. New York: W. W. Norton, 1999.

Keegan, John. *The First World War*. New York: Alfred A. Knopf, 1999.

Kratsas, James. "*The Great War: World War I and the American Century—A Ford Museum Exhibit*." The Record, September 1998. https://www.archives.gov/publications/record/1998/09/the-great-war.html.

Potter, Constance. "World War I Gold Star Mothers Pilgrimages, Part I." *Prologue*, Vol. 31. No. 2, NARA, Summer 1999. https://www.archives.gov/publications/prologue/1999/summer/gold-star-mothers-1.html.

Potter, Constance. "World War I Gold Star Mothers Pilgrimages, Part II." *Prologue*, Vol. 31. No. 3, NARA, Fall 1999. https://www.archives.gov/publications/prologue/1999/fall/gold-star-mothers.html.

Yockelson, Mitchell. "They Answered the Call: Military Service in the United States Army During World War I, 1917-1919." *Prologue*, Vol. 30. No. 3, NARA, Fall 1998. https://www.archives.gov/publications/prologue/1998/fall/military-service-in-world-war-one.html.

World War II

Gawne, Jonathan. *Finding Your Father's War: A Practical Guide to Researching and Understanding Service in the World War II US Army*. Philadelphia, PA: Casemate, 2006.

Knox, Debra Johnson. *World War II Military Records: A Family Historian's Guide*. Spartanburg, SC: Mie Publishing, 2003.

Mulligan, Timothy P., ed. *World War II Guide to Records Relating to US Military Participation*. Washington, DC: National Archives, 2008.

"Records of Military Agencies Relating to African Americans from the Post-World War I Period to Korean War," National Archives and Records Administration, Reference Information Paper 105. https://www.archives.gov/files/publications/ref-info-papers/105/index.pdf.

Records Relating to Personal Participation in World War II: American Prisoners of War and Civilian Internees. Washington, DC: National Archives and Records Administration, 1992.

Korean War

Blair, Clay. *The Forgotten War: America in Korea, 1950-1953*. 1st edition. New York: Times Books, 1987.

Wehrkamp, Timothy. *Records Relating to American Prisoners of War and Missing-in-Action from the Korean Conflict and During the Cold War Era*. RIP 102. Washington, DC: National Archives and Records Administration, 1997.

Vietnam War

Karnow, Stanley. *Vietnam: A History*. 2nd edition. New York: Penguin Books, 1997.

Schamel, Charles E. *A Finding Aid to Records Relating to American Prisoners of War and Missing in Action from the Vietnam War Era, 1960–1994*. Reference Information Paper 90, Washington, DC: National Archives and Records Administration, 1996.

"The Vietnam War." *Goodreads*. Accessed June 1, 2017. http://www.goodreads.com/work/best_book/1366379-the-vietnam-war.

Chapter 6: Ethnic Research

African American and Caribbean Resources

Burroughs, Tony. *Black Roots: A Beginners Guide To Tracing The African American Family Tree.* Original edition. New York: Touchstone, 2001.

Everly, Elaine C. "Freedmen's Bureau Records: An Overview." *Prologue*, Vol. 29, No. 2, Summer 1997. https://www.archives.gov/publications/prologue/1997/summer/freedmens -bureau-records.html.

Frankel, Noralee. "From Slave Women to Free Women: The National Archives and Black Women's History in the Civil War Era." *Prologue*, Vol. 29, No. 2, Summer 1997. https:// www.archives.gov/publications/prologue/1997/summer/slave-women.html.

Lane, Geraldine. *Tracing Your Ancestors in Barbados. A Practical Guide.* Baltimore: Genealogical Publishing Company, 2009.

Reidy, Joseph P. "Slave Emancipation Through the Prism of Archives Records." *Prologue*, Vol. 29, No. 2, Summer 1997. https://www.archives.gov/publications/prologue/1997 /summer/slave-emancipation.html.

Woodtor, Dee Palmer. *Finding a Place Called Home: A Guide to African-American Genealogy and Historical Identity.* New York: Random House, 1999.

Native American Resources

Carpenter, Cecelia Svinth. *How to Research American Indian Blood Lines: A Manual on Indian Genealogical Research.* Orting, WA: Heritage Quest, 1991.

Lennon, Rachal Mills. *Tracing Ancestors Among the Five Civilized Tribes: Southeastern Indians Prior to Removal.* Baltimore: Genealogical Publishing Company, 2002.

Kirkham, E. Kay. *The Native American Records That Established Individual and Family Identity.* Salt Lake City: Church of Jesus Christ of Latter-day Saints, 1980.

Krauthamer, Barbara. *Black Slaves, Indian Masters: Slavery, Emancipation, and Citizenship in the Native American South.* Chapel Hill: The University of North Carolina Press, 2013.

Malinowski, Sharon, and Anna Sheets. *The Gale Encyclopedia of Native American Tribes.* Detroit, London: Gale, 1998.

National Archives Guide to Bureau of Indian Affairs Records. https://www.archives.gov /research/guide-fed-records/groups/075.html.

Swanton, John Reed. *The Indian Tribes of North America.* Washington, DC: Smithsonian Institution Press, 1974.

Waldman, Carl. *Atlas of the North American Indian.* New York: Checkmark Books, 2009.

Waldman, Carl, and Molly Braun. *Encyclopedia of Native American Tribes.* New York: Facts on File, 2009.

Walton-Raji, Angela Y. *Black Indian Genealogy Research: African American Ancestors Among the Five Civilized Tribes, An Expanded Edition.* Bowie, MD: Heritage Books, 2007.

Five Civilized Tribe Resources

Gibson, Arrell M. *The Chickasaws.* Norman: University of Oklahoma Press, 1972.

Goss, Joe R. *A Complete Roll of All Choctaw Claimants and Their Heirs: Existing under the Treaties between the United States and the Choctaw Nation, as Far as Shown by the Records of the United States and of the Choctaw Nation.* Conway, AR: Oldbuck Press, 1990.

Littlefield, Jr., Daniel F. *Africans and Seminoles: From Removal to Emancipation.* Reprint edition. Jackson: University Press of Mississippi, 2001.

Porter, Kenneth W., ed. *The Black Seminoles: History of a Freedom-Seeking People.* Reprint edition. Gainesville: University Press of Florida, 2013.

CHAPTER 7: EUROPEAN RESEARCH

Overview of European Research

Alzo, Lisa A. *The Family Tree Polish, Czech and Slovak Genealogy Guide: How to Trace Your Family Tree in Eastern Europe.* Cincinnati: Family Tree Books, 2016.

Baxter, Angus. *In Search of Your European Roots.* Baltimore: Genealogical Publishing Company, 2008.

Dolan, Allison, and editors of Family Tree Magazine. *The Family Tree Guidebook to Europe: Your Essential Guide to Trace Your Genealogy in Europe.* Cincinnati: Family Tree Books, 2013.

Dolan, Allison, and editors of Family Tree Magazine. *The Family Tree Historical Maps Book - Europe: A Country-by-Country Atlas of European History, 1700s–1900s.* Cincinnati: Family Tree Books, 2015.

England, Wales, and Scotland

Baxter, Angus. *In Search of your British & Irish Roots: A Complete Guide to Tracing Your English, Welsh, Scottish & Irish Ancestors.* Fourth Edition. Baltimore: Genealogical Publishing Company, 2006.

National Archives of Scotland, *Tracing Your Scottish Ancestors: The Official Guide.* Sixth Edition. Edinburgh: Birlinn, Ltd, 2012.

Rowlands, John, and Sheila Rowlands, eds. *Welsh Family History: A Guide to Research.* 2nd Edition. Baltimore: Genealogical Publishing Company, 2008.

Ireland

Grisham, John. *Tracing Your Irish Ancestors: The Complete Guide.* Fourth Edition. Baltimore: Genealogical Publishing Company, 2012.

Santry, Claire. *The Family Tree Irish Genealogy Guide: How to Trace Your Ancestors in Ireland.* Cincinnati: Family Tree Books, 2017.

Italy

Carmack, Sharon DeBartolo. *Italian-American Family History: A Guide to Researching and Writing about Your Heritage.* Baltimore: Genealogical Publishing Company, 1997.

Colletta, John Philip. *Finding Italian Roots.* 2nd edition. Baltimore: Genealogical Publishing Company, 2008.

Holtz, Melanie D. *The Family Tree Italian Genealogy Guide: How to Trace Your Family Tree in Italy*. Cincinnati: Family Tree Books, 2017.

Germany

Baxter, Angus. *In Search of German Roots: A Complete Guide to Tracing your Ancestors in the Germanic Areas of Europe*. Fifth Edition. Baltimore: Genealogical Publishing Company, 2015.

Beidler, James M. *The Family Tree German Genealogy Guide: How to Trace Your Ancestors in Germanic Ancestry*. Cincinnati: Family Tree Books, 2014.

Beidler, James M. *Trace Your German Roots Online: A Complete Guide to German Genealogy Websites*. Cincinnati: Family Tree Books, 2016.

Minert, Roger Phillip. *German Census Records 1816–1916: The When, Where and How of a Valuable Genealogical Resource*. Orting, WA: Family Roots Co., 2016.

Jewish Ancestry

Kurzweil, Arthur. *From Generation to Generation: How to Trace Your Jewish Genealogy and Family History*. New York: Jossey-Bass, 2004.

Rottenberg, Dan. *Finding Our Fathers: A Guidebook to Jewish Genealogy*. Baltimore: Genealogical Publishing Company, 1998.

CHAPTER 8: ADOPTION RESEARCH

Carangelo, Lori. *The Ultimate Search Book: Worldwide Adoption and Vital Records*. Bountiful, UT: Heritage Quest, 1998.

Carp, E. Wayne. *Adoption in America: Historical Perspectives*. Ann Arbor: University of Michigan Press, 2002.

Hinckley, Kathleen. *Locating Lost Family Members and Friends*. Cincinnati: Betterway Books, 1999.

Tillman, Norma Mott. *How to Find Almost Anyone, Anywhere*. Nashville: Rutledge Hill Press, 1994.

CHAPTER 9: DNA

Bettinger, Blaine T. *The Family Tree Guide to DNA Testing and Genetic Genealogy*. Cincinnati: Family Tree Books, 2016.

Bettinger, Blaine, and Debbie Parker Wayne. *Genetic Genealogy in Practice*. Arlington, VA: National Genealogical Society, 2016.

Dowell, David R. *NextGen Genealogy: The DNA Connection*. Westport, CT: Libraries Unlimited, 2014.

Nelson, Alondra. *The Social Life of DNA: Race, Reparations and Reconciliation after the Genome*. Boston: Beacon Press, 2016.

Sykes, Brian. *DNA USA: A Genetic Portrait of America*. New York: Liveright Publishing, 2012.